I'll live 'til I die

The Delia Murphy Story

*To my wife Joyce, and children,
Kathleen, Seán, Brian and Conor*

I'LL LIVE 'TIL I DIE

The   Delia Murphy Story

Aidan O'Hara

First published in Ireland by
Drumlin Publications, Nure, Manorhamilton, Co. Leitrim, 1997.

ISBN: 1 87 3437 17 X

Cover Design: Terry Bannon, *The Layout Pad*.
Cover Photo: Delia in the 20s *Capuchin Annual* 1940.

Printed by ColourBooks

Contents

Illustrations

1. Delia Murphy, the 8-year-old schoolgirl, 1910.

2. Delia's husband, Dr. T.J. Kiernan; Delia; her sister, Angela; and "Turf girl", a Harry Kernoff woodcut.

3. Delia in 1920s, Capuchin Annual 1940.

4. "Athlone's three compères", John Burgess, Ian Priestly-Mitchell, and Leslie Thorne.

5. A Gramophone Co. (HMV) advertising poster of duet recordings by Delia and Richard Hayward.

6. Cover of the Walton music sheet, The Spinning Wheel.

7. Farewell presentation to Dr. Kiernan and Delia, October 1941; and Arthur Darley.

8. Newspaper advertisement of a concert by Delia in Co. Leitrim, April, 1941; Fr. Tom Twomey OSA; and German soldiers fleeing Rome, June, 1944.

9. Delia and her husband boarding an Aer Lingus flight, 6th October, 1945.

10. Concert programme, St. Colman's College, Claremorris, Co. Mayo, 5th June, 1950.

11. John Count McCormack; Éamon De Valera; Donagh MacDonagh; and Most Rev. Dr. Daniel Mannix, Archbishop of Melbourne.

12. Éamonn De Valera; Delia and her husband at dinner with friends in mid-1940s; Delia with a group of friends in Dublin mid-1940s.

13. Leo Maguire.

14. Delia and author, Jasper, Smiths Falls, Ontario, Canada, August, 1968; Delia and Seán Ó Cillín, winter of 1968-69, at Jasper.

15. Delia's farmhouse in Jasper; Delia recording for Canadian Broadcasting Corporation radio programme, May, 1969.

16. Delia on stage at her last major concert, Camp Fortune, Quebec, Canada, July, 1969.

Acknowledgements

When talking about the extraordinary life she had led, Delia Murphy said that memories should be shared, because in doing so, some of the pleasure, excitement and gaiety can be shared, too. She said she had tried to be worthy of the great honour of being Ireland's hostess abroad as wife of an ambassador, and the instrument through which was communicated the wealth of Ireland's great store of songs and ballads. "I hope I succeeded," she added. "Only others can judge."

I had been in broadcasting just over a year when Delia died in February, 1971. Months went by and when nothing was done to note her passing, I compiled a documentary tribute to her on RTE radio which went out the 4th June 1972. Then, after many more years I proposed to RTE that maybe it was time to do a TV documentary, and that was eventually transmitted in 1988. And the book? Well, since nobody else had written anything, many of those I interviewed for the documentaries encouraged me to write her story. Eventually, in the summer of 1995, I decided it was now or never. Anyway, I had little doubt that towards the end of her life, Delia was hoping to tell her story herself, but she died before she could tackle it.

One of Delia's close friends in her last years in Canada was the late Barbara Hutchinson, a librarian from Smiths Falls, Ontario. She knew that Delia was anxious to tell her story to the world, and being the good librarian that she was, she sat Delia down and recorded a number of conversations with her. I am most grateful to her for allowing me to use her transcripts of those chats with Delia.

There are many people to whom I owe a great deal for giving of their time in sharing with me their memories, opinions, and thoughts of Delia, that a mere word of acknowledgment seems totally inadequate. Many of those with whom I spoke for the RTE radio and television documentaries are no longer with us, but their contributions are sincerely acknowledged. I am most grateful to RTE for granting me permission to quote from those taped conversations.

I wish to express my deepest gratitude to Dr. Colm Kiernan, Delia's son, for all his help. Colm not only supplied me with a great amount of information and advice in his letters from Australia, he encouraged me when the going was not easy. I realise that any opinions I have expressed, or interpretations I have made, might not necessarily gain Colm's endorsement. However, as an author and historian himself, he will understand better than most the obligations and imperatives of the biographer.

The following people were especially helpful with details on Delia's young days in Hollymount, Co. Mayo, and her years as a student in Tuam, Dublin and University College Galway: Mrs. Margaret Doherty, a schoolmate of Delia's at Roundfort National School; neighbours of the Murphys: Mr. Nolan, Mike and John Killeen, Pac Hereward, Fr. Eamon Concannon, formerly C.C. at Roundfort, and Mary Cassidy, who worked for the Murphys at Mount Jennings House; Ger Flanagan, a friend of the Murphy family; the Sisters of St. Joseph's Presentation Convent, Tuam, especially Sr. Fursey, Delia's music teacher; the Dominican Sisters, Griffith Avenue, Dublin, for giving me access to *The Lanthorn*, the yearbook of the Dominican Convent, Eccles Street; Bríd Ní Bhroin, a fellow–student of Delia's at UCG, and her daughter, Fionnuala.

For details on the years Delia and her husband, Dr. T.J. Kiernan, spent in London: Liam Ó Riagáin, former Secretary at the Department of Posts and Telegraphs; Noel Dorr, former Secretary at the Department of Foreign Affairs, and the staff at the Department. For help with the years Delia was in Dublin in the thirties and early forties; Martin Walton of Walton's Musical Instrument Galleries, and his friends, singer and broadcaster, Leo Maguire, and bandleader, Billy Carter; artist, Harry Kernoff; Leslie Thorn who worked for The Gramophone Company HMV (His Master's Voice) actor, Liam Redmond, and his wife, Bairbre; Mary Darley, niece of Dr. Arthur Darley, musicians/singers, Albert Healy, Stella Seaver, Seán Ó Síocháin, and Hubert Valentine; Tadhg 'Kerry' O'Sullivan, Paddy Kiely, and Patrick McMonagle, Killarney; Chris Curran and Jack Horgan, Dublin, for their information on the film, *Islandman* ; and historian, Leon Ó Broin.

For information on Delia's years in Rome: Most Rev. Dr. Thomas

Ryan, late Bishop of Clonfert, Fr. Tom Twomey, OSA, Fr. Michael Lee, OFM (Br. Humilis), Dr. Don Carr, and Fr. John 'Spike' Buckley, OSA. and for details on Delia's years in Ireland in the early fifties: Dr. Ivor Browne, Delia's son-in-law; entertainer, Pascal Spelman; the late Joseph Mooney, Drumshanbo, Co. Leitrim and his wife, Eva; Fr. Jarlath Waldron, Claremorris; Leo Cullen, Delia's nephew, and Leo's sister, Carmen Roddy, and their late aunt, Eve Cullen.

For details on Delia's life in Canada and the U.S.: Dr. Kenneth S. Goldstein, former Professor of Folklore, University of Pennsylvania; Seán Ó Cillín, now of the Department of Geography, UCG; Dr. Michael Brennan, London, Ontario; Jimmy and Margi Sheridan, Montreal, Quebec; Marni Buckley, and Teresa Brennan, Smiths Falls, Ontario; and my brother, Mel O'Hara, Ottawa, Ontario.

For help with general research: Dr. Benedict Cullen, OFM Cap, and An tAth. Pádraig Ó Cuill, OFM Cap, St. Mary of the Angels, Church Street, Dublin; Alf Mac Lochlainn, former Librarian at UCG; Nicholas Carolan, Director of the Irish Traditional Music Archives, Dublin; Don Kennedy, RTE Sound Librarian; Kathleen Gill and Chris White, Claremorris library; the staff of the Ballyroan Library, Rathfarnham; John C. Gray, Librarian, The Linen Hall Library, Belfast; Gerard Delaney, Family Research Society, Hollymount, Co. Mayo; Tom McNamara of the Valuations Office, Dublin; and Maura Kennedy, Librarian at the Gilbert Library, Pearse Street, Dublin.

Thanks, too, to those who wrote to me at RTE Radio I. They include: B. Acton, Thomas Donoghue, Kathleen Duffy, Gregory Dunne, Larry O'Dowd, Elizabeth Fogarty, Diarmaid Ó Broin, Gerard O'Connor, Bridie O'Rourke, Noreen O'Sullivan, and P.J. Ryan.

To my wife, Joyce, who has shown great understanding and forbearance throughout the months of writing, and encouraged me at all times, I am most grateful. To my good friends Jim Kelly, Carmel Wynn and Colman Cassidy who 'marked my cards' and helped me dot my i's and cross my t's; to Terry Bannon, *The Layout Pad* who designed the cover and also the Scanning Shop who helped with the photographs– many thanks. I am grateful to my friend, Diarmaid Ó Cathasaigh for bringing the book, *The Real Klondike Kate* to my attention.

Aidan O Hara

Foreword

Delia Murphy was a very significant talent, and a very important personality in the cultural history of this century, whose biography is long overdue; and I greatly welcome this book by Aidan O'Hara which salutes Miss Murphy's life, and will, I hope, introduce her generous personality and absorbing story to a younger generation – and revive her memory once more for those who recall her wonderful musical gift.

Delia Murphy was, in her time, an adored singing star whose voice frequently adorned the airwaves of early Radio Eireann broadcasts in the 1940s, and, as Mr O'Hara so well illustrates in this work, although she was a woman of her time, she was also, perhaps a woman before her time. She sang with great warmth, and with an unmistakable catch in her delivery that evoked memory and feeling; like Edith Piaf, her style was absolutely her own. She had learned her repertoire listening to the travelling folk in Co Mayo during her childhood– she was born in 1902– and she always had a special affection for Travellers and their traditions because of that childhood closeness. But although Delia herself was admired as a musical personality, her espousal of the 'the tinkers' style' was not always understood in her lifetime, at a time when many Irish people (and people in other societies, too) were more inclined to esteem the American dance-band styles, or international 'sophistication', than music based on a grass-roots folklore. In that sense, the time was out of joint for Delia Murphy: in the 1990s, when we have a much stronger sense of rescuing nomadic cultures, her understanding of Travellers' singing styles would be the subject of much scholarly attention.

As a woman too, Delia Murphy had her conflicts. Although she knew much happiness in her marriage to the academic and diplomat, T.J. Kiernan, and her final thoughts were for him, her marriage did demand duties which obviously sometimes stifled her artistic yearnings. She experienced that strong creative urge to be writing and performing music which could not always be heeded when her responsibilities as a diplomat's wife (or, it might be added, for a creative artist, as anyone's wife) weighed. To be a wife, a mother and home-maker requires time and commitment; to be an artist requires, really, to make the work, the *opus* a priority. It is, it must be said, a strain to try and do both, though Delia carried out the role of the diplomat's wife with brio, if sometimes a little unconventionally. Yet her lack of conventionality was also matched by her fortitude and courage when, during the Second World War, in Rome, she ignored some of the finer formal points of Irish neutrality and helped save those escaping from the Nazis, including Allied prisoners, and indeed, persecuted Jews. It was, I felt, typical of Delia that her humanity came before any sense of protocol.

Mr. and Mrs. Kiernan, enjoyed their years abroad, and they had the joy of seeing their children grow into accomplished individuals; the couple were often lionised, particularly in Australia, which took Delia and her husband especially to its heart. But in her later years, Delia Murphy's life as an artist did not develop as it should have done. (This might also be said of her sister Angela, who sang most beguilingly, and who died prematurely, in tragic post-childbirth haemorrhage).

Delia was, as Liam Clancy says in this text, a pivotal figure; she took up the ballad and turned it into something of their own; she transmitted an essential element of Irish traditional music and interpreted it in the transmission. Our main regret must be that she did not record more, or that television took so little opportunity to capture the essence of the woman, and the artist, on camera.

But we are thankful to have what there is, that full, rich voice, the musical narrative which she could adapt, sometimes piquantly, to either gender, the irreplaceable yearning register of wistfulness and melancholy, as with the Portuguese *fado*, mixed with that old Connacht sweetness. And now we have the story of Delia Murphy's life, captured for history by Aidan O'Hara, and from so many witnesses who knew her; it is, I would predict, the first of a whole new wave of studies on Delia Murphy as a woman of our century, a significant Irish cultural figure, and a musical artist who brought great delight during sometimes hard times.

Mary Kenny, Dublin and London: February 1997.

Prologue

It was a hot humid Ontario day in August 1968, when I headed out from my home in Ottawa to visit Delia in Jasper, a small village formerly known as Irish Creek, fifty miles to the south. She was already a legend when I was a boy, and I was more than a little excited, even nervous, at the prospect of meeting her. After all, it is not every day one gets to meet a figure from one's childhood who was as near to being a 'star' as anyone in the Ireland of the 1940s could claim.

Jasper is located in rolling farmland country, and it was the last place on earth one would expect to find an Irishwoman in her mid-sixties farming on her own, never mind one who had mixed with and heads of state, and was used to being addressed as 'Your Excellency'. A friend had given me Delia's telephone number, and when I rang her to ask if I might call and see her, she gave me a cheery invitation to come and visit her any time.

"Can you make your way to Smiths Falls?" she asked. I said I could. "Right then," she went on, "just ask anyone you meet on the main street where Delia Murphy lives, and you won't go wrong."

It was not that I doubted her word, but I took the precaution of checking precise directions with my friend who had been to see her several times. And I was glad I did, because Delia's farm was in as isolated an area of Southern Ontario as you will get.

I have few recollections of my thoughts that day as my wife, Joyce, and our one-year-old daughter, Kathleen, travelled along Highway #15 to Smiths Falls, but as we approached the turn-off for Delia's farmhouse 'way out in the sticks', as Ottawa folk described it, I clearly recall thinking, who would believe that the Ireland's most popular woman singer was living on a farm in this out-of-the-way spot?

Most people who remembered her would most likely have said, "Delia Murphy! Sure, I thought she was dead long ago." But it was a very lively Delia that I encountered As I drove into the short drive-way to her stone farmhouse, she was reclining on a canvas lawn chair, at the gable end of the house under the shade of a tall maple tree. With her was an old man who helped out on her farm, and both were drinking cold beer to help them cope with the heat. "Well, you're very welcome," she announced in that broad Mayo accent I was to become so familiar with over the next year. There was no awkwardness or formality in our meeting. "Grab a chair there and sit down, and help yourself to a beer."

As Joyce and I set up the playpen for our infant daughter, Delia asked us about ourselves. I told her I was born in Donegal, but that I had lived in Dublin and later in British Columbia before moving to Ontario. She made observations about each place, commenting on Dublin as 'dear ould dirty Dublin', and adding, "But, sure, I'm from Mayo, God help us, where the crows ate the man." And chuckling away to herself she continued, "I always say that to people who ask me where I'm from in Ireland, and I enjoy the reactions I get."

Then she said: "I've just been thinking about my husband, Dr. Tom Kiernan. He died last year, you know. And I'd like to sing you this song which reminds me of him." It was, *Cold Blows the Wind*, a variant of the ancient ballad, *The Unquiet Grave*. And there and then she sang it, a most plaintive, moving song with words which matched her reminiscent mood exactly.

> *..I'll go and mourn on his graveside*
> *For a twelve-month and a day.*
> *A twelve-month and a day had gone by*
> *When my true love he arose,*
> *Saying, "Why weep you on my graveside,*
> *I can't take my repose.*
>
>
> *Ah, what want you of me, dear love,*
> *You will not let me sleep;*
> *Your salty tears they trickle down*
> *And wet my winding sheet."*

When shall we meet again, dear love?
When shall we meet again, dear love?
"When the autumn leaves that fall from the trees
Are green and spring again."

I was quite stunned by Delia's remarkable control and delivery of the song which obviously held a great deal of meaning for her. She recalled happier days with her late husband, and spoke fondly of their friendship and love for one another.

After that she reminisced about her life and singing, and told several stories about her travels abroad as the wife of an Irish ambassador and of her encounters with the humble and the mighty. The Delia I got to know that day remained the same friendly outgoing Delia until her sudden death eighteen months later. During that time and in the following years I was to become more and more familiar with the story of Delia Murphy, 'Ireland's Ballad Queen', and I learned a great deal about one of the most remarkable figures ever to emerge from the world of entertainment in Ireland.

Aidan O' Hara

I

'I will go an seek my fortune in far Amerikay'

Writing about rural Ireland shortly after the turn of the century, poet and writer, Pádraic Colum, said that there were few centres of interest or amusement in the country. He had travelled across Ireland from the Midlands to the West, mostly on foot, lodging with the people – the Irish Catholic peasantry, he called them – observing how they lived, and later, publishing his findings in a series of 'studies' for *The Manchester Guardian* and *The Nation*, which appeared in book form under the title, *My Irish Year*, in 1912.

On one of his walks in the West, Colum fell in with an earnest young student who "talked with the gloom of a Russian intellectual". The young man railed against the people's attitude to marriage saying they lacked will, that the dowry was everything and that the institution was just a bargain. The children of such marriages, he said, can have little passion for life, and he added: "And there is little freedom. No social freedom you may say."

The young man went on to tell Colum about a recent incident in his locality where a priest announced from the altar his intention of putting down dancing in his parish. "And this, after a sermon against emigration," he declared. "And yet this priest is sincere and hard-working, seeking to create a tolerable economic situation. It's strange that he does not understand that a desirable social life is as necessary as a tolerable economic life."

Writing about life at the turn of century, Padraic Colum's wife Mary, also noted the depressed state of the people. She wrote in her *Life and the Dream:* "The country I grew up in had all the marks of a conquered country and some of the habits and manners of an enslaved country."

When Delia's father, John Patrick Murphy, was growing up in Co. Mayo in the eighteen-seventies and eighties, life was pretty dismal. There was a failure of the potato crop in 1879, the year John "Jack" Murphy turned nine, and while it was not a total failure, it was severe enough to bring the memory of the horror of the 1846- 47 famine to mind. In places like Mayo the crop was just one fourth of the previous year, and the corn yield, too, was under average.

The difference this time however was that there was almost immediate help from outside and relief was prompt and well organized. Charles Stewart Parnell, the Irish political leader, and his colleagues formed one relief committee, and the Duchess of Marlborough another. Subscriptions were raised in Ireland, in England and Scotland, in places abroad, especially in the United States.

It was at this time that the 'champion' potato was introduced into Ireland. The Board of Guardians went to Scotland for the new seed, and in two years no other seed but the 'champion' was planted. Even though the tenant farmers had obtained a certain security of tenure in 1879, the rents they were compelled to pay for land on which to plant and sow were exorbitant. "The people had been forced back to scramble for a livelihood on the land, and they were prepared to bargain for the soil as people in a besieged city bargain for bread," Pádraic Colum wrote.

The effect of the crop failure of '79 was to make people believe that the will of God was against the people of Ireland. For years afterwards the marriage register in many parishes was a blank. Abnormal emigration, abandonment of tillage, contempt for agricultural employment; these were the effects of '79.

But the people of Mayo had decided that enough was enough, and discovered a weapon with which to challenge the landlord who charged too high a rent. The Land League had been formed, and to its armoury the people added the highly effective tool of the boycott, named after the Co. Mayo landlord, Captain Charles Boycott. Landlordism was attacked with resolution and intelligence.

The year 1881 marked an advance towards tenant liberation. In that year an act was passed which gave the tenant his land at a 'fair' and not at a competitive rent. And still the land agitation went on. But all the while America and Britain beckoned, and the young women and men, with few prospects of earning a living or entering into marriage, left Ireland's shore in their thousands every year.

This then was the world in which young Jack Murphy grew up in the late eighteen hundreds. His family were small farmers from the townland of Cloondinnaire in the parish of Crossboyne and Taugheen, near Hollymount, Co. Mayo. They were a large family, and there were few prospects for any of them other than the emigration ship.

Jack Murphy, or Papa as he was known in later life to his children and grandchildren, worked for a while on the docks in Galway City. The work was back-breaking and he often told how he had to wade into the water along the strand and carry bags of salt ashore from boats anchored in the bay. If the salt got wet it weighed a ton, he would say. One of Jack's shoulders was permanently drooped, and he blamed it on the work he did in Galway.

Jack used to tell how he stood and looked at Mount Jennings House in the neighbouring townland of Roos just before he and five of his brothers emigrated, and he promised himself that if ever he made enough money he would return and buy the house and estate. He had heard from friends and neighbours in America about the many opportunities the New World offered to young men like himself, and he was determined to go there and make his fortune.

He was particularly keen to try his luck in mining for gold because he had heard so many stories about Irishmen who had struck it rich out there. If he was aware of the fact that for every one who made it big in America there were thousands who did not, he never said. He was young and determined, and nothing was going to stop him. His plan was first to go to England to earn enough money for his passage to the United States.

Some time before Jack Murphy arrived in America, out on the Pacific coast, George Carmack and his brothers-in-law Skookum Jim and Taglish Charlie had heard from an experienced prospector that they might find gold in Rabbit Creek, a tributary of the

Klondike River in the Yukon Territory in north western Canada. Carmack and his pals found gold on 17th August, 1896, the biggest gold strike in North America. But word of their find did not emerge for another eleven months, and then newspapers like the *Seattle Post-Intelligencer* and the *Vancouver Sun* broke the news to the world.

When word got out about the gold strike, Jack Murphy and his brothers joined thousands of others from all over North America and, indeed, from all around the world, and headed for the goldfields. They formed part of the flood of 18,000 who trekked to the Great North West in the year 1898. They represented a cross-section of the human race, and came from every walk of life and from the four corners of the globe. Very few of them were genuine prospectors and only the latter knew what lay in store.

We do not know what route Jack Murphy travelled to get to the Klondike. It might have been the overland route chosen by those from the east, like Donegalman, Micky McGowan, who wrote of his experiences in his book, *The Hard Road to Klondike*. Like Micky, Jack might then have taken the sea route from Seattle or Vancouver on the Pacific coast, the same route taken that same year by the famous Katherine "Klondike Kate" Ryan, a young woman of Irish parents from eastern Canada who tackled the hard road to the Klondike all on her own. But whichever route Jack Murphy took, either journey was long and arduous, and very dangerous.

Klondike Kate's and Micky McGowan's accounts of the journey to the North West leave one in no doubt about the severity of conditions young hopefuls like themselves had to face. Micky tells how he and two other Donegalmen made it to the Yukon River in September and began the journey by skiff up river. They were rowing against the flow and met hundreds of people in boats going in the opposite direction, escaping south to avoid having to spend another winter in Arctic conditions. "They thought we were mad," he said.

Later when the river froze over they had to take to the trail and if they thought they had never experienced cold like the cold they endured on the river, they were in for a surprise. "The cold would catch you unawares," Micky wrote. "You were never properly warm even when walking, and if your feet were wet or if you were perspiring, that was where the danger lay. In the twinkling of an eye, you'd freeze as soon as you'd stand and you wouldn't know it until the cramps hit you. If the frost got you while you were sleeping, you were done for. You wouldn't waken up at all." Through a combination of extraordinary good luck and help from friends they met along the way, McGowan and his pals made it to their destination.

The amazing 19 year old Klondike Kate, daughter of another Donegalman, made her way entirely on her own at first along the Stikine Trail. Eventually she met up with a group of North West Mounted Police and travelled with them a good part of the way. Later she would have a career herself as the first ever woman member of the North West Mounted police, going on to become an important political figure in the North.

Many, of course, never made it to the Yukon at all, defeated by the severe conditions along the icy trail that led through the wilderness of northern British Columbia and southern Alaska, and they headed back home much chastened by their dreadful experiences, and even poorer than when they set out. But remarkably, both Micky McGowan and Jack Murphy would both survive and prosper from their hardships and deprivations. Each returned home and bought the local Big House.

Mary Cassidy who worked as housekeeper in Mount Jennings House in the 1930s recalls hearing from Jack Murphy about how hard the work in the Klondike was. "There was a man there – he was a ganger, or whatever – and one day he gave John a belt of a shovel and he had to walk nine miles to see the doctor. The doctor told him to return home and report it in the morning. He did, and the engineer told him to go home and when he was well enough again to come back. The end result was the ganger was got rid of and Mr. Murphy got his job. He worked hard all his life y'know. When he was only twelve, he told me, he began work bringing turf into the town and that sort of thing."

Jack Murphy stayed long enough in the Klondike to realize that there was going to be little in it for him, and eventually he made his way south to Leadville, Colorado, 10,000 feet high in the Rocky Mountains, where gold and silver had been mined from the 1860s. He had been preceded a few years earlier by another, though very different sort of Irishman, who was on 'a grand procession of one' across the United States. According to Oscar Wilde himself, his stay in Leadville was one of the high points of his American adventure. It was there he claims to have read a sign over the piano in The Casino: "Please don't shoot the pianist; he is doing his best."

When asked if he found the miners to be a rough and ready lot, Oscar replied: "Ready, but not rough. They were polished and refined compared with the people I met in larger cities farther East ... There is little chance for roughness. The revolver is their book of etiquette. This teaches lessons that are not forgotten."

Wilde visited the silver mines and impressed the miners – so he claimed – with his ability to drink whiskey after whiskey. Later he lectured to them about the 16th century sculptor and silversmith, Benvenuto Cellini. "I was reproved by my hearers for not having brought him with me. I explained that he had been dead for some little time which elicited the inquiry, 'Who shot him?'"

Whatever about Oscar's rather amusing views of the Leadville miners being polished and refined, it is a fact that life in the mining town was rough and ready at the time, and not much different when Jack Murphy arrived fifteen years later. According to the records in the Denver Public Library, he was only one of a score or so of John or Jack Murphys working in the mines there in the late 1890s. And whether or not he was one of the gun-toting miners of the kind described by Mr. Wilde in the 1880s, Jack certainly did have to defend himself from the rough and ready types with his fists on at least one occasion.

This was at a place called Cripple Creek where he had been appointed foreman because of his dependability and his capacity for hard work. It seems a Mexican objected to some command or other issued by Murphy and there was a fight. Jack delighted in telling how it lasted the best part of a day as they slugged it up and down the creek. Jack, of course, emerged the victor and he had the respect of everyone afterwards. But however well Jack

Murphy defended himself with his fists, he could not avoid becoming a victim of one of the many hazards of mining work, resulting along the way, in the loss of a finger.

He did much better in Leadville than he did in the Klondike, it seems, and when he had put away enough money, he headed back east. Some time during this period he met a young Irish woman named Anna Agnes Fanning, and he married her. She had emigrated to the United States with her family some years earlier from near Roscrea in Co. Tipperary.

Some of the people in the Hollymount area of Co. Mayo said she was a young widow with lots of money and that she had a child named Lizzie. Mary Cassidy says that Mrs. Murphy told her one day that some locals were even putting it about that she had married 'a black' and that he had lots of money!

"When they moved into Mount Jennings House they had Mass there," Mary said, "and Fr. Begley, the parish priest was there. When he came to the house Mrs. Murphy answered the door. He asked, 'Is Mrs. Murphy in?' She said, 'I'm Mrs. Murphy.' He didn't believe her, and she said, 'Well, I am.' 'You look very young to me,' he said. 'Weren't you married before in America.' 'I was no such thing,' she said. I'm sure she was very fit for him. Anyway, he believed her. She told me that she was married very young and that she was just twenty when Lizzie (the eldest of the Murphy children) was born. Her father, she said, died when she was only fourteen and her mother then went to America. There was a big farmer near where they lived in Tipperary, and her mother thought that if she got a bit of money, maybe she could marry into this farm. But she met Jack Murphy and that finished her with the farmer at home. The Murphys would tell you everything, and there was nothing they would deny at all."

The newly-married couple returned to Ireland in 1901. For the best part of two years they lived in Ardroe, Claremorris, where Delia was born. She was baptised at Kilcolman Parish Church, and according to Mary Cassidy, Delia Hanley, who became Mrs. Clarke later, 'stood for Delia' at her baptism. Later they lived for a short time in Cloondinnaire before moving into Mount Jennings House.

II

'Children & chicken must be always pickin'

Growing up in Hollymount, Delia heard stories about Mayo's historic past from house visitors to Mount Jennings and from one of her favourite people in the village, the Tailor Mooney. The old people spoke about the glorious past when there were ten ancient churches and eleven Norman castles in the area, and of more recent sadder events, like the Great Famine of the late 1840s, when an estimated 25-30% of the population of Mayo were lost either through hunger or sickness. They would have told her, too, about great Mayo men like Michael Davitt, who founded the National Land League in 1879, James Daly, who organised a protest meeting over demands for rent arrears near Ballindine, not far from Hollymount, and Fr. John O'Malley, parish priest of Kilmolara, who suggested the use of the word 'boycotting' because the local people could pronounce it more easily than 'ostracisation'.

Writing in *Mayo* about the land war period in Ireland, Bernard O'Hara said that almost half of what were termed 'agrarian outrages' (maiming of cattle, destruction of property, wounding and even killing of land agents, landlords, and those who were considered 'land grabbers') in the early 1880s, occurred in Mayo, Kerry, and west Galway. By 1882, the fight for the land was virtually won, although various later land acts increased the pace and scope of the transfer of ownership from landlord to tenant.

The period between the death of Charles Stewart Parnell, in 1891 and World War I, was one of ferment and of fundamental change in Irish culture and politics. The Liberal Chief Secretary for Ireland, Augustine Birrell, said he began to see the developments in Irish literature and drama as having even more significance than the material contained in the RIC's (Royal Irish Constabulary) monthly reports. The activities of the intelligentsia were seen as having greater importance than the actions of politicians and the small group of so-called 'agitators'.

John Redmond, leader of the Irish Parliamentary Party, represented the tenants at the 1902 Land Conference, and this resulted in the 'Wyndham Act' of 1903, which arranged for the sale of entire estates to the occupying tenantry. Money was advanced by the state on very easy terms – repayable over sixty–eight and a half years at three and a quarter per cent, and landlords were further tempted by a special bonus payment from the state on each sale.

Coinciding with the general disillusionment with politics following the Parnell split in the early 1890s was the 'literary movement' of people like W.B. Yeats, Lady Gregory, Douglas Hyde, J.M. Synge, and others, whose poetic, romantic vision for Ireland fuelled the growing nationalist movement where ideals counted far more than votes. The literary revival and the rapid growth of the Gaelic League from its foundation in 1893, brought about a widespread interest in the Irish language, and caught hold of the popular imagination. Political groups who were influenced by the Gaelic League included, Sinn Féin, the IRB, and James Connolly's socialist movement.

This was the world Jack Murphy's young family grew up in, an Irish-Ireland where Home Rule was rejected and the aim was the abolition of the illegal Act of Union of 1800.

The Murphys' first daughter, Lizzie, was a year and nine months old when Delia was born, on 16th February 1902. Jack Murphy had been looking out for a property to buy at the time, and when an opportunity presented itself of purchasing Mount Jennings House and a portion of the estate around it, he jumped at it. He paid Charles Benjamin Jenings £1,750 for the dwelling and 134 acres, 2 roods of good farmland.

A local man said that the Jeningses were 'jumpers', and he explained what it meant: "That word comes from the Irish - *d'iompaigh siad ina bProtastúnaigh* (they turned Protestant). And they say that's why they dropped an 'n' from the name after that, y'know? Because all the Jenningses in Mayo are Catholics."

The other Murphy children in order of birth were: Paddy (1903), Laura (1904), Mary, who was known as 'Baby' (1913), Helen, known as 'Nell' (1915), Angela (1916) and Teresa, known as 'Tess' (1918). Mrs Murphy had a number of miscarriages and gave birth to other children who died at birth or in early infancy. Nell died in her teens following an operation.

Delia loved her Mount Jennings House, a beautiful spacious home, and was forever flitting about from room to room, upstairs, downstairs, and down to the basement where the kitchen was, "lookin' for excitement" was how Mary Cassidy put it. "She was that way when she was a youngster, and the same way when I met her later on in the thirties. Always on the go."

Mount Jennings was a large period two-storey house with a basement, of Georgian design, built in the early 1800s. It was the type of house only the more wealthy could afford, and the previous owners, the Jenings family, were of the minor gentry. The front entrance was through a high panelled door which had a fanlight above it. There was a chandelier in the hallway, and the coved ceiling had an elaborately decorated centrepiece. At the end of the hall was a large double door which was set into an archway. Behind this was the staircase made of mahogany. To the right of the hall was the sitting room with another room off it, which might at one time have been used as a study. To the left of the hall was the living room which the Murphys also used as the dining room. The bedrooms were all on the second floor. There was also a small room upstairs which the children used as a spare room. The servants' living quarters were in the basement. Mary Cassidy did all the cooking and washing there.

"It was a beautiful house with the finest of furniture," she said. "There was a room for everybody. There was Lizzie's room, and Mary's room, and Angela's room, and Tess's room. Then in the cellar there was a store room, Mick's room, Johnny's room, Jimmy's room, and a breakfast room. Every room in the house had a name."

At the rear of the house there was a large enclosed orchard surrounded by high walls. The main entrance was through a gateway and there were a number of smaller side entrances. Outside the orchard walls there was an apple store. As well as the stables and a barn, there were kennels in which, for several years, the Murphys kept the beagles of the South Mayo Hunt. All around the grounds were trees large and small. Oriental trees and shrubs lined the driveway; the remainder were Elms, Oaks, Ash, Sycamore, Beech, and Chestnut. The Dawn Chorus was a deafening cacophony of querulous crows, chirping sparrows, and a myriad of other kinds of small birds.

Delia described herself as the Murphys' harum-scarum daughter and said that as a child she was always the odd one out, always in trouble. Throughout her life, she would say, she had "her own troublesome and romantic self to deal with". She was always quite open about herself with friends and acquaintances, always ready to laugh at her *faux pas* and childish rebelliousness. It was all due to the fact that she was high-spirited and fierce-tempered. Delia laughingly recalled that her father once told her, "You're capable of anything from pitch-and-toss to manslaughter." She was regularly in trouble over her romantic attitude towards the Travellers, and with one of them in particular. He was Tom Maughan, to whom she owed a lot, she said, because he stirred up in her a great fondness for 'the ballads'. She loved to tell how she used to sit around 'the tinkers' camp fires at Featherbed Lane, a few hundred yards from the Mount Jennings House, and listen to them "sing like blackbirds".

This caused her parents a few headaches and heartaches. The people of the parish, she said, forever talked about "the rebellious Murphy girl, the one who mixes with the tinkers". Featherbed Lane ran along the edge of the Murphy farm and got its name from all the discarded mattresses the Travellers left behind them when they moved on. "I believe bedlam was the word for the noise coming out of Featherbed Lane at times," says Delia's nephew, Leo Cullen, "but it never worried Mr. Murphy."

Throughout her life Delia spoke with great delight and affection of Tom Maughan, one of those who had nothing yet everything, she would say. "Perhaps that is why this tinker's brat – for that is what he was – became my childhood sweetheart. His clothes were ragged and torn, yet to me he was a prince, and his mother's raw dough suppers were a delicacy that make me smack my lips to this day."

She recalls how they first met. 'The tinkers' were camped once again on Featherbed lane. "I well remember the day I was on my way to school when a huge tinker woman stuck her tousled head out from the back of a caravan and yelled, 'Delia Murphy, come here.' I turned and saw her coming towards me, pushing a small boy ahead of her. 'Here,' she said. 'Let you take Tom Maughan by the hand and bring him with you to school. That way he'll know what to do when he gets there.' I did as she told me."

This was an early instance of the rebellious Delia doing her own thing – even if it meant running foul of the neighbours' attitude to the Travellers – and ignoring the consequences. "People said I must not mix with the tinkers," she said. "But that was of no importance to me and as well it wasn't. Except for me, the daughter of a well-to-do farmer, Tom Maughan was friendless at school. Such snobbery in the hearts of young children! I never shared their snobbery, then or since. Ever since then I have always tried to make rules elastic, and a smile, I discovered early in life, shuts many a blind eye."

She readily admitted that she was her own greatest challenge, and that she was unruly. "I was a handful," she confessed. But even when she was not making trouble for herself, Delia could still run foul of her parents. When she was about eight or nine she had a pet dog called Captain, an Irish Red Setter. One day she said, "If only he could talk back to me and tell me what he's thinking about."

Her mother was listening to her, her face covered in suds from the washing. She gave Delia a clip on the ear and the dog moved towards Mrs. Murphy, putting both paws on her shoulders and growling. Her mother was scared out of her wits, and told her husband about it when he came home. Delia did not realize that her mother was pregnant. That night J.P. took out a gun and whistled the dog outside the house and shot it. Delia was very upset, and for the rest of her life she never allowed herself to grow fond of a pet.

She frequently told stories about local people which showed

26

their uniqueness and their individuality. One story she related to Dr. Ivor Browne, a psychiatrist, who was to marry her youngest daughter, Orla, concerned an old lady near Hollymount who was very poor and had only one sow. Ivor chuckled as he remembered Delia's telling of the story, and how she reproduced the old lady's pronunciation of the word, 'where', which was pronounced with an *f* (fwhere): "The sow got out one day," Delia said, "and ate all a neighbour's cabbages, and the neighbour was furious. She came in to complain to the old lady who listened and then responded: 'My sow she goes fwhere she likes; she don't get invited nofwhere.'"

"That sort of story delighted Delia," Ivor said, "and she loved that sort of independence."

Delia went to school for the first time on 8th April, 1906, shortly after her fourth birthday. She was enrolled at Gortskehi National School, a few hundred yards across the fields from Mount Jennings House. "I used often get my feet wet crossing those same fields," she recalled, "and we had to take a sod or two of turf with us under our arms for the school-teacher's fire. You would always have to make sure the turf was dry no matter what happened to yourself on your way through wet fields in rainy weather."

She was to remain at Gortskehi N.S. until her transfer to the grey-stone oblong-shaped Roundfort National School late in 1912. According to the records at Gortskehi N.S. she was twice struck off the register, first on 31st October, 1908, when she was in High Infants, being re-admitted three days later on 3rd November, and again, on 6th December, 1912, four days before her transfer to Roundstone N.S. Yet the Gortskehi register shows her being re-admitted a second time on 6th August, 1914. That date is strange since children should have been on their summer holidays then.

We know from Delia herself that the reason she was transferred to Roundfort was that a teacher there, Miss Sweeney, was a good musician and Delia's parents were keen that their daughter should be encouraged to develop her musical talents. But the real puzzle is why was she re-admitted a second time to Gortskehi N.S. Could it have had anything to do with what Delia used to refer to as "her own troublesome self"?

She admitted herself, "As a student discipline went against the grain!" Her general attendance record over the years was not good either, and perhaps it is because of this she was kept in fifth standard for two years – 1915 and again in 1916.

The school register even shows that she spent another thirteen days in sixth standard in 1917. Delia was fifteen years old then. She said, however, that she had one thing to thank the schoolmaster for – which teacher, she did not say – and that was, that he taught her "to distinguish between verse and rubbishy rhyme". We get an insight into how Delia's mind worked in a statement she made later in her life about her schooldays in Co. Mayo.

"Like so many other children we were forbidden to speak Irish in school, but at playtime, or on our way home from school, we used to break into our native song. And as well we did, because much of the spoken beauty of our land, its romantic fantasies and spellbinding fairy tales, would have been lost for ever if we'd all been good little boys and girls." Imagination, it has been noted, is the prime agent of all human perception, and whatever the truth or accuracy of what Delia says about what was forbidden her as a child, she certainly seems to have carried a torch for the underdog throughout her life, and revealed indeed a great deal of imagination and more than just a modicum of feistiness in bringing the ballads to a wider Irish public at home and abroad.

Mrs. Margaret Doherty of Islandmoor near Kilmaine, Co. Mayo, remembered Delia with a great deal of affection. They were at school together, and Delia was popular with the teachers. Even then Delia had 'a low tone' and they both sang 'seconds' in the choir. She recalls Mrs. Murphy asking the two of them to sing some of the Benediction hymns for her and when they failed to sing one of them through to the end she remarked that, with all the choir practices they were having, they should have had at least the *Tantum Ergo* off by heart.

The music teacher, Miss Sweeney, also taught Delia to play the piano and the harmonium, Mrs. Doherty said. The games they played were those played by children the world over. Skipping was very popular, and Delia was good at it. They also played Jack Stones, sitting in the middle of a dusty side road and then breaking off to play a game of 'hide and seek' through the fields and bushes, or around the 'plantation' that surrounded the Murphys' house.

Mrs. Doherty recalled the day that Delia arrived at the school with Tom Maughan in tow. "He accompanied her to school for a week," she said, "until he knew the way himself." Delia ignored the fact that Tom had a problem with lice, and even sat next to him in class because, she said, they were "childhood sweethearts". She admitted that it was probably because of the lice the other children shunned him.

A few years later the same Tom Maughan was the cause of yet another school transfer for Delia. Following another few months on the road, Tom and his travelling family were camped once again on Featherbed Lane. He had acquired a penny whistle. Meanwhile, Delia was the proud possessor of a melodeon worth about ten shillings. Tom wanted the squeeze-box. According to Delia , "he used all his tinker guile to get me to part with it. 'Sshh,' he would whisper on the way home from school. 'Can you hear my magic whistle? Just play a tune on this and you gets any wish you wants.' One day he held his hand over the tattered pocket of his jacket. We stopped and listened, but there wasn't a sound. 'You can only play it after midnight,' Tom went on. 'This is what we'll do. I'll trade you my whistle for your melodeon. Not tonight – tomorrow, because that's the lucky day.'"

The following night Delia crept down to the Travellers' camp to make the swap. "Don't attempt to blow it until after midnight," Tom warned. "I was afraid it would take wing," said Delia, "and I held it tight in my hand. I crept home again and hid the whistle under my pillow."

Tom had told her: "When the two hands meet at the top of the clock, then you can play it." Just as the clock struck midnight she took the whistle out from under the pillow and blew. Nothing. The whistle was broken. "A piece of wood was missing," Delia recalled.

Next day one of Mr. Murphy's best milch cows took sick and died. The vet was called for and the cause of the trouble was discovered when he found a piece of the melodeon in the animal's

stomach. "Stamped on it," said Delia, "was, 'Made in Germany'."
Tom Maughan had taken the melodeon apart to see what made
the sound. Then he threw the pieces over the hedge into the field
where Mr. Murphy's cows were.

Mary Cassidy heard the story of the melodeon from Delia, too,
but there was no mention of Tom Maughan. According to Mary,
Delia had saved the few shillings for the instrument but was afraid
to bring it into the house. "So she hid it abroad in the field and
the cow ate it."

"My father decided it was time to take drastic steps," said Delia.
"Not only had I contracted lice from the tinker boy, but now his
prize cow, the one he had proudly shown at the fairs, was dead. He
packed me off to the Presentation Convent in Tuam as a boarder."

Delia and her older sister, Lizzie, shared a room at St. Joseph's
Presentation Convent with another girl and a young music
teacher, a Miss Morris from Headford, Co. Galway who joined the
community a few years later and took the religious name, Fursey.

In 1986 when she was ninety-two, Sr. Fursey recalled in some
detail, and with great affection, her memories of the schoolgirl,
Delia: "She must have been about fourteen or fifteen in 1916
when I first knew her as a boarder at St. John's, a building which
was part of the Presentation Convent. It faced the Cathedral Road
and was a National School one time, with some rooms converted
into a dormitory for the boarders. I was a past-pupil myself and I
entered the convent in 1920. We were in a room off the main dormitory, and myself and the girls were very pally."

Sr. Fursey was also anxious to let people know that she had
taught the rudiments of Gaelic football to the renowned Galway
footballers, Frankie Stockwell and Seán Purcell, when they were
mere youngsters!

She taught singing, piano, and violin, and Delia was one of her
favourite pupils. "She often sat at the end of my bed and sang and
sang. We'd talk music and sing some more. Delia had the loveli-
est smile. She was a most pleasant girl and I always liked to see
her coming into the room. She loved music. It was like she had-
n't really grown up at all. She was very popular with all the girls."
She said that Lizzie was a different sort, much quieter, smiled and

joined in, but she hadn't the same taste in music as Delia. Sr. Fursey often played the piano for the boarders at recreation time. She herself was more like one of the boarders than a member of staff.

She remembered that the young Delia sang songs like *Carrigdoun* and *Home, Sweet Home*, songs that were popular at the time. She took piano lessons, but not violin. "I did a lot of concerts with the group I was teaching music to, and others, too. These were concerts to pass the time for the nuns and the school. Delia was terrific on stage, especially as a comic. We did a lot of Stephen Foster's songs, and in one of our concerts Delia sang *Poor Old Joe*. She blackened her face for the part, and it didn't bother her in the least. She sang *Way down upon the Swanee River*. We did comic songs and duets and she took down the house. Whatever had to be done she did it. She was at home on the stage."

Sr. Fursey recalled seeing Delia taking off her stockings in her room one time, and she noticed a scar on her leg. She asked her what happened. Delia said that when she was a child, they were cutting the hay and she rushed out into the field and ran against the scythe. However, Delia who always had at least two versions of every story gave the tamer version to Sr. Fursey out of schoolgirl cautiousness, perhaps, not wishing to portray herself in a bad light. The true account of what actually happened is a lot nastier.

About a year before her move to Tuam, she remembers her younger brother, Patrick, going with her to the orchard for apples. "I'll strike the tree and you'll catch the apples," he said to Delia, "and get me the whetstone, too."

"Get it yourself! What did God give you legs for?" was Delia's brusque response.

"No, you'll get it," said Patrick.

"No," said Delia of the uncertain temper, "you'll get it." And she picked up a billhook.

"I don't want that," Patrick said.

"No, but you're goin' to get it," she said, and made a drive at him with the implement. But Patrick had grabbed a scythe lying nearby and made a swing at Delia, catching her on the leg with the razor-sharp blade.

"It cut through sinew and muscle in my leg," Delia said, "and to this day the scar, livid on cold days, is there." She even said that the shock of it caused her mother to have a miscarriage. According to Delia, as a result of the injury from the scythe, she herself was in bed for two months or more. "In my nightmares I saw the billhook cut off Patrick's head. I swore then that I would never lose my temper like that again."

At the Presentation Convent the junior boarders had Mass every morning at 8 o'clock. They walked in pairs in an orderly fashion from St. John's to the convent chapel. Sr. Fursey recalled the story about a Miss Kelly who had worked in France for a number of years, and who had a knowledge of making the altar breads. She had been recommended by nuns in Dublin, and helped start that work in the convent in Tuam.

Miss Kelly stayed in St. John's House, too, and had charge of the juniors to make sure they got to Mass in time. Delia, like all the other girls, was well aware of the fact that it would be a serious thing to miss attending Mass. Miss Kelly was a prim and proper sort of woman and the girls used to make little comic verses about her. One of these pieces had two lines which went:

At the last seat in the chapel, Miss Kelly sits in state,
With her eye on the watch-out for the girls who come in late.

"I used to share their little secrets and I laughed at it," Sr. Fursey said. "I might even have given them a hand at it! Anyway, I was in the music room one day and Delia burst in, her face a white as a sheet."

"Oh," she exclaimed, "the head nun has demanded that poem whoever it was that told her. Will we tear it up, or what will we do?"

"I said not to because there was nothing in the poem that anyone could be ashamed of. Nothing. Do not tear it up. Hand her that poem."

"Oh, will I be killed?" asked Delia breathlessly.

"I said there's nothing to be ashamed of. It's all fun. Anyone who would see anything wrong in it would have very strange minds. Hand it up to Sr. Gertrude and watch her face."

Delia did as she was told, and after a while she returned, smiling all over.

"I asked her what the Sister Superior said when she had read it."

"She handed it back to us," said Delia, "and she said, 'There's nothing in that at all that anyone could be offended with. In fact, it's very smart.'"

"I knew Sister Superior had a sense of humour," said Sr. Fursey.

And what was Sr. Fursey's opinion of the young Delia Murphy's singing voice? "There was nothing extraordinary in her voice at all, but she used it to the full." There was just one note of regret in her voice as she added, "But she never came back to the school and I would have been delighted to see her again. I never did."

When Delia was still a boarder in Tuam, the chaplain asked her one day to sing a song for him. She replied that she did not know any. He said, "None at all?" Delia replied less than candidly, "I don't know any songs at all, Father. None at all." She said the lie nearly choked her.

Years later when she had gained notoriety as a singer she sang at a concert in Mayo. "And who was there but the Archbishop of Tuam, the same young chaplain from my school days at the Presentation Convent. I had to confess to him that I was a terrible liar."

During holiday time at Mount Jennings Delia had time to herself to indulge in all the fantasies of childhood. One of her favourite past-times was to go visiting with the neighbours round about. One of those she spent a lot of time with was Mooney the Tailor. "I used to sit on the table and listen to him talking," she said. "And there I heard all the lore of the world. He was a good musician, too."

According to local man, Pac Hereward, Mooney knew the history of the landlords and evictions and 'the Big House'. "He was the one who had all the folklore and all the stories about the place, the suppression of the language, the radical teachers and the radical thinkers. Delia spent a lot of time there."

From all accounts it would seem that Delia was a happy and contented girl at Tuam's Presentation Convent. However, after a year or so her father and mother decided to send her for the remaining years of her secondary education to the prestigious

Dominican College, Eccles Street, Dublin. What the reason for this change was is not clear.

Perhaps the Murphys felt that here was where she would be made into 'a young lady', mixing with girls from some of Ireland's wealthiest and established families. Maybe they hoped that some of their refinement would rub off on their much-loved but undisciplined daughter. "I was sent to the Dominicans," Delia said, "to learn discipline and to be taught to read and think. But they couldn't break my spirit. I missed so much. Forever I was giggling, diddling and fiddling. The tunes Tom Maughan had taught me buzzed in my head instead of prayers as I walked the stone corridors of the convent to early morning Mass. Time and time again the sisters warned and scolded me for talking on the way to breakfast when there was a rule of silence. I was always starving at breakfast time."

She joined the college choir under the renowned Dr. John Larchet. "I was smaller than most of the girls and I was put at the back of the choir. I believed I had the finest voice in the world, and I wasn't afraid to sing out loud and lustily. I couldn't believe my ears when one day the choirmaster bawled out, 'You in the back row! Out, out, out! Yes, you. That girl there at the back.' The girl next to me nudged me in the ribs. 'It's you. He means you.' And as I made my exit he announced in front of everyone, 'You've a voice like a crow'. Of course, there was another girl from Co. Mayo in that same choir a couple of years earlier who was the apple of the music director's eye. She became one of my dearest friends when she had gained world renown as a great opera singer. Margaret Burke Sheridan was her name. And later, too, I became friends with Ireland's greatest tenor ever, the famous Count John McCormack. I mightn't have been a great classical singer, but those two were my friends."

The Dominican College Eccles Street published a Year-Book called, *The Lanthorn* which contained photographs and articles on the year's activities. The issue for the year 1919 shows seventeen year-old Delia among fifty-five girls in the Senior Debating Class. Delia was never stuck for words, and one wonders what her contributions might have been like in the cut and thrust of debating. She would probably have put forward a few unorthodox opinions and played it to some extent for laughs, if not for the shock effect.

The year-book reported that Delia was a member of the Sodality of Mary and had recently been admitted to the Sodality of the Sacred Heart. Perhaps she was accommodating herself to the 'discipline' and ethos of the College and learning that 'belonging' to such worthy religious groups helped her get along better and won her valuable points in the end-of-year progress reports.

She admits herself that she went overboard somewhat in her valiant efforts to 'fit in'. "Whatever made me put my hand up, when five hundred other girls had sense enough not to move a muscle, I'll never know. We had regular talks about the great work of Irish nuns in 'the foreign missions'. Well, a number of visiting Dominican nuns from 'the missions' came to the college one day and told us about their work in the mission fields and leper colonies. They finished their talk and said they were looking for postulants – recruits to join the nuns, you know. I stepped forward. At six o'clock that evening one of the visiting nuns called me to her cell, and after hearing me repeat my desire to help, she handed me a pen, notepaper, envelope, and a stamp. She stood over me as I wrote: 'Dear Dad, this is to say good-bye. I'm going to the leper islands to help those poor sick people who are covered in sores. ...'"

Mr. Murphy was not impressed. Delia laughed as she continued the story. "No sooner had he read the letter than he came storming up to Dublin, arriving at the convent in the early hours of the morning. He told me later how he arrived just as the lights were going on for matins. How he must have frightened the little lay sister who opened the door to his angry knocking. There he was, this giant of a man with thick black hair, and shouting, 'Don't Mr. Murphy me! Get my daughter, Delia, right now.'

"I was busy scrubbing my nails when the Reverend Mother told me my father was waiting to see me. I rushed into the office, tears in my eyes at the thought of seeing him in the middle of term. I knew then I could never say good-bye. I wanted desperately not to go to the leper isles. I'd never heard him use such language. So strong, and with so many nuns within earshot. 'I'll knock the soulcase out of you,' he roared. 'They're full of sores, are they? And you are going to help them! Over my dead body.'"

Delia was in floods of tears and rushed into his arms. Very quickly Jack Murphy's anger subsided. "I knew I was safe, and he knew that his dear daughter would never leave for the mission islands. But it had been close," Delia laughed. "In another day or two maybe, I would have been whisked away to become a postulant, destined for a life among the lepers."

Father and daughter then went out for breakfast. It was a real treat for Delia and a welcome change from plain convent fare. "But he bawled me out good and proper," she said. "And he warned me that my mother would tan my hide if I ever mentioned lepers again. Then we returned to the convent. There he told Reverend Mother: 'Don't ever let me hear any more talk about the missions or lepers.' And that was end of any daft ideas I might have had about becoming a nun. Some nun I would have made."

In the 1918 issue of *The Lanthorn,* the Junior Grade Intermediate Examination results for that year are given. Delia is listed as having passed in English, French, History and Historical Geography, Arithmetic, Algebra, Commercial Course, Experimental Science and Drawing (first year's course). Interestingly enough, Irish is not listed. She was actively engaged in games, debates, and sodality activities, and if she gave any thought at all to her future, there were plenty of articles in *The Lanthorn* to guide her. One wonders what she would have had to say about an article that appeared in an edition a few years earlier, entitled, "What shall we do with our girls?" Under a sub-head were listed job areas where there were "openings for girls": the Civil Service, the banks ("but influence is important here, not competition"), teaching, drill mistress, nursing, instructresses in poultry-keeping.

In her Middle Grade Intermediate Examination in 1919, Delia is listed as having passed in English, Arithmetic, Algebra, Irish, French, and Hygiene (third year's course). She passed in her Senior Grade in the same subjects the following year. Delia passed her National University of Ireland Matriculation Examination that autumn and she gained entry to University College Galway. She was eighteen years of age.

Bríd Ní Bhroin was in Second Year Commerce at UCG when Delia arrived in 1920 and they met shortly afterwards. She was impressed with Delia's appearance and manner right from the start.

"She was very attractive and great fun at hoolies and sing-songs. She was a very fine singer even then. I remember she sang all sorts of ballads and mostly light songs. She taught me one of them. I think it was called, *Under the Lilac*. The words went something like this: 'Under the lilac he smoked a cigar, smoked a cigar.' There's a great deal of repetition, a sad jokey kind of song, and it ends up by the romance being a complete fiasco. Part of it went: 'He told her he loved her, but Oh, how he lied, Oh, how he lied. And he went to hell, and oh how he fried,' etc., 'And she went to heaven and flip-flop she flied,' and so on. She had a great store of songs and taught them to anyone who wanted to learn them. She was great company and very generous, very open."

Delia stayed for a while in some of the hotels in Galway and also at the house of a friend of her father's. But for most of her time at UCG she stayed in digs at 10 Dominick Street. Bríd was there many times for hoolies. "It was famous for parties," she said. "Everyone had to do a party piece on these occasions, and she was always a star turn. I stayed there one year myself, and I recall someone telling me that it was there Delia met her future husband, Tom Kiernan. He was staying in the same building and heard the sounds of partying and joined in. Delia sang, of course, and I hear that it was then he fell in love with her."

Dr. Colm Kiernan, Delia's only son, has a different account of their first meeting. "My father did some part-time lecturing at UCG, and my mother came to a birthday party at the place where he was staying, and she wanted to sing. Well, my father was very good with the piano and the violin, so he played for her while she sang and then they realised that he was the teacher and she was the student and they had that in common, too, because they were both interested in the subject that he was teaching – economics."

But whichever occasion it was, Delia's own account of her meeting with Tom Kiernan was always told with great relish, and she gives yet another location and an entirely different set of circumstances for that first meeting.

"My father was determined to make a scholar out of me, and at last it reached the stage where I had to bury my head in some stuffy books, in particular, one called, *British War Finance and the Consequences*. I'm never likely to forget it. T.J. Kiernan was the author! A fortnight before our exams Professor McBryan, I remember, told us to read Chapter Four. 'Mark it in the lining of your hats,' he warned us. But another girl beat me in the rush to get the book in the library, and kept it for a week. I like to think that was why she won the scholarship worth £50. I had the book for only a few hours and was soon sick to death of it. But the girl with the £50 threw a party for some of the students at one of Galway's best hotels.

"Soon after it had begun, the manageress came upstairs: 'There's a gentleman here who is the new inspector of taxes,' she announced, 'and he would like to meet the students causing all the row. Will I let him up to your party?' If he's good-looking and young, let him in, says I. And when he walked in through the door, I remember thinking to myself, I never thought they made our tax inspectors so young and handsome! Our eyes met across the room. He played the piano later, and I called out, 'I'll dance with the pianist.' I remember him saying, 'Indeed, and who'll play the piano?' I caught him by the arm and laughed: 'Let the devil play a tune, if you like. We'll dance.' And we did, for most of the night.

"When he told me his name, I said, 'If you're anything to that fella who wrote that book on British War Finances, I don't want to know you.' But next day we met up in church. He knelt beside me at Mass and walked me home. Casually he said, 'I expect I'll be marrying you soon.' He was right!"

They were indeed a contrasting pair. She was outgoing and effervescent; he was a quiet, shy man in his late twenties, and of an academic turn of mind. On the face of it they would appear to have absolutely nothing in common. But then, "Bliss it was in that dawn to be alive, But to be young was very Heaven!" They were indeed a most handsome young couple and romance quickly blossomed.

Tom Kiernan was born on 9 November, 1897, in Dublin, the son of a civil servant in the Land Commission who hailed from Co. Longford; his mother was a Hurley from Dublin. Following his secondary school studies at St. Mary's College, Rathmines, he went to University College Dublin. When he became a clerk to Inspector of Taxes at the Inland Revenue, in March 1916, Tom Kiernan was just eighteen years old. In late January, 1920, he was appointed Assistant Inspector of Taxes, and became Inspector of Taxes for Galway in November, 1922.

He had joined the Civil Service at a time when the Administration at Dublin Castle was in some crisis. Britain was coping not only with the Great War on the continent but with the Ulster situation *vis a vis* Home Rule, the existence of thousands of men in volunteer organisations North and South, the attendant threat of German interference, and all compounded by an inefficient and inept administration in Dublin Castle.

A few weeks after young Kiernan joined the Civil Service the Easter Rising occurred. Afterwards the Under Secretary for Ireland, Sir Matthew Nathan, asked all members of the civil service employed in Dublin to supply him with a full statement of their movements during the week of the Rising. Some ninety officials from various government departments who were members of 'the Sinn Féin Society' were arrested.

One of those apprehended prior to the Rising on suspicion, and charged with making notes and sketches of Lough Swilly – a defended harbour and protected district – was Pádraic Ó Conaire, a writer in Irish. His refusal to speak English, the authorities asserted afterwards, had nothing to do with his arrest. Delia said that she and her friends would spend hours chatting with Pádraic on a low wall in Eyre Square, Galway. He talked at length about his travels, and his stories had them enthralled.

"He reminded me of a leprechaun," Delia said, "sitting on the wall or by the canal bank with his shapeless hat on the back of his head, smoking his pipe and chewing sometimes on an apple. He gave me the plot for a play set in Jerusalem that would certainly have offended all the bishops in Ireland. He was full of ideas and talked with leisurely ease. 'If you don't use ideas,' he'd say, 'it doesn't matter. The important thing is to put the thought on the ether. Someone will use it later.' Until we learned better we used to take him back to our digs and feed him bread and cheese."

They must have made a curious pair as they wandered around Galway – the attractive, raven-haired young economics student, her head full of ballads and romantic ideas, and Ó Conaire, wandering master of traditional legends and stories. Delia claimed that he wrote poems to her. "And he'd tell me long, rambling stories of his days in the tinkers' camps. Ailled – my name spelled backwards and with an extra 'l' – was how he always wrote to me. 'One day,' he used to say, 'you'll write a book.' We would spend hours discussing titles. He said I reminded him of the lines from Francis Thompson's poem, *The Hound of Heaven*: 'Across the margents of the world I fled, and troubled the gold gateway of the stars.' How true that was to be!"

Delia also recalled hearing Pádraic's story of how he went to Liverpool University to take a paper in Irish. "He told me that he set the paper, answered it, corrected it, and earned a 100% mark!" Pádraic Ó Conaire was in his late thirties when Delia knew him, and she was not yet twenty.

"He's a man I'll always remember for the tunes he taught me, for in his heart he was a true musician."

She claims, too, to have spent time in Galway City's famous fishing village, the Claddagh, listening to the songs of its fiercely independent people, and adding several more ballads to her growing repertoire. And while Delia always made sure that a good story was never lost in the telling, we may have to take with a grain of salt her claim that she often went with the Claddagh fishermen in their boats. There was a tradition among fishermen that it was bad luck to bring a woman on board when going to sea.

And yet, Delia told Martin Walton, founder of the famous Waltons' Musical Instrument Galleries on North Frederick Street, Dublin, that while she was in Galway she had roamed the Claddagh and sailed with the fishermen in Galway Bay where they talked and sang in Irish. "In a short time she had acquired a repertoire of seafaring songs that she said would have satisfied a bosuns' reunion," Martin said. "Men like the Galway pilot, Tom Smith – who had sailed the seven seas and incredibly had brought back Irish songs from every port – taught her."

Bríd Ní Bhroin recalled the difficult times during the War of

Independence while she was in UCG. Everybody was for 'the movement' and many of her fellow students were 'involved'.

"Delia was one of those who would have been interested in it. I remember British soldiers coming into the Quad one day while a band was playing and lining up all the lads to get them to salute the flag. All of us women students were standing along the side of the quadrangle looking on, and we didn't know anything about standing to attention while the band played *God Save the Queen*, or anything like that. There was an English student who was doing a course at UCG at the time and she told us what we should do was to sit down. So I sat down while the anthem was being played, and some of us started to sing *The Soldiers Song*. Some of the students who had caps in their pockets took them out and put them on their heads. One of them who was a great friend of mine afterwards gave his to Professor Larkin. They were hauled off by the soldiers to a factory they had taken over. Nothing much was done, and next day they were back. They were great heroes, of course."

On her time off from college, Delia was happiest visiting with the neighbours and learning songs from people like The Tailor Mooney. Mike Killeen's family ran the local post office, a favourite visiting place for anyone who wanted to catch up with the latest news and gossip. He says the Murphys were all great sports.

"You could say the girls, Lizzie, Mary ('Baby'), Angela, and Laura were tom boys." On the farm there were men hired to do the work of planting and sowing oats, barley, and vegetables and when the sugar factory opened in Tuam, they planted beet. "Mulligan, Hughes, Henry and King worked on the farm. Jack Murphy himself worked as hard as the men. The Murphys had a ball alley at the house where people went every Sunday to play after dinner time. The orchard was an added attraction. Mrs. Murphy often gave the players a bag of apples, even feed them if they were at the house."

The Murphys' nearest neighbours were the Nolans, and old Mr. Nolan had nothing but praise for them. "If you ever wanted anything they'd give it to you. They had a big kitchen with a flag floor and they had country house dances there nearly every Sunday night. An accordion playing, set dances and step dancing. And they sang. I often heard Delia sing in the kitchen. I knew

Jack Murphy well, and he was a real gentleman. I used to help him out on the farm with the crops, and he had about sixty cattle and a hundred sheep. The son, Paddy, had no interest in the farm, and he went to the U.S."

But inevitably Delia had to face the mundane routine of student life. There were classes to attend and exams to do. When it came to studying, Delia readily admitted that she lacked discipline. In many ways she was still the schoolgirl student.

"One of the university professors heard me giggling in class one day and he said, 'You are making a braying noise which is the sound you would have if you crossed an ass with a bullock.'"

The 1921 issue of *The Lanthorn* reported that two Eccles Street past pupils, Bridie Gardiner and Delia Murphy, had passed their first year exams in UCG. In 1922 Delia was one of nine women and three men who were taking a Bachelor of Commerce Degree in second-year. Her subjects were English, French, Commercial Law, and Commercial Geography. The following year she was one of eight students who graduated with a Bachelor of Commerce Degree from UCG. Two of them got honours and Delia was one of the six who received a pass.

On the day of her conferring Delia participated in the students' traditional rowdy high jinks by way of letting off steam and celebrating the end of years of study. Bríd Uí Bhroin says that there was a long-established custom at UCG of students pelting each other with flour after the ceremony.

"I don't know where it came from, or how long it was the practice, but on degree day, when all the students emerged from the Aula Maxima after the conferring, all the others were waiting outside with bags of flour which they threw at the new graduates which, of course, destroyed the gowns which were on hire from Moons of Galway. They had to go back to them and be cleaned. And some of our own clothes, too, were pretty-well ruined by the flour."

As Delia's time in Galway came to an end, she could look back on an important period during which she had steadily built up her repertoire of songs and ballads and before long she would have the opportunity of showing her talents as a singer to a very different audience in the capital ciy of the British Empire.

III

London 'the golden years'

Following Dáil Éireann's ratification of the Treaty on 7th January 1922, the administration at Dublin Castle handed over the reins of power to the Provisional Irish Government. The setting up of an Irish exchequer was entrusted to an able young civil servant, Joseph Brennan, acting as the new Free State's first Comptroller and Auditor General, a title that did not represent his actual duties, which were those of a financial advisor and administrator. He had been given the task by Michael Collins a month after the ratification in acknowledgement of invaluable advice given when Collins was negotiating a settlement in London.

Tom Kiernan's appointment as Inspector of Taxes for Galway came ten months after the Treaty was passed in the Dáil. Around this time there were protests from people who did not get their tax forms in Irish, among them people from the Galway area, and Tom Kiernan would have passed on their complaints to the Chairman of the Revenue Commissioners, William O'Brien. His instructions were, "Tell them we're not running a branch of the Gaelic League here."

While Delia was still at UCG her father was contacted by the Inland Revenue regarding tax. According to Mary Cassidy, "He was stung for income tax because he had all this land, y'see. So Delia said to him, 'Papa, I know this man who might be able to help you get out of it.' She landed him up to Kiernan and Mr. Murphy put it to him that he might be able to help him with his returns."

Jack told Mary that when he saw Kiernan he said to himself, "Sure, this lad wouldn't get me out of anything."

"Dr. Kiernan was a small thin man, y'know," Mary remarked. "But he got him out of it alright." Delia would have enjoyed that – her boyfriend, the Inspector of Taxes for Galway helping her father, a man from his tax district who was behind in his payments. An opportunity of cocking a snook at the authorities would have appealed to her rebellious nature.

Many people inside and outside the civil service were deeply unsettled by the Treaty, of course, and for some it was a disaster. But most saw it as an opportunity, and the more nationally-minded among them set about learning Irish which was regarded as essential for advancement. However, Tom Kiernan was already reasonably proficient in the Irish language, and certainly by 1937, while he was Director of Programmes at Radio Éireann, he was sufficiently competent to be appointed extern examiner in economics, economic history and commerce, through the medium of Irish, to the National University of Ireland.

As regards Delia we have no details on what she did immediately after graduation but it appears that she became engaged to Tom Kiernan in late 1923 or early 1924. An engagement picture taken by Lafayettes, the photographers shows an extremely youthful couple. Neither set of parents was in favour of them getting married, and according to Delia's son, Colm, each had high expectations of their respective children. "They thought each was marrying beneath the other, so to speak. They were, no doubt, considered an unlikely pair," he says, "because they were somewhat at opposite polarities. My father intended doing a Ph.D. and perhaps at that time map out an academic career. It turned out instead that he was going into the diplomatic service. My mother didn't really have any aspirations for an academic career and therefore there was no possibility of a clash there. But she was interested in the social side of things – singing and entertainment, and it wasn't known then that she'd be outstandingly good at it. And so, although they were different people – one was city, one was country, one was intellectual, one was a singer – this was more of an advantage than a disadvantage in their case."

Mary Cassidy said that Delia's mother, too, was opposed to the match. "But her father was ragin', because as he said himself, he lost everything he had educating her, and now what had he to show for it. No, and the Kiernans didn't want her, and she didn't deny it at all. If they didn't want her, sure she wasn't the type to let it bother her."

All this is confirmed in a story Delia's sister-in-law, Eve Cullen tells. "Delia and her mother-in-law to be had some little falling out. 'I went out there,' Delia told me, 'and I took my diamond engagement ring off my finger, and I flung it out into the long grass in the orchard just to show her how little I cared.' Now, I'm a very practical person, and so I said, 'But Delia – your diamond ring! Was it found?' 'Oh, you needn't worry about that,' she said. 'On the way through town I stopped at Woolworth's and bought a ring and put it on my finger and put my engagement ring in my bag. I just wanted to make the gesture,' she said. And that was Delia – making gestures. And she knew how to make them."

In any event on the day Tom and Delia got married, neither family attended. Delia had just celebrated her twenty-second birthday. The following announcement appeared in the 1924 edition of *The Lanthorn*:

> *Kiernan and Murphy – February 27, 1924, at University Church, Stephen's Green (with Nuptial Mass), by Rev. J. O'Dea, Diocesan Secretary, St. Mary's, Galway, assisted by Rev. J. Sherwin, Thomas J. Kiernan, M.A., Inspector of Taxes, Galway, second son of Francis and Mrs. Kiernan, 123 Upper Rathmines, Dublin, to Delia Murphy, B.Comm., second daughter of John P. Murphy and Mrs. Murphy, Mount Jennings House, Hollymount, Co. Mayo.*

> *Mr. Thos. J. Kiernan, M.A., formerly Inspector of Taxes at Galway, and a well-known writer on economic subjects, has been appointed secretary to Mr. James MacNeill, Saorstát High Commissioner in London, in succession to Mr. P. McGilligan, T.D., now Minister of Industry and Commerce.*

When one looks at the charming engagement photo it is easy to imagine that they must have felt more than a pang of regret not to have had their parents and families present to share their joy and happiness.

In the first paragraph in *The Lanthorn* announcement, it wrongly states that Thomas J. Kiernan, M.A., is "Inspector of Taxes"; but in the second paragraph it states correctly that he was "formerly Inspector of Taxes", and had been appointed to London. He took up that appointment two months later, on 22 April, 1924.

Professor Denis Gwynn of University College Cork, a friend of Commissioner McNeill's, once asked him why he had chosen T.J. Kiernan as his secretary, and he replied that as a former member of the Indian Civil Service, he had developed a high opinion of capable young tax collectors, and Kiernan had started life as an inspector of taxes. His faith in Kiernan was well placed, as time would show.

These early years were full of incident as the new Free State government struggled to establish law and order following a bloody and destructive civil war, and to get the country's economy up and running again. On top of all that, the Army Mutiny and the Boundary Commission affair resulted in ministerial resignations. Then there was the revocation of Article 5 of the Treaty and the substantial waiving of the Free State share of the British National Debt. Meanwhile, the Shannon Electrification Scheme was launched under the new Minister for Industry and Commerce, Patrick McGilligan.

It was a very new and a different world in which Delia found herself in her new home at 93 Lewin Road, Streatham. The country girl from Mayo was now a wife who was expected to share her husband's job as a diplomat, entertaining distinguished guests at parties and receptions. When she announced to her UCG classmate on the train that she thought, in fact, that she might have found a position, she can hardly have imagined anything like the job she found herself doing in the capital city of the British Empire.

"Life in those early years was extremely hectic," says Colm Kiernan. "My father's work at the High Commission required him to do a lot of socialising, and he and my mother would attend lots of parties, and that would draw the attention of the Irish. He became a sort of focal point for the Irish in London at that time, because they never really had one before 1921. There was a party virtually every night."

Colm says that these were important years for his mother, too, because at those occasions where there were a lot of Irish present, she did what she liked doing most – singing songs at impromptu sessions around the piano. "She was finding an audience, learning what kinds of things they wanted to hear. They were chiefly exiles songs," he said.

Toward the end of their first year in London, in December 1924, the Kiernan's first child, Blanaid (Blon), was born. Delia was entering yet another new role, that of mother, one that would engage her fully for many years to come. Aisling Fionnuala (Nuala) was born in October 1928; Colm, in November 1931; and Orla, in July 1933.

"Orla and I had the same godmother," Colm said, "Lady someone or other, whose name I forget, who gave us each a silver christening cup." A photo taken 12 July '33 shows the week-old Orla, and another photo taken on the same occasion, includes his father's close friend, the Irish poet D.L. Kelleher who lived with the Kiernans, and his girlfriend, Hilda, whom he later married. Delia said that over the next few years she did most of her singing and composing in the kitchen or the nursery, and while it was a busy time for her husband, for her, family concerns predominated.

In addition to his duties at the High Commission Office, Tom Kiernan worked toward his Ph.D. at London University, and was the prime mover in setting up the National University of Ireland Club in the city. He soon showed his ability in helping to organise the Irish office and becoming acquainted with all useful Irish contacts in London. Because of this he conceived the idea of founding the NUI Club as a centre for its graduates who had gone to live in England.

The proposal was to establish 'a Dining Club for graduates of the National University of Ireland', and an announcement to this effect appeared in English and Irish papers in December 1928. But following a couple of dinner get-togethers, this notion was dropped and it was decided instead to go for a club with premises instead.

Visitors and guests in the early years included Augustine Birrell, former Chief Secretary for Ireland (invited to the club because of his part in the University Bill), Lady Gregory, Professor Stephen Gwynn, and Robin Flower, who brought the Irish literature of the Blasket Islanders, Peig Sayers and Tomás Ó Criomhthainn, to the notice of the world. Kate O'Brien was the club's first librarian. Sara Allgood and the Abbey Players appeared there, and W.B. Yeats and T.S. Eliot first met at a luncheon arranged by the club's manager, Ned Kennedy, an old Abbey actor.

In those early years, too, NUI Club members were entertained by distinguished visitors, including the music arranger and folksong collector, Herbert Hughes, and writers, Liam O'Flaherty, and Seán Ó Faoláin. Professor Stephen Gwynn attributed the success of the club to the perseverance and enthusiasm of Dr. Kiernan. Writing on the occasion of the club's silver jubilee celebrations, he said: "It has become one of the recognised institutions of the National University and an invaluable centre for Irish interests in London."

Of course, Delia enjoyed the social aspect of life in London. It was a break from housework at their home in Lewin Road, Streatham. "As a young mother of four the monotony of housework and nappies dragged while the songs I was to write and sing screamed inside my head to be unleashed."

She attended the NUI club regularly with her husband and was a frequent contributor at impromptu singing sessions there. "She found her métier there among the middling orders," Colm Kiernan says, "and developed her singing technique. To my knowledge she didn't sing on stage at this time."

Because of his work at the High Commission and at the NUI Club, Dr. Kiernan was a central figure for all things Irish in London, and many distinguished people from all walks of Irish life made their way to his door. The world-renowned tenor, John Count McCormack was to become a close friend; so, too, the composer, Sir Hamilton Harty, and Herbert Hughes. One of Delia's favourite photographs, which she kept prominently displayed in her living room down through the years, was one of John McCormack. It was signed, "To Musha, with love, John."

She told Billy Carter, a band leader in Dublin, the story behind the signature, when he visited her at her home on Elgin Road

Dublin in 1937. Carter noticed the photograph, which showed John McCormack standing over a little girl sitting on a stool at a grand piano, and he asked Delia about it. The occasion, according to Delia was a reception given by the Prince of Wales in London.

"My husband was there, too, and there were waiters going around with White Ladies, and Pink Ladies, and sherries, and champagne, and a man said to me, 'Would you like something to drink, Madame?' No thank you, says I. And this voice behind me said, 'Arrah do have a drink.' Musha then, says I, I won't. And with that he burst out laughing. This was my first introduction to John McCormack. From then on I was Musha to John."

That was not Delia's only nickname, because her husband always referred to her as Murphs, and she in turn called him Mac. "I called him Mac because, I told him, his family were originally Mac Thiarnáin, or McKiernan, but that they had dropped the Mac part of their name because they were too grand – pulling his leg, of course."

It was almost inevitable that somewhere, some time, Delia's talents as a singer would be recognised. Throughout her years in London, she met famous people from every walk of life, and not only at official High Commission functions, and at the NUI Club; the Kiernans received innumerable invitations to parties and social occasions all over the city. If there was a sing-song, Delia would often sing. All that was required therefore was to have someone from a record company present on one of these occasions and the rest would follow. And that is indeed what happened; but when, and exactly where, is difficult to say.

Delia herself gives two different accounts of how this came about. There are elements common to both versions – principally, that it happened in London and the same people are named. Version number one has it that John McCormack and the violinist, Fritz Kreisler were at a musical evening given by Herbert Hughes, and someone sang the beautiful Irish love song, *Úna Bhán*. "It was terrible," Delia said. "The world's worst."

After a polite round of applause, Kreisler, who had overheard Delia's comment, turned to her and said, "And how should it have been sung, Mrs. Kiernan?" The outspoken Delia never put a tooth in it. "In Co. Mayo we'd be thrown out for singing it like that," she declared bluntly. "Come now, Mrs. Kiernan, show us how it should be sung," coaxed Kreisler, and John McCormack who was standing nearby, overhearing what was being said, added his voice in persuading her to show how it should be done.

"Then and there," she said, "I demonstrated where the singer went wrong. I told them that the phrasing on the words, "Féach, a ghrá, cé acu b'fhearr den dá chomhairle," was all wrong, and showed them how it should have been sung, all in one breath. McCormack and Kreisler lavished praise on me for my singing." It was as a result of that effort she was introduced to a record company, she said.

In her second version the location is different and the singer of the song, *Úna Bhán*, is named. It was none other than John McCormack himself!

"I went to hear John McCormack at a recording session at the HMV studio on King's Road, Chelsea. When he'd finished singing, I said, John, that's awful! Hadn't I the nerve to put him right? But it wasn't his singing. That was as beautiful as ever, but the phrasing was all wrong. He hadn't the traditional *nyaah*. She went on to say that the HMV man who was in charge heard her singing and he was impressed.

"Come over to the studio in the morning," he told her, "and you'll make a recording." I sang him *The Spinning Wheel*, and as soon as it was released everyone in England and Ireland was singing it. It became a top pop, and the first of some four hundred I recorded."

If it happened as she tells it, then the sight of Delia Murphy trying to teach John McCormack to sing with the right *nyahh* would certainly have been something to see. McCormack never recorded the song, nor did he ever record any song in the Irish language. As for the HMV man telling her to pop round for a recording the next day, well, that need not be taken quite literally, of course, but the earliest reference we have for two of her early recordings, *The Spinning Wheel* and *Three Lovely Lassies*, on an HMV 10" 78rpm record, number IM646, 1939, we find that it had been previously issued in England as HMV BD1256. But were the recordings made in London or Dublin? All of the evidence seems to show that they were made in Dublin.

There is yet a third and more plausible account of where and when it all began for her. According to Leslie Thorn, HMV's man in Ireland from the mid-thirties, he was invited along to hear Delia singing at a party in Dublin early in 1937, and on the strength of her performance on that occasion, he offered her a recording deal. More about that later.

Among the famous people Delia claims she met in London was the writer, James Joyce. She says she could never figure out *Finnegan's Wake* or *Ulysses*, and so, one day, she said to Joyce, "Now, you'll tell me about it or you'll never get out of my house. So he read aloud many passages to me and suddenly shouted, 'Kiernan, I've got it! You mustn't read *Ulysses* like a book. There's music in it'." According to Delia Joyce went on to say that as you don't look for the composer's meaning in a Beethoven symphony, so you musn't look for logic or meaning in his (Joyce's) words.

Colm Kiernan told about the time James Joyce and his father were taking a stroll in London, and as they were passing a public toilet, Joyce asked to be excused for a moment, and went inside. Dr. Kiernan waited outside, and after a couple of minutes he heard yelling and screaming coming from inside the public toilet. He was very frightened, and wondered if Joyce was in trouble. Suddenly the noise ceased, and Joyce emerged shortly afterwards. "Ah, that's better," he said. Dr. Kiernan asked him what on earth was going on, and Joyce replied, "Oh, nothing. I just like to scream and yell a bit now and then. I feel much better afterwards."

The movie actor, Liam Redmond, a lifelong friend of the Kiernans, told of how Delia met the poet, William Butler Yeats, and how she put her foot in it. When her husband was Inspector of Taxes in Galway, he had helped Yeat's friend, Lady Gregory, with her tax affairs. She appointed him her executor. She invited the Kiernans to spend a weekend at her house in Coole Park in Co. Galway. Yeats was a house guest, a formidable figure who took himself and his work very seriously. Delia knew that she would have to be on her best behaviour.

"After dinner on Sunday night," said Liam, "they were sitting around, listening to the pearls of wisdom that fell from the lips of the great poet. When darkness descended, Yeats rose slowly from his seat and made his way to the bookcase. He searched among the vast volumes. 'At bedtime,' he said, 'I always find the need of a little Trollope to help me to go to sleep.' Well, it was too much for Delia. Her laugh was loud and raucous. 'God, Mr. Yeats,' says she, 'you're a howl!' Lady Gregory raised an imperious hand, 'To bed, child,' she said. 'To bed.'"

Delia often spoke about how she could never rid of herself of a childlike giddiness that would overtake her when she found herself – as she frequently did – in the presence of great men and women, some of whom were pompous and full of their own self-importance. Most people would have been cowed by them or at least would pretend to go along with the charade of deference imposed on them by convention . And while Delia, as the wife of a diplomat, did what was required of her on these occasions, there were times when it was too much for her. She certainly was not afraid of them; it was simply that she found their behaviour and that of their flunkies just plain silly.

"Delia was an extrovert," Liam Redmond said. "She liked people who had the same openness as herself, and they liked her. Women with social pretensions and prissy men didn't care for her. She just thought such people ridiculous and, typically, she would seek out someone who was less hidebound by convention with whom she would have a bit of 'craic'. If possible at all, she would start a sing-song, and soon she would have everyone around her singing along in the chorus……. She couldn't stand meanness, and she couldn't stand mean men. I remember there was a character in Radio Éireann who had a terrible reputation for meanness. Delia described him to me. 'Aw,' she sighed, I can't stand mean men. He wouldn't give you the itch for fear you'd have the comfort of scratchin' it.'"

Of course, there were some who thought she was not sophisticated enough for the role of a diplomat's wife; 'lacking in chic' was how one Cork woman, who met her at a gala evening in the city by the Lee, described her. Author and former Secretary at the Department of Posts and Telegraphs, Leon Ó Broin, said he often wondered at what an odd pair T.J. and Delia made. "I found him to be gentlemanly, courteous, and desperately discreet. He was a retiring, quiet man who smoked incessantly and, I would say, highly strung. He was very good-looking, almost effeminate; and she was handsome, too, but bustling, almost rough. I wondered how they fitted into the embassy scene abroad."

But appearances can be deceptive, and Delia proved to be a welcoming, generous hostess, and very well organised. Her husband was not all that keen on playing host and preferred to leave the entertaining largely to Delia. He found the tedious task of standing in line at receptions very difficult. Small talk did not come easily to him. Dr. Ivor Browne who got to know Delia well in the early 1950s when he was studying medicine in Dublin, said of her:

"She didn't tolerate humbug in anyone else. If someone was being dishonest in a human sense, she'd be likely to rip into them. She was well able for the entertaining side of diplomatic life and I could imagine her taking on anything. I could imagine, however, stuffy formal occasions being very trying for her, but then she could get a laugh out of those. She was totally unaware of any social or class distinction. She would particularly go towards any travelling people. I don't know whether in a lot of Irish people that that's in some way looking for the exotic, but she genuinely loved them. I just think the only thing she couldn't tolerate was boredom or being stifled in any way. She had an absolute need to be free."

At a reception in London in the early thirties Delia recalled seeing a stunning redhead in a green dress coming down the stairs. At the very same moment the Prince of Wales came up to her. She pointed to the redhead and said, "Isn't she a lovely-looking girl; with hair like that she must be Irish." The Prince replied, "She's probably somebody's dressmaker from Clerkenwell!" They laughed, and then had a long conversation, she said.

But, of course, as with other stories she liked to tell, she gives another version of what took place that evening, and one that is equally plausible. Impossible and improbable as it may seem to some, she says she did not know that the man who spoke to her was, in fact, the Prince of Wales, and treated him the same way she would anyone else.

The same conversation takes place, but then following HRH's remark, Delia says she walked off laughing. She adds that shortly afterwards her husband came up to her and said in an exasperated voice, "For God's sake, Delia, did you not know who you were talking to just now? That was the Prince of Wales! You can't turn your back on royalty like that."

Novelist Leo Cullen, son of Delia's sister, Angela, grew up in Tipperary, and although he never met Delia, he was very aware of his famous aunt. He used to visit the family home in Hollymount during the summer holidays and he got to know how the family viewed Delia and her husband.

"You see, she was married to 'Mac' Kiernan, and he was held a little bit in awe because of his status. And they knew the sort of person Delia was, and maybe people were afraid that, God, she could easily blot her copy book, that she could easily go over the top. There was always that fear; and she did, too. Well, there are stories about her, that she was quite rude on some occasions – or what some people regarded as being rude – in the embassies. There was the occasion when she was sitting in St. James' Palace in London. She got fed up with the carry-on, and she spat into the fire, and one of the porters came around with a golden spittoon and presented it to her and told her that she could use that, and she said: 'Get away, boy, it was far from spittoons I was reared.' Those were the kinds of stories that were told about her. You see, it was to do with her lyrical expression, because her expression was of a lyrical nature. She was a song-writer, and she was a singer, and she liked singing in concerts, and she liked being on stage. But she was completely curtailed in the situation in which she found herself; she was constricted. It had to burst out some place. She couldn't contain herself, I think. The workaday situation wouldn't have allowed her much outlet for singing. She wasn't on stage, and she wasn't getting the feed-back that she loved, I imagine. Anyone who is of a creative nature and has to forego it – it would have crippled them really, I'd imagine. So it was shown in her theatrical nature. She was always aware of herself."

Marni Buckley, one of Delia's most intimate friends in Smiths Falls, Ontario during the 1960s was afforded a remarkable insight into Delia's character. Delia was in the habit of visiting Marni after Sunday Mass and on one such occasion, when she noticed change on the breakfast table she said, "You know, Marni, when I see change like that it always reminds me of the time when we were in London and were invited to the Russian embassy. Everything was laid on. I think it was after the ballet or something. Gold trays with all kinds of drink, anything you wanted to drink. And once when the waiter came around with a tray, I put my empty glass on it. There was a lot of change on the tray and I scooped it up, much to the surprise of the waiter. The next day I looked in my bag and I wondered where all this money came from, and I realised what happened." Delia said that there must have been all of sixteen pounds in change. "What did you do with it?" Marni asked. "I didn't know what to do. I couldn't send it back," was the reply.

"You could never be quite sure what she was going to do," Marni went on. "She was masterful at hiding her emotions but never really let you know what she was thinking. She showed me some of her photographs when she was younger, and she showed me her lovely clothes. She drank a lot. Her drinking was only limited by the amount on hand, and it didn't matter what it was. Delia may have been her own worst enemy. She drank a lot after her husband died."

Marni said Delia knew everybody around the area; she helped them and they helped her. She never saw her angry. She said to her one time, "Delia, you always agree with me." And she said, "Well, now, Marni, and why would I be wantin' to make you feel bad?"

Marni was fascinated about two quite contrasting characteristics in Delia. "She took some of my clothes," Marni said, "and traded them off to farmers, and when she was going on a visit to Washington, she borrowed several of my hats. But then, on the other hand, if you admired anything of hers, she would tell you to take it, and would insist that you take it.

"She had great charm and enunciated beautifully and you can see that on her recordings. She had great dignity, but she could also trail her skirt in the manure. She'd say, 'Marni, I was at church and Dr. John Hogan was there, and there I was with shit on me boots and a rent in me dress.' You don't forget people like that. She could also speak the language of the labourer. I always felt she was banished up here because she didn't always behave most decorously."

One evening in London, Delia received an unexpected visit from her younger brother, Paddy. He had left home in 1920s, saying he was off to such-and-such a place and would see them later. The next thing anyone heard from him was when a letter came from America telling the family where he was and that he would be staying there.

Delia recalled their meeting: "Pat, you devil, me own sweet brother, where's the £20 you stole from me when you ran away?" Pat was not phased one little bit. "I'm sure sorry, Delia, that I had to borrow that dough, and here's the twenty pounds, and twenty more, and here's a hundred, and another hundred. I've made my fortune in America,"

"Thatchin' sky-scrapers, I suppose," laughed Delia. Paddy grabbed her, turning her round and round. "Yes," he said, and looking her up and down, observed, "The chassis's sure okay, but the clothes are goddamn awful!"

Keeping up the banter, Delia said, "Patrick Murphy, that's me best frock, and how dare you criticize it in your Yankee language. If it wasn't for the nightmares I had from that attack you made on me with the scythe, I'd tear into you."

In 1934 the famous American movie producer, Robert Flaherty, made his remarkable film documentary, *Man of Aran*. The studio shots were done in London and the Aranmen came to London and, of course, they met Delia. In her typically generous fashion, she arranged for some of them to stay with her in Streatham.

Ivor Browne recalls an amusing story Delia told him about the Aranmen. "They were very lonesome," she said, "and they were making this mash in the house over two or three days. The smell was very powerful, and they noticed this big policeman walking up and down. So they got a bit nervous. Anyway, he came back the next day and eventually he walked up to the door, and they thought the game was up. But he asked, 'Is the shtuff near ready?' He was a West of Ireland man, and he'd been waiting patiently. On another occasion one of the Aranmen – it may have been Pat Mullin– was in the London Underground, and he must have stood out in the Aran gear. A man came up to him and asked if he was a Boer. And Pat, thinking it was an insult, lashed out and levelled him."

Delia described another amusing incident involving another Irish policeman. "I was watching a man with a monkey playing a hurdy-gurdy on Shaftesbury Square, and this big Irish policeman came up to him, and I overheard him saying, 'With your tarrutherin' and your tarrantherin', your tin whistle, and your dirty foreign cat ... will you get the hell out of here.'"

Delia was certainly champing at the bit toward the end of Dr. Kiernan's term of office in London, because, she said, "I had a bee in my bonnet about the stage, something that always taunted me." The songs inside her head were 'screaming to get out'.

Ivor Browne has a theory of how Delia's confidence in her musical ability developed during her time in London. "She seems to have been very quiet and shy as a young girl. Many Irish people experience a release phenomenon when they leave Ireland. They suddenly seem to be able to break free of the restrictions of Irish life and realize themselves. Now, I think this must have happened to her in a very full way. It probably happened very early on in the first period in London. So, then she was able to have all the colour you can associate with Irish people.

"She was very proud of being Irish, and she had an extraordinary devotion to everything Irish. She hadn't really very much interest in people of other nationalities. She'd be fine with others, but bring in a few Irish and she would ignore the others. She genuinely loved Irish music. I could put on any Irish record and she'd sit quietly and listen. And this is not always true of a lot of Irish singers. You could bore them in five minutes with the (uilleann)pipes. She would listen to them for four and five hours and she'd lap it up. And she loved books about the music or literature and history ......"

"The fact is that John McCormack seems to have taken her seriously, even though he'd joke with her about her singing. Delia said John once told her that there were a hundred things that went to make a singer; that she had ninety-nine of them, and the only thing she lacked was a voice. But he took pains to help her with her singing. I understand he helped her with her diction, and she had beautiful diction. She said he did, anyway. But he must therefore have seen her as unique, and she must have seen herself as such, too."

In 1935, Dr. Kiernan's career took yet another turn. Firstly, in the twenties, he had been transferred from Finance on secondment to Foreign Affairs; then, eleven years later, he was transferred to another department, Posts and Telegraphs, when he was appointed Director of Programmes at Radio Éireann.

Was this the opportunity Delia needed? Would her role as the wife of a radio station executive provide her with the means of testing the waters in the entertainment business perhaps? How would a mother of four, in her early thirties – who had known no way of life other than that of 'the kitchen and the nursery', as she said herself, and the more rarefied world of the diplomatic cocktail circuit – succeed in the rough and tumble of showbiz? Delia would shortly find out.

IV

'The talent of success - doing what you can do well'

The Kiernans moved back to Dublin in 1935, and rented a house at 32 Elgin Road, Ballsbridge. It was a large premises, and had to be heated by two anthracite stoves. The owner was Countess Plunkett who lived where the American Embassy is today. Nuala, Orla and Colm went to Pembroke School nearby, while Blon went to the Loreto Convent on St. Stephen's Green. In London the children had a governess, who was only known as 'Mademoiselle', but she returned to France soon after the family moved back to Ireland. The Kiernans then hired the first of a number of maids, almost all of whom were Irish speakers from the West of Ireland. The decision to rent rather than to buy a house, according to Colm, was due to the fact that his parents lost money on the sale of their home in London, and they never owned a home again. "Theirs was a rags and riches life which is now usual, but was uncommon then, namely, a sharp contrast between their public life, which was glamorous, and their private life, when money was scarce....But the time at 32 Elgin Road was precious, as was the time in London."

It is important that we should understand the sort of Ireland Delia Murphy and her family returned to in 1935. By getting a perspective on the circumstances prevailing at the time, we can better understand the impact her singing made on the public, and it will help explain the huge popularity she enjoyed for the next thirty years and more. Because the fact is that it was primarily through her recordings that she came to prominence as a singer.

Up to the time of her return to Ireland Delia had not sung in public, nor was she known as a singer outside her circle of friends and acquaintances, and there was no agent to promote her as an entertainer. There must therefore have been something very special indeed about her singing style and her choice of songs that explains the sudden growth of her popularity and the huge impact she made on the Ireland of her time. And she was already past her mid-thirties at the time she made her first recording.

The condition of the Irish economy in the thirties was grim. Mr. de Valera's Fianna Fáil Party won the 1932 election and formed a government whose declared policies included plans for the removal of the oath of allegiance to the British crown from the Free State constitution. Irish farmers had been paying twice-yearly instalments on land annuities which the Cosgrave government had collected and forwarded to London. The capital costs had been advanced by the British government and went to buying out the landlords.

Soon after taking office, de Valera decided to withhold these annuities and some other payments, amounting in all to £5 million a year. Britain retaliated by taxing imports of Irish cattle into Britain and the Free State replied with duties on British goods. The so-called Economic War had begun and lasted for six years and it intensified the harmful effects on Ireland of the world economic depression of the 1930s. In 1938 the annuity dispute was settled by payment to Britain of a capital sum of £10 million and the treaty ports were handed over to the Irish government.

According to Fergal Tobin, in his book *The Best of Decades,* the old struggle with England had meant that nationalism "in its resistance to Anglicization set its face against a wider world." This attitude was summed up by Mr. De Valera when he set out his vision for the sort of Ireland he wanted for the mid-twentieth century. In his famous broadcast for St. Patrick's Day, 1943, he stated:

> That Ireland which we dreamed of would be the home of a people who valued material wealth only as the basis of right living, of a people who were satisfied with frugal comfort and devoted their leisure to the things of the spirit — a land whose countryside would be bright with cosy homesteads, whose fields and villages

would be joyous with the sounds of industry, with the romping of sturdy children, the contests of athletic youths and the laughter of comely maidens, whose firesides would be forums for the wisdom of serene old age. It would, in a word, be the home of a people living the life that God desires that man should live.

In his *Modern Ireland*, the historian, Roy Foster, refers to this period as the 'De Valera Dispensation', and he contends that "Fianna Fáil embodied two aspirations: one was to redefine Ireland's relations with the Empire, and the other was to institute a state of 'protectionism', both economic and cultural.... 'Protection' might also be linked to the introspection and conservatism of a state where those whose interests were not met by the status quo tended to leave instead of trying to change it."

Social conditions in Ireland – particularly in rural Ireland – in the 1930s were primitive. According to Foster, "...much in 1930s rural Ireland would have been recognizable to a reincarnated Victorian traveller. Housing remained dominated by the single-storey cottage; living conditions were basic; families large; emigration and tuberculosis part of life." However, he concedes that changes were being made, and the two-storey slated farmhouse was appearing alongside the thatched cottage.

"Land Commission dwellings were raised in considerable numbers through the 1930s, as part of the same policy that encouraged state-sponsored urban housing programmes. De Valera's vision of Ireland...was of small agricultural units, each self-supporting a frugal family; industrious, Gaelicist and anti-materialist. His ideal, like the popular literary versions, was built on the basis of a fundamentally dignified and ancient peasant way of life." But even while the electrification of rural Ireland was being carried out (by the war the programme had been largely completed) the fundamental reality behind the image of rural Ireland remained that of an emigrating population.

But regardless of conditions in the country, the Kiernan family reacted with considerable pleasure at the prospect of moving to Dublin. "They'd been in London eleven years," Colm Kiernan said, "and felt it was time they were getting back. The fact that my father was moving back as Director of Programmes was a promotion under the circumstances, and they had remained very Irish and nationalistic while in London – partly because of the job, but also that was the kind of culture they experienced. The children, too, were happy, and my parents wanted them educated in Ireland, if that was at all possible." Dr. Kiernan's secondment to Posts and Telegraphs was to be for one year only before he would return to work in Foreign Affairs, but his position with Radio Éireann was extended yearly until 1941.

Bairbre MacDonagh, the wife of Liam Redmond, tells of her first meeting with Delia which took place in the mid 30s ,

"I was staying over in the middle island in Aran, and one afternoon we were having a marvellous time on the beach, and suddenly we heard the sound of an outboard motor which was very unusual there at that time. Naturally, we all headed up to a high point to have a look, and we saw a tiny currach in the distance, and the islandmen all came running to see what it was all about. Now, as you know, the currach is a light boat covered with canvas, and one of the men said, 'Oh, that's a very dangerous thing to do. You should never put an outboard motor on a currach.' And with that the motor stopped. We could hear it spluttering for a while, and then we saw oars coming out. As it came nearer we could see two men and a woman rowing. And when it pulled into the beach, here was Delia pulling away mightily. That was the very first time I ever saw her. The islandmen were absolutely astounded. They had never seen a woman rowing a currach before."

In Dublin, Delia was soon attending parties and functions and, of course, singing at every opportunity. Liam Ó Riagáin, told a story he heard from a friend concerning Delia at this time. "This friend was coming through Dublin Airport, and his colleague who met him said that there was a party that evening at the British Embassy, so he was invited to come along. He was given a lift in a car into the city with some others, and he suggested that they should try and get Delia Murphy to come along and sing a few songs. A voice from the back of the car said, 'The difficulty is getting her to stop.' My friend found out later that the voice in the back was that of Delia's husband, Dr. Kiernan."

After almost two years back in Ireland, Delia was ready for the one venture she had been consciously or unconsciously preparing for: "The children were still young, but not so young their mother couldn't find some time to record a few of her songs..." she said. She was all set to go.

In 1936 a young Londoner named Leslie Thorn who had been with the Gramophone Company, or HMV (His Master's Voice) as it was more generally known, since 1923, arrived in Dublin with a colleague, Jock Farmer, to promote and develop the company's interests in Ireland.

According to Leslie: "HMV had been toying for some years with the idea of starting a factory in Ireland, because at that time there was duty on HMV goods and they had to get around that in some way. The country was developing from an industrial point of view and we felt we should be there to help." Leslie had visited Ireland regularly for HMV for weeks at a time, and his knowledge of the country and the gramophone trade was well established. It was largely on his recommendation therefore that the company decided to set up a factory in Waterford, with offices and stores in Eustace Street, Dublin. Some time before, I had been sent to Waterford to survey the place, because it was the most strike-free port in Ireland at the time. I took the ferry over and took photographs of the factory and reported back favourably on the site. When they looked at the photos I had taken, my chief pointed at one of the them and said, 'Well, that's a good start,' he said, and I looked and saw a sign on a wall which said, *Boycott British Goods*."

Once he got the office established in Dublin, and had got the feel for things, Leslie felt they should start recording. Equipment for pressing records at the HMV plant in Waterford was brought over from London. "We were afforded every possible assistance by the authorities, which included a protective duty on importations, and all our products were then made in Ireland. This enabled us to lay plans for exports to world markets. I was Record Sales Manager and Recording Manager. Jock Farmer, a Scot, looked after the radio side of things for HMV."

A young pianist and piano accordion player named Albert

Healy was just coming into the concert and recording scene at the close of the thirties. As Albert recalls it, Jock was the boss, and Leslie was his assistant. "They worked as a team," he said, "and together they toured the country talent-spotting. I just did their Dublin season. The auditions were held in an upstairs room in Jurys Hotel."

Leslie was the ideal man for the job. Not only was he a good administrator, he was also a first-rate musician and had his own 'big band' in London and they played regularly at the famous Piccadilly Hotel. Leslie played the violin and made a number of recordings himself for HMV in the twenties. He wore a neatly trimmed moustache, was a dapper dresser and cut quite a figure in his distinctive plus-fours and bow-tie. Most importantly, the slightly chubby Leslie was of a cheerful disposition – bordering on the 'jolly fat man' type, in fact – and was the ideal man to deal with artistes and performers in a kindly and sensitive manner.

Leslie remembered well how he first came in contact with Delia: "Besides Paddy Beades, there were other *Come all ye* singers recorded, but they didn't sell all that well. But soon I was to meet the woman who would help to bring about a change in the fortunes of HMV in Ireland, the first popular female singer of traditional ballads ever recorded in Ireland, and perhaps the most popular Irish woman singer ever. There was a paper called *The Irish Radio News* which came out weekly, edited by a cheerful man named Jimmy Kitchen. Some time in 1937, Jimmy suggested to me that I should consider recording Delia. I had never heard her sing, so Jimmy brought me to a party where she was singing one evening. I was flabbergasted, I thought she was absolutely magnificent, and I knew she had what it takes - her own way with Irish songs, and the right amount of *nyaah*." Don Carr, a young UCD student, said that the occasion was the second meeting of the Irish P.E.N. club in Jury's Hotel in 1937. Martin Walton agreed on the date and location in an inerview with the author. According to Don Carr, "the Club had just been formed the previous month, and it was decided to have a ballad night on the occasion of the next meeting. I was invited by my friend, Andrew E. Malone, the former literary editor and dramatic critic of *The Irish Times*. I remember that the writers, Maurice Walsh and Lynn Doyle, the singer, Richard Hayward, and Delia Murphy were present. She and Richard provided most of the evening's entertainment, and I distinctly remember that the first song she sang that night was *Three Lovely Lassies*. Whether the song was well-known then or not, I've forgotten, but of course, it later became 'the rage' – to an extent that it was said, unkindly, that it had become compulsory to play it in every programme broadcast by Radio Éireann! True or not, I do know that eventually most people were very fed up indeed with the lovely lassies from Bannion."

The chorus of that song finishes with, "There are three lovely lassies in Bannion, And I am the best of them all." Some years later, Delia and Dr. Kiernan were at a reception in Drogheda just before leaving for Australia, and as they were leaving, one of the women said to her, "Don't forget to remember us to the other two." A perplexed Delia asked,"The other two?" "Yes," the woman replied, "the other two – when you're back in Bannion."

For quite some time after his arrival, Leslie Thorn had no means of recording in Dublin, and because he did not want any delay, he immediately set up a series of recordings for Delia at the company's main studios on Abbey Road, St. John's Wood, London. Richard Hayward was going there to record at the same time, and so, in addition to the half a dozen or so songs Delia recorded, Leslie had her and Richard record a few duets.

He did not remember Herbert Hughes nor John McCormack at any of her recording sessions in London nor was he aware of any previous interest in Delia from HMV. But Delia's son, Colm Kiernan, says that the recording company in London were interested in her before she returned to Ireland in 1935.

"Her singing (at functions and parties in London) drew on her the welcome attention of HMV, and she probably recorded some duets there during this period, though certainly no solos." Whether or not she actually recorded in London before 1935, is difficult to say, but most of the evidence seems to indicate that her recording career really began in earnest after she had returned to Dublin.

Delia herself said that the first songs she recorded were, *If I* were a *Blackbird*, *The Spinning Wheel*, and *Three Lovely Lassies*, and they were an instant success. The records of HMV's matrix cards are incomplete, but it seems that her first recording sessions took place in 1938 or 1939. Certainly, the first reference we have to her in the HMV catalogues and their monthly or bi-monthly supplementary catalogues, is in the July-August 1939 listings. Listed are those three songs Delia mentioned, and a fourth song, *Down by the Glenside*. Also listed are two songs she recorded with Richard Hayward: *What will you do, Love*, and *Molly Bawn and Brian Og*.

In the listings for October that year, there is a new duet with Richard, *The Lovely Sailor Boy*. HMV ran an advertisement in December the following year which offered among others, four new songs from Delia: *The Moonshiner*, *The Roving Journeyman*, *The Girl from Donegal*, and *On the Banks of my own Lovely Lee*. By November the following year, she had added ten new songs to the listings, and had begun the first of seven duets with baritone, Michael O'Higgins (these duets included, *Thank you, Ma'am, says Dan* and *The Peeler and the Goat*). That year, too, she recorded *The Star of Donegal*, a duet with George Walsh, their only musical collaboration.

The only studios available in Dublin in the late thirties were those at Radio Éireann in Henry Street, so Leslie consulted with Dr. Kiernan, and he gave permission to record Delia there – about a dozen songs were involved. When Leslie realised that there was considerable potential for the recording business in Ireland, he hired the Bohemian Room at Jurys Hotel. One of those who accompanied Delia on the piano then, he thinks, was Arthur Thornton of the singing duo, Thornton and Earles.

But this question of who accompanied Delia, on what instruments, and when, is a vexed one. Colm points out that his oldest sister, Blon, who was a good accordionist, accompanied Delia on a number of recordings. Albert Healy says he used to give Blon lessons at her home.

"But my mother didn't generally like accompaniment," Colm says, "because obviously she was making up the songs and she would vary them if she felt like it, so she was very difficult to accompany even when she was recording. Unfortunately HMV would often give her accompanists that she didn't like, especially violinists. She hated the whole race of violin players because their scratchy music would cut through her voice like a knife. Most of her good recordings have no violin in them, and in those early ones, there are only two accompanists –Arthur Darley on the guitar, and my sister, Blon, on the accordion. If there are other claimants they would have to establish that they were there, because many people make such claims that they accompanied her."

The one name that appears on almost all of Delia's matrix cards is that of the guitar accompanist, Arthur Darley. He is also regularly credited as arranger. Albert Healy said he himself never accompanied Delia on any of her recordings. "I did for lots of other singers, including Delia's sister, Angela, who recorded one or two songs. I don't think Angela was a stage performer. Angela's son, Leo Cullen, said his mother had voice training, and that this was noticeable in her recordings. "But her voice lacked the personal folk touch, the atmosphere of Delia's. My mother's problem, my father said, was that she did not have stage presence. "

In his dealings with Delia as a recording artist, Leslie Thorn said his impression of her was that she was a great character, full of fun, and a great professional. "She'd come to the studio with everything ready. She was always cheerful and never nervous, and she didn't seem to be bothered at all about wearing headphones and singing in an empty studio. She was just a 'natural'. We never had to do a retake of any of her records. Some artistes made lots of mistakes, but not Delia."

It is interesting to note that someone else who accompanied Delia at that time has quite a different account of how well these recording sessions went. She was Stella Seaver, an accomplished accordionist who used to play céilí music and had already done some recordings for Regal Records. She played regularly on Radio Éireann and had started broadcasting on children's programmes. Stella said she provided accompaniment for Delia in Jurys Bohemian Room. "She spoiled more recordings because she'd lose her breath maybe and we'd have to go over it and over it, I don't know how many times." Information on the HMV matrix cards shows that Stella's memory is quite accurate about

Delia's retakes. Each card states precisely how many 'takes' there were in each song, and in Delia's case, it was almost always three.

Albert Healy explained why it was so important for the recording artiste at the time to get it right as soon as possible. Recording methods then were quite primitive, and audio tape was only being developed around that time by BASF in Germany. "If a mistake was made in the words or in the singing, the little wax discs were totally spoiled and had to be discarded. The discs were expensive, and they could carry around only so many."

Stella Seaver said that there was no written music for most of the songs Delia sang, but Dr. Arthur Darley, who was on the guitar, and Frank Kelly, a violinist with the Radio Éireann orchestra, jotted down a few notes. "They were great. We'd run over the tune and when we were ready we'd do it." She remembers recording *Three Lovely Lassies, If I were a Blackbird*, and *Dan O'Hara*.

A strange thing is that, Albert Healy – who said he never did accompany Delia on her recordings – remembers Stella at these sessions, but Leslie Thorn does not. Yet Stella remembers that Leslie and Jock Farmer were there as producers. There are those who put forward the explanation that perhaps HMV, or Delia, or both, were unhappy with some of the recordings made, and that it is possible they were redone either in Dublin or London, and, to avoid hurting people's feelings, nothing was said about any change of accompanist.

In any case, Stella Seaver's memories of her involvement in the recordings are quite vivid both in colour and detail. She was visiting her sister in Dalkey for a few days, she recalled, when her brother arrived with a telegram from Jock Farmer telling her to come to Jurys with her accordion the following morning for a recording.

"I thought it was something on my own because I had done recordings before this. I arrived and was told I would have to play for Mrs. Dr. Kiernan. Well, I nearly died....I was afraid of me life." She could not recall if it even registered with her who Delia Murphy was , "but when she came in she was marvellous. She was so friendly and homely. We were there for the whole day and had all our meals there; a week *in toto*, and I returned to Dalkey each night. Everyone got along great," Stella remembers, "there was no friction. I felt happy and at home once I found out what sort of person she was. She was very open, no airs and graces."

One evening during the week she and Delia took the No. 8 bus out to Ballsbridge. Stella was on her way to Dalkey, and Delia was getting off near Elgin Road. "When we came to the pub opposite the RDS, she said to me, 'Come on, we'll go in here for a drink.' We did, and I think we had wine. Before we parted Delia said, 'Will you call for me in the morning?' I said I would, and then we parted. Next morning, I arrived at an elegant house with a huge drawing room on Elgin Road. Delia was standing at the grand piano swallowing raw eggs out of a tumbler, for her throat. And this nice little man came into the room – came in from behind me. 'Did you ever meet him?' Delia asked me. 'That's my husband,' she says. I thought he was a butler. Like, the way she said, 'Did you ever meet him?' I forget if he said anything. He shook hands with me alright – very friendly. But I thought it was very funny. She never took a drink or smoked a cigarette for that whole week."

Leslie Thorn remembers that after recording some of Delia's best songs in the Bohemian Society Music Room in Jurys, he sent her and Richard Hayward to London to record six more titles at the HMV studio on Abbey Road. Their duets enjoyed great popularity with the record buying public, and one of their most popular songs was *Molly Bawn and Brian Óg*. She and Richard did concerts together around the country, north and south.

"I was deeply involved in the Irish Hospitals' Trust Sweep Programme then," Leslie said, "and Ian Priestly Mitchell was using Delia in his Radio Luxembourg presentations which were fairly elaborate. They were mostly recorded in London, and as a result, Delia appeared at many social occasions and became a really popular broadcasting figure, well-known wherever she went."

He recalled what he said was 'a risqué story' Delia told him about a trip she made to London in the late 1930s. "She'd been recording some programmes there for the Hospitals Sweeps people and others – for Radio Luxembourg – and it had paid off very handsomely. Delia decided to treat herself to a pair of the very latest high-heel shoes. She was standing at Piccadilly Circus station waiting for the next west-bound train, when a lovely rich

Dublin voice said, 'Jasus, Delia, where'd you get the whore's shoes?' She told me that with great glee."

According to Colm Kiernan, Delia was not all that keen on recording duets and wanted to concentrate on her solo singing. "So her aim was to use the early duets as a platform from which to launch herself, and this is what happened, because she became at least as well known as Richard Hayward." However, Leslie Thorn is quite certain that HMV released Delia's solo recordings first and these immediately began to do very well.

Before Leslie Thorn established HMV's office in Ireland, there was a dearth of Irish traditional material available to record buyers. Indeed, it is probable that in most Irish homes there were more recordings of this kind of music on American labels than on anything produced in Ireland. Leslie felt that Delia's singing would go a long way to rectifying the situation. And what was the reaction to her recordings when they first came out?

"She got along well with 'society types' in Dublin, but most of them did not care all that much for her songs. They were inclined to look down on the sort of songs Delia sang, but then they began to be less snooty about it all after Delia came on the scene. But at the start it was thought by some that some of her songs were very low-class indeed, and that is one reason why her husband didn't like Delia performing in public. He felt that it 'reacted against' his job as Director of Broadcasting. He also knew he'd be going into the Diplomatic Corps at some stage. He didn't like it at all. Her type of song was considered to be very rough one time, but that all changed in time and she had a terrific following. Her record sales were far ahead of her nearest rival and this was reflected in demands for her talents. She was tops."

Colm Kiernan disagrees that his father was opposed to his mother's singing in public. "He always supported her in her musical career," he stated emphatically. But he agrees with Leslie's assessment of how 'society types' reacted to her songs: "It would be fair to say that in 'polite' circles in Dublin she was scathingly referred to as either a tinker or as someone who sang their music; as a mother who was neglecting her home duties in favour of trailing her coat, or in some such disparaging terms."

"These absurd charges were all false, he says, and although the constant travelling around Ireland was inconvenient for her, it did not distress those who remained at home. We always had a maid from the West of Ireland who was trained to cook and to mind the house." However Colm thought that his sister, Blon, who was a schoolgirl at the time and often played accompaniment for her mother, might have found traipsing around the country a bit inconvenient.

Colm also points out that his mother received support and encouragement from two famous people who were adored by the musical establishment of Dublin, which had so little time for Delia's singing: "Count John McCormack and Ireland's greatest ever soprano, Margaret Burke Sheridan, also from Mayo, were my mother's good and close friends." Colm says he is reasonably sure that McCormack – who was noted for the clarity of his diction when he sang – taught his mother how it should be done. But whether this is true or not, as a singer she was universally praised for the clarity of her enunciation.

Colm Kiernan is certain that his father's position in RÉ did play a part in Delia's success: "The fact that my father was Director of Programmes had a bearing on the outcome. While he never influenced anyone to play her music, and while there were thousands of letters that requested her music, the fact that he was Director doubtless influenced programme selection in Henry Street." He added that HMV were hopeful that her records would be promoted 'on air' by Radio Éireann, their thinking being that Dr. Kiernan's position there could only help her advance in her career.

Albert Healy offered an interesting insight into how those in the entertainment and society circles viewed Delia and her singing at the time she was emerging onto the recording scene. The Come all ye's were completely frowned on, he said, – they were totally unacceptable in entertainment circles, nor were they appreciated in society circles. "There were two well-known singers on the scene then," he recalled, "the baritone, Joseph Crofts, and a great circus character named Johnny Patterson. Johnny wrote a lot of good ballads, including *The Stone Outside Dan Murphy's Door, Shake Hands with your Uncle Dan*, and *The Garden Where the Praties Grow*.

They both tried very hard, but the point is, they didn't have the same clout Delia had to bring it off, and this is where she scored."

Albert said that on occasions like big dress balls, important functions in places like Dublin Castle, Áras an Uachtarán, the American Embassy, and so on, Delia would be there and she'd get up and sing. "They had to like it because of who she was," he claimed. "Reactions varied, of course. Some didn't care for her, but the majority of people liked her singing, because they liked her as a person. She was charming."

Colm Kiernan, has an interesting view on the historical significance of his mother's music: "It appeared to show Irish people a way forward... It proposed the homely virtues upheld in Ireland, such as honest industry. These were the values of a pre-industrial society where human beings predominated over machines. It wasn't Beatle music, but ballad music, intoned in an authentic Mayo accent, and was recognised as being Irish in its orientation. It appealed to Irish nationalism. Delia's music filled the deep and long void left after the Civil War, which it was intended to do. As such, it was historically important."

Martin Walton the music publisher, expressed a similar view regarding Delia's importance: "During the bad times, the War of Independence, in our spare times and in prison with men like Peadar Kearney, who wrote our National Anthem, we discussed Irish music and its prospects and its almost near demise, and we formed plans. The Civil War came along – that cursed Civil War – and everything Irish seemed to flop. People lost interest and heart in it. I made several attempts with Kearney to start the publishing of Irish ballads and songs. But it was useless. There was no response. After about twenty years of fruitless efforts, Delia Murphy suddenly came on the scene and her songs were an immediate success. The beautiful simplicity and superb interpretation given by Delia to these songs proved irresistible, and a new status was accepted for simple Irish songs. I have no doubt that the revival of the interest of true Irish folk songs that we see today (1972) had its start and its success in the efforts of Delia Murphy."

The folk singer Liam Clancy also sees Delia as a pivotal figure in the Irish ballad tradition. "I grew up during the height of what could be called The National Inferiority Complex in Ireland. Irish people were very sensitive to the 'pig-in-the-parlour', 'dirty Irish' image, and they even became ashamed of their own music and songs. But what we must remember about Delia Murphy was the context of the times when she started recording. We were coming out of desperate poverty, and it wasn't fashionable any more to sing the ballads, or Come all ye's, as my mother used to call them. Cut out them old Come all ye's, people were told. Everyone was getting a piano in the house; that famous story epitomises it all: Where is the such-and-such? Oh, it's behind the piano in the dining room with the ass's winkers. So, my early memories were of Bing singing on the radio, Vera Lynn with her, *We'll meet again*, the war bulletins, the sound of sawdust sausages frying in the pan, the hiss of wet turf, the talk of ration books, black bread, shamrock tea – they were all mixed up together. The Come all ye's weren't to be heard and we were up to our tonsils in tenors, light opera and heavy sopranos were the order of the day. Ireland was bursting blood vessels all over the place with songs like, *Good-bye to the White Horse Inn*. But in there among them all like a breath of fresh air, was Delia Murphy. And it gave all of us a feeling of confidence and a feeling of value that there was something to our own traditions, and that we had been ashamed of it, and that there was no need to be ashamed of it, because she wasn't. And she became a heroine and the most popular singer in the country."

Seán Ó Síocháin, a former President of the GAA, sang with Delia at concerts around the country during these years. "Her singing was close to what I had grown up with in Co. Cork. Very few others had that way with the ballads, especially the ladies. If there was anything conscious in her presentation of herself and her songs, it was that she wanted to recreate on stage the background from which she came - the style of singing, that nothing was going to curtail that, nothing would in any way cut down on her way of expressing a ballad. It was very genuine. She was one of our own who wasn't cramped by convention. The themes of her songs struck a chord with the people. She had enormous appeal."

Band leader, Billy Carter, and broadcaster and baritone, Leo Maguire had no doubts about the huge impact she made at the time. Billy Carter heard Delia for the first time when he was listening to the radio at lunchtime one day.

"What struck me was her natural West of Ireland voice, perfect diction and sincerity. The song was *Three Lovely Lassies*. I thought this was marvellous, because up to then we only had the ballads that were popularised by John McCormack. The lady singers we had doing Irish ballads were trained singers whose diction was, you know, absolutely perfect, singing with absolutely correct pronunciation. But here, with Delia, we had this genuine ballad style of singing, which I'm sure ninety-nine per cent of the people of Ireland had never heard on record before. I was working for Martin Walton at the time, and he gave me permission to interview her. I was very graciously received by Delia who spoke in the same accent she sang in.

"She invited me in and I told her that the firm would be interested in publishing some of her songs. I introduced her to Martin Walton, but I don't believe at the particular time that she was interested in money. If Delia Murphy had an agent, I'm sure she could have made thousands out of her singing then. She told me that on one occasion she was approached by the management of the Royal to do a week there. Previous to that, Gracie Fields had been in Dublin, and got a thousand pounds for a week. And the management were always afraid – like at an auction – of bidding against yourself. They were feeling about, trying to find out what Delia would want for a week. So Delia said, 'Well, Gracie Fields got a thousand pounds, so I'll take a thousand pounds.' So that was the end of that. She never did her week in the Royal.

Mary Gaffney of Hollymount thought that Delia was under contract for a time. In an *Irish Press* article on 24th April, 1982, she said: "It was not until she toured Ireland for Lorcan Burke (of the well-known theatrical family) that she received any payment for her singing." Whether that was true for the late thirties and 1941, the year she left for Rome, or later, could not be ascertained. But Delia always said she never made money from her singing and that it was her own fault for not being good at managing her affairs as an entertainer.

Leo Maguire, composer of popular songs like *The Gypsy Rover* and *The Dublin Saunter*, was a regular guest singer at variety and charity concerts around the country. He is best remembered for his Walton's Programme every Saturday lunchtime on RTE radio and for his parting line at the end of every programme, "If you feel like singing, do sing an Irish song." He appeared with Delia on many occasions, 'always playing second fiddle', he said. He got to know her very well.

"Delia was a primitive in the very best possible way. All her instincts were straightforward, childish. She was basically a very innocent person. Quite unworldly, perfectly natural. If Delia said something you knew she meant it. She had tremendous personality. Completely extrovert. I honestly believe Delia never worried in the whole course of her life. She took life as she found it. It might be forgotten, too, that she was always ready to sing for charity. She loved bringing joy to people. She brought tears also with some of her songs like *Dan O'Hara*, a most poignant little song. But mostly she brought you laughter. And strangely, Delia was more at home in a male gathering. She was always a lady, but she could be a man among men. In company, you forgot that she was a woman."

The first record HMV pressed at their Waterford plant was that of the up-and-coming young tenor, Hubert Valentine. He had come to prominence a few years earlier and was marked out for great things. He was even described by some as 'the next McCormack'. Leslie Thorn regarded him as HMV's greatest 'find' in their search for new talent. He was also aware of attitudes to Delia's singing.

"Leslie Thorn sent me to England to record a number of songs, including, *My Mary of the Curling Hair*, and *Rose of Killarney*. Other artistes recorded then were baritones, Robert Irwin and Michael O'Higgins, Cecily Kenny, Renee Flynn, Máirín Fenning, Máire Ní Scolaí, Joseph Crofts, Richard Hayward, Jimmy O'Dea, Noel Purcell, and, of course, Delia Murphy."

He made one recording with Jimmy Campbell's Band from the Royal Theatre in the old Radio Éireann studios and he made other recordings later on in Jurys. Hubert listed a number of accompanists at these recordings: "Lucey Linnane was one I remember, and there was Julia Grey, Kitty O'Callaghan, Jennie

Reddin, Vincent O'Brien on special occasions, and accordionist, Albert Healy, who was just starting out."

The first time Hubert Valentine met Delia was in the offices of HMV in Eustace Street when they were making arrangements to record her. "The Come all ye's were not popular. As far as I was concerned, that sort of singing was what you'd hear from a fella who was half-drunk. I had never heard them. I liked and didn't like the quality of her style of singing. I was 'legit' classical, you see. But she grew on you, and she could do the folky song. She wasn't considered by most of the singers in those days as a singer, let's face it. She started the trend in folk music that came on in later years. At first people said 'isn't she awful', but as she became popular she was wonderful. " Delia and Hubert also performed together at Herald Boot Fund concerts.

Others who sang the more traditional type songs were Denis Cox and Seamus Hughes, but light opera and variety concerts were the popular form of entertainment then. To get some idea of the sort of material that was typical of the variety-type concerts which were so popular in the thirties, and who the performers were, it is useful to look at the programme of a concert hat was held at the Mansion House, Dublin, on Tuesday, 23rd November 1937 at which Hubert Valentine performed.

The concert was in two parts, and opened with dancing by the "Clann na nGaedheal Troupe". They were followed by Máire Ní Mhaoil Bhrighde playing "Selections on the Violin"; Seán Fitzpatrick (Tenor) sang *God Save Ireland*; Máirín Fenning (Contralto) sang *Clare's Dragoons* and *The Battle Hymn;* there was a harp selection from Mrs. Cahalan; Michael O'Higgins (Baritone) sang *Cath Céim an Fhiadha* and *My Dark Rosaleen*; Aine Ní Chonaill (Traditional) sang *Seoladh na nGamhna* and *Oro Bhuachaillín, seol do Bho;* Rory O'Connor danced a hornpipe; Eamonn de Barra gave a recitation (*The Rebel*); Aindrias O Muineachain (Traditional) sang *Rosc Catha na Mumhan* and *Boolavogue*; Hubert Valentine sang *The West's Awake* and *Step Together*; and finally, Giolla Criost O Broin contributed *Fir an Iarthoir* (sic) and *The Harvest Worker's Hymn*.

Part Two opened with "A Lecture on the Manchester Martyrs"

by Tomás Mac Curtain; then there was a one-act play, "The Gaol Gate" by Lady Gregory, produced by one of the actors, Aoife Taaffe; next, Joseph Crofts sang *Allen, Larkin and O'Brien*; there was a dance by Cumann na gCailíní; Máirín Fenning sang *Déirín Dé* and *For the Green*; Eamonn de Barra gave another recitation, *When I was Twenty-One*; and the evening finished off with Hubert Valentine singing *She is Far from the Land* and *The Minstrel Boy*.

Most people who saw Delia Murphy on stage were struck by her relaxed and easy-going style. When she was introduced she would walk slowly out on to the stage, grinning for ear to ear, and as she waited for the applause to die down, would stand at the microphone – where there was one – looking around the hall, and when the clapping had just about stopped, she would say something like, "How are ye?" Her patter was brief and to the point.

"I'm delighted to be here, and I'd like to start with a song you might have heard on the radio which I recorded a few months ago. It's all about a girl who thought she was the bees knees, and it's called, *Three Lovely Lassies from Bannion*." And then she would turn to the accompanist who would start to play.

According to Albert Healy "she was larger than life. She was a fine buxom woman. Now I'm not taking from her in saying that because she had a personality to match, almost overpowering. Delia was very pleasant to work with and was most appreciative of everything you did for her. I remember at one concert she sang *The Rose of Mooncoin*. When she came to the lines, 'Flow on, lovely river, flow gently along,' and the one with the words, '...and the lark's merry song...,' I played the appropriate effect on the piano, imitating these sounds, y'know? Singers don't notice these things as a rule, do y'see? Now, I was very young at the time, very green, and just starting off, but at the end of the evening I asked her to sign my autograph book, and she signed it, 'To my dear friend, Albert, who made the rivers flow and the birds to sing for me tonight.' It was a typically generous and thoughtful Delia gesture, and all through her life, there were many who received such simple marks of appreciation from her."

Before a major performance however, Delia was usually quite nervous, according Colm Kiernan. She practised with or without accompaniment every day, and on the day of the recording or the performance she was uncharacteristically irritable. "But she would quickly take control of herself, and by the time of the performance she appeared to be well in control of her nerves." Mrs. Bridie O'Rourke who was a neighbour of the Kiernans on Elgin Road in the thirties and used to play with Colm and the girls on the street, often heard Delia practising her singing.

And all this time she continued in her role of wife and mother. Even though she had a maid to help her, Delia did all the shopping, and drove the car to the shop to load up with groceries and provisions. Dr. Kiernan never learned to drive, Colm said. She sometimes did the cooking – which she hated – especially when entertaining. "My father's position required him to do a lot of entertaining, and she kept a close eye on everything that was happening on these occasions. The general standard of living wasn't very strong and my father was supporting his mother and various members of his family. So living was quite tight, and that tends to unite a family all the more than if they were more affluent and freer with money. There was very little money for holidays on the continent or anything like that."

He also recalls that the children were very taken with what he called 'the mystique' of his parents. "My father seemed to be a great success in his work, and my mother made a go of it as a singer at a time when no other woman in Ireland at the time could do that." But when he was seven or eight, other small boys at school would tease him about his mother's singing, saying hurtful things like, "Your mother's a tinker, isn't she?" It reflected what those children were hearing at home – that Delia Murphy's style of singing was in the style of the tinkers.

V

Where she got her songs

In describing one of Delia's many acts of generosity, Bairbre MacDonagh throws some light on the sources of her songs. Bairbre was a daughter of Tomás MacDonagh, one the signatories of the 1916 Proclamation. Delia was talking to some friends of hers about the MacDonagh's two children, Bairbre and her brother, Donagh, and wanted to know how they had fared after the death of their mother who had never really got over her husband's death following his execution in 1916 and who died not long afterwards.

"Delia learned that we were not doing too well, and she set about making arrangements to look us up. Don's young wife had died tragically a few months before this, and he was trying to raise his children on inadequate Bar earnings. He had always been interested in ballads, so Delia decided this was somewhere she could help. She encouraged him a lot by singing, and talking about ballads to him, and it was typical of her generosity that she gave him a lot of her own books of ballads, and even copied out ballads she herself had collected. The result was that he got a programme on Radio Éireann called, *Ireland is Singing*, which kept the wolf from the door for many's the year."

So it appears that Delia already had a library of books on folk-song and had built up her own manuscript collection of songs. There are several instances of how generous she was with her books, and her library must have been sufficiently large that she felt able to part with some of them. She possibly had already trawled through the books she parted with and had extracted from them those songs she wanted for her own purposes. What she did with these and other songs, and how she made use of them will be seen later.

Apart from her own library of books, what were the other sources of the songs she sang, from whom did she collect them, and most importantly, were any of those she recorded her own compositions, wholly or in part ? Because it was not just her distinctive singing itself that made her a phenomenon. The uniqueness of the songs she sang also guaranteed her immediate popularity.

It requires a lot of sifting and searching to find out just where, when and how the songs entered her repertoire, but it will be a worthwhile exercise, as will be seen. It reveals yet another aspect of her talent which has been recognised by very few people indeed, one which, arguably, was the greatest of all her gifts

In the course of a conversation one day about traditional songs at her home in Jasper, Delia said, "I have a rhyme for every sort of tune you can imagine, and I don't know where I heard them or where I got them, but I seem to have them." Then she added almost as an afterthought and quite emphatically, "Every Irishman has, of course."

Delia was not of an analytical cast of mind, and gave no great deal of thought to when or how she acquired her songs; but it is probably safe to say that what she meant by saying, "Every Irishman has...", was that Irish people from the same background as herself who grew up at the start of the century, had absorbed the songs and tunes from a tradition that was still very much alive.

She did not care a lot about examining the past to explain the present, nor bother about being precise about dates and times, or figures. "I recorded over four hundred songs," she would say, when, in fact, it was only a fraction of that – less than one hundred. Her father had a farm of four-hundred acres, told her Canadian friends, when it was one third that size.

When I asked her in 1968 when it was she showed John McCormack how *Úna Bhán* should be sung, she said, "About 1945...about twenty years ago." In fact, it happened much earlier while she was living in London, and that was prior to 1935. And McCormack died in 1945.

But what she lacked in preciseness when dealing with dates and figures, she more than made up for in the marvellous facility she had for picking up songs, and an unerring instinct for picking words and tunes that would appeal to 'the real people of the gods'. In any case, it can be inferred from her statement in Jasper that she was steeped in the oral traditions of her native place.

"When I was a child I used to go down to the village, and there was an old blacksmith there, his mouth full of tacks. His name was Mickeen Cunningham. He'd sing for me all day if I'd go and buy him a loaf of bread in the evening on my way home from school. Well, one day I was very hungry, and I went and bought him the loaf, but along the way I ate half of it." And she laughed at the memory of it as she continued: "He fired a hammer at me and out the door I ran, and I didn't go back for a few days after. But he sent me a message that he'd have more songs for me if I'd come back. And I came back, very meek and mild, and that was that. I was great friends, too, with the tailor in the village. He'd sit up on the table with his legs crossed, and I used to thread the needles for him. I had good eyesight as a child, and I'd sit there pretending I wasn't listening, but I heard all the lore of the world."

Once again, Delia's attention to detail fails her, because the tailor whom she named as Pat McNamara on this occasion, is called Tom Mooney in a later telling. In an *Irish Press* article on 23rd April, 1982, the day before the unveiling of a Memorial to Delia in Hollymount, reporter, Mary Gaffney, spoke to some local people. One of them, Michael Connolly (83) of Davris, Hollymount, remembered Delia as a young girl "singing her heart out" at Tailor Mooney's, a neighbour's house. "She would sing local ballads, many of them learned from the itinerants who camped on Featherbed Lane." And this is confirmed by Delia herself when she was asked where else she got her songs. "Tinkers, of course – Tom Maughan. And my father. But you'd have to coax them out of him. He used to be in bad humour sometimes, sometimes in very good humour. 'Twas he sang me *The Fenian Song* – y'know, 'The Queen's Own Regiment was their name, From fair Toronto town they came...'"

(In 1866 twelve hundred Irish-American Fenians under the command of General O'Neill, a U.S. Civil War veteran, crossed over from Buffalo, New York, and invaded Canada. They wrote *The Fenian Song* following their successful routing of The Queen's Own Rifles from Toronto. In later years Irish sailors sang it on Great Lake ships, and Mr. Murphy possibly picked it up in America.)

At a crossroads, a few hundred yards from Mount Jennings House was the local post office which was run by the Killeen family, and the junction was always referred to as Killeen's Cross by the local people. The Murphys were frequent visitors, and the two Killeen brothers, Mike and John, were very friendly with Delia's younger sisters who were about the same age as themselves. When researching my television programme for RTE, I asked them if they could throw any light on the question of where Delia got her songs? Did she, for example, get any of her material from the Travellers? John said most emphatically that she did.

However, after listening to John, and pausing for a moment before speaking, Mike said, "I don't believe at all that she learned them from the tinkers, because I never heard a tinker singing any of those songs. Not that I heard tinkers singing a lot, but I don't think that's the kind of song they used to sing. Mary Cassidy who worked for the Murphys used to sing the kind of songs Delia said she heard from the tinkers – the old Irish songs. Old fashioned songs."

However, both agreed that Delia's recordings did not contain songs from the locality. Mary Cassidy agreed with John that she did get songs from 'the tinkers', and said that Tom Maughan was a great singer. I asked her who else might have given her songs.

"She got a few from a local man called Jamesy Mellett, a postman," she said. "And I gave her a few. She got the words of the song, *Combing her hair by candle light* from Jamesy. We all helped her out as best we could. I gave her a song called, *The Sailor Boy*."

Another childhood neighbour of the Murphys, her school chum, Mrs. Margaret Doherty, thought that Delia 'invented' the songs herself. And yet, many people who knew Delia personally say she gave 'the tinkers' the credit for her songs. She would not qualify her statement by saying 'some songs' or 'all of her songs'. We have already heard what she said about Tom Maughan. In fact, she said that it was Tom who gave her *The Moonshiner*. She also said she would "forgive the tinkers anything for saving the traditional tunes".

Colm Kiernan categorically denies that she owes them anything, or very little, anyway. "Lies, rumour and gossip surround those who have a public life. Delia Murphy was no exception. People wondered from where she secured her music. As theories were legion, she invariably answered, 'What do you think?'" He says she would usually laugh at the reply to the question which was generally some absurd theory. "She never answered, 'I got the music from the tinkers', because she did not take refuge in so obvious an absurdity." But Delia did not need to be asked where she got her songs to launch into an account of "evenings with Tom Maughan under starlit skies, with him spinning me yarns of magic and fantasy", as she used to say to me and to others within my hearing. So what does Colm think she was doing?

"She was selling this as an Irish cultural tradition at a time when Ireland was trying to find a cultural tradition. She did not want to say she invented it or made it up. It was easier to say something like, 'Well, where do you think I got it from?' And they'd all say, 'You got it from the tinkers, we know you got it from them.' She'd say, 'Alright then, from the tinkers it came.' But anyone who knows anything about the itinerants knows they contributed nothing to music of any kind. They were too busy trying to make a living."

The strength of the Travellers' music tradition is well known, and a great many Traveller families have gained renown as traditional musicians, among them, the Doran brothers, John and Felix, John Cash and his son, James, all of whom played the uilleann pipes. They had their fiddlers, too, like the Doherty brothers, John, Mickey, and Simon, the McSweeneys and the Gallaghers. The famous piping and singing Furey Brothers – who got their music from their father, Ted – and Paddy Keenan, the uilleann piper, are all from settled Traveller families.

Up to the last war, and perhaps even later, it was quite a common sight in small Irish towns to see Travellers singing ballads on the street and selling their ballad sheets for a penny each. When gathered together round the fire in the evening, singing was a common form of entertainment among the Travellers, and the Traveller women had a delivery that was strong and vigorous. Until very recently, one could still hear well-known singers like Pecker Dunne and Margaret Barry, performing on the street at festivals and fleadhanna around Ireland, both of whom also made records.

While the Travellers in Scotland have gained fame for their great song tradition through renowned folksong collectors like Gavin Greig, and academics from the School of Scottish Studies, Travellers in Ireland – at least until fairly recently – were largely ignored. This has now been rectified by collectors like Tom Munnelly of Roinn Bhéaloideas Éireann, University College Dublin.

Fr. Jarlath Waldron, who hired Delia to sing at a concert in Claremorris in 1950, had heard about Delia and 'the tinkers', so he decided to try her out. "The only tinkers' song I ever knew was one sung by a young classmate of mine – he was from the tinker class. He tried to teach me one called *The Ould Rigadoo*, but I failed because there were so many grace notes in it. So I asked Delia if she knew it, and she said of course she did. So she grabbed a car rug that was there, put it around her shoulders like a shawl, and with her feet placed far apart, she sang it – just perfect. It was obvious she had picked it up from the tinkers because nobody sang it like that except them." Delia recorded *The Ould Rigadoo* in 1940 under the title, *The Roving Journeyman*.

Folk singer Liam Clancy, too, wondered where she got her material. "It seems to me that a lot of it came from vaudeville or the stage. Donagh MacDonagh may have had a part in it, because he was the only other person I can remember at the time who was presenting ballads or folk music –the Donagh MacDonagh *Songbag* and *Ireland is Singing* programmes on Radio Éireann on Saturday nights .But what Donagh was doing, which was also very valuable, was he was taking a lot of American songs which had counterparts in the Irish tradition. And by playing them he was making us think about what we had. Like, my mother used to sing a song called, *The Frog in the Well*, and we were totally amazed when we heard Donagh MacDonagh playing Burl Ives singing, *Mr. Froggy went a-courtin'*. To think that somebody else had the same song – different tune, but the same song – was great. " Delia and Don certainly collaborated on one song at least – *The Tinker's Drinking Song* – which was published by Martin Walton.

In July 1969, Delia sang at a concert recorded for the CBC (Canadian Broadcasting Corporation) attended by about one thousand people, in the Gatineau Hills, Quebec, north of Ottawa. It was her first big concert in many years, and the last before her death a year an half later in Dublin. The host was the Canadian folk singer, Tom Kines and when he asked her where she got

The Spinning Wheel. "Well," said Delia, "I found the words, which were written by a professor of English in Trinity College a couple of hundred years ago. So, I had an old Irish tune and just married them, and that's the way it happened." She sang *The Moonshiner*, and Tom said, "Didn't you have something to do with that song, too?" She replied: "Yes, I got one verse and made up the other three." In his *Comic Songs of Ireland,* James N. Healy says that *The Moonshiner* is "Traditional, nineteenth century", and his version of the song is substantially the same as that sung by Delia.

The author of *The Spinning Wheel* was the lawyer and Trinity scholar, John Francis Waller, LL.D. (1809-1894), a native of Castlewaller, Newport, Co. Tipperary. In the 1974 edition of *Ceol Tíre*, the Newsletter of the Folk Music Society of Ireland, Alf Mac Lochlainn, former Director of the National Library in Dublin, says that a song called *La mere aveugle* by Béranger, published in Paris in 1867, seems to be the original of *The Spinning Wheel.* He quotes the following lines in translation: *While spinning your flax/ Just listen to me, dear. Already your heart is beating/ At the very name of young Colin./ Beware of what he puts into your head./ I may be blind, but I can see what's going on;/ I listen to everything,/ And I can hear you sighing to yourself./ Your Colin is a deceiver.../ But you're opening the window;/ Lise, you're not spinning.* Mac Lochlainn says: "Waller was a regular contributor to the Dublin University Magazine, and the words of *The Spinning Wheel* occur in his *Poems*, 1854 (second edition, McGlashan and Gill, 1863). The *Poems* include a number of translations but *The Spinning Wheel* is not acknowledged as one of them." Incidentally Chris Curran, the actor says, that his sister Eileen gave the song to Delia.,

Ivor Browne says that her knowledge of Irish folk music was a lot deeper than might have been suggested by the songs she sang herself. "Some might say her songs were not in the same category as the pipes and sean nós, but she had a great knowledge of the songs. She found that a certain kind of song suited her, some of them English songs like *If I were a Blackbird*, and they particularly suited her style. But that doesn't in any way mean that she wasn't totally devoted to all Irish music."

Delia was always looking for new material from friends and

acquaintances. Among them Dr. Arthur Darley. Darley came from a musical family, and his father, also called Arthur Darley, played the violin, and was one of Ireland's most prominent music teachers and an adjudicator at feiseanna. Colm Kiernan has no doubts about the young doctor's contribution: "The one who helped her most was an unknown musical genius, Arthur Darley."

Albert Healy confirms this, "I think her principal source was a man called Arthur Darley who was very interested in the music scene, particularly in the Irish trad. He had a great store of songs and I think he passed on a lot of them to her."

A collection of songs published some time in the 1940s by The Parkside Press, Dublin, *Ballads with Music*, was compiled and edited by Donagh MacDonagh,with music (staff notation & tonic solfa) by Arthur Darley. In the Preface – which it is probably safe to assume was written by MacDonagh or Darley, or both – it says, "These (local) songs were written by the score in every county in Ireland, and the best of them survived ....The majority of songs in this selection belongs to this class..." There are thirty songs altogether including some which Delia recorded. But no song is credited to her; nor is her name mentioned anywhere in the book.

In fact, there are only two songs where the authors are given credit: *The Spinning Wheel* (John Francis Waller), and *The County of Mayo* (Translated from the Irish by George Fox). *Seán Ó Duibhir a' Ghleanna* is, in fact, in English, but MacDonagh does not say whose it is. It is,in fact, Canon Sheehan's ballad, which was based on another English translation of the Irish language song, and it was recorded by Delia under the title, *After Aughrim's Great Disaster*, from the opening line in Canon Sheehan's song. The first song in the book is *The Moonshiner* a nd other songs in the volume which we know Delia recorded or used to sing at her concerts, are: *The Rose of Mooncoin, The Enniskillen Dragoon, If I were a Blackbird, Three Lovely Lassies, The Bright Silvery Light of the Moon, Thank you Ma'am, says Dan, The Peeler and the Goat, The Green Bushes, The Lowlands of Holland, The Bantry Girl's Lament,* and *The Jackets Green.* So, twelve of the songs in Donagh MacDonagh's volume were recorded by Delia.

There is a revealing sentence at the end of the Preface which shows that the authors assume that the songs in the volume have been around for a very long time indeed: "Many of these songs have never been published with music, some of them have never been published at all, but all of them have passed the sternest of all tests – that of Time." So, was this book one of Delia's sources, or did she contribute some of them herself from her own collections? Otherwise, if she adapted any of them in any way – in words or music – why was she not credited by MacDonagh and Darley, both of whom had worked closely with her and were familiar with her material? The Walton music sheet of *The Spinning Wheel* – "as sung by Delia Murphy and played by Arthur Darley" – states that the song is "by Seamus Kavanagh". There is no mention of Waller. In his article in *Ceol Tíre*, 1974, Alf Mac Lochlainn says that in two other of Walton's printings of the sheet music of the Delia Murphy number, the credit is given to Delia and Waller.

Around the time Delia made her first recordings, Colm Ó Lochlainn of the Three Candles publishing house in Dublin, brought out his famous *Irish Street Ballads*. It contains several songs which Delia recorded: *Coortin' in the Kitchen, If I were a Blackbird, Thank you Ma'am, says Dan, The Peeler and the Goat,* and *The Star of Donegal*. Ó Lochlainn had been collecting his Irish Street Ballads for more than twenty-five years, so along with this new book, songs from her youth, others she collected herself, and her own book collection, Delia had lots of sources for her recordings.

It is probable, of course, that she already knew many of the songs in these publications. But to what extent she 'tinkered' with them is hard to say, because songs that are transmitted orally are inevitably changed as they pass over generations. Several of the songs where she is credited with "words and music", were published by Waltons around 1950, and include, *The Connemara Cradle Song, Dan O'Hara, The Fairy Lullaby, If you will marry me,* and *The Captain with the Whiskers*. In most cases it is quite obvious that she got her inspiration from the folk song and ballad tradition. A version of *The Captain with the Whiskers,* for instance, was collected by Sam Henry from John Henry Macaulay of Ballycastle, Co. Antrim, and printed in *The Northern Constitution* on 18th July, 1936. It is almost identical to Delia's version, but the air is only a 'distant relation' of the traditional tune she uses.

Colm Kiernan remembers his mother composing songs in the drawing room of their home on Elgin Road. "The words came first," he said, "and then she would hum a tune to go with them. A number of them she developed out of her own experience, out of what she thought would be useful for the market. She borrowed some, she sang some that were there already, but a lot of them didn't pre-exist her. Those that she borrowed were from songs that were already published, but she got little from songsters, or tinkers, or Don MacDonagh. Whatever she got came out of Ireland."

Albert Healy also thought that she wrote songs. "She collected a lot of songs from around the country herself, as I say. She'd come to me and ask, 'What do you think of that?' and would ask me to write down the tune for her which I did on many occasions."

Delia herself said that when she was still at school she discovered she had a talent for writing songs. "I found out I had this gift of being able to piece together bits of old ballads, filling in missing portions and straightening out the tunes when they, like the words, had been battered by time. I tinkered with ballads the way men of the roads tinkered with cans, and I sometimes got a shining new ballad for my pains."

Even during the war years in Rome where her husband was Irish Minister to the Holy See, Delia collected songs. When the Allied forces entered Rome, there were many Irish among them. She got songs from Irish-American soldiers , and she even made up a song, cobbled together from some of them, which she called, *If you and I were two fine birds*. Irish soldiers in the British Army brought out a booklet of their favourite songs, called, *Songs of the Irish Brigade*, which was printed in English. They gave Delia a copy.

Delia did two free concerts for Fr. Joe Flanagan in Woolwich, to help in raising funds for the church. While there, she sent a card to his mother in Co. Galway asking for the words of the song, *The Wake in Kildare*, also known as *Coming Home from the Wake*. Delia recorded the song, and Fr. Joe's brother, Ger, said his mother would play the record but not when anyone was around because of the words, "And I slipped a kiss to Nellie coming home from the wake." However his was the 'sanitized' version of the song. Delia's unexpurgated version was not for 'polite people'.

VI

'They're gonna put me in the movies'

One day in 1938, quite out of the blue, Delia was offered a part in the film, *Islandman*, which was being made on the Great Blasket Island off the coast of Co. Kerry. The script for the hour-long movie was written by Kerryman, Donal O'Cahill, who had also been involved in the 1934 film, *The Dawn*, which was produced by T.G. Cooper of Killarney. The original plan was that Delia would help out the film company, Butcher Films of London, by bringing her children to Kerry to take part in some of the crowd scenes. However, the producers needed someone to play the part of the mother in the film, and they asked Delia if she would do it. She agreed, and her fourteen-year-old daughter, Blon, took part in some of the crowd scenes. Writing in the 1940 edition of the *Capuchin Annual*, she described what she felt when she first met the film crew: "My fantastic ideas of a high-falutin' grandiose film colony were shattered. Instead, I found just a handful of technicians, the leading lady, a gentle retiring Cork girl, her opposite number, a modest quiet Kerryman, who had a principal part in *The Dawn*. I decided there and then that I would have to tone myself down considerably if I were to make myself fit in."

"I was covered in greasepaint, a shawl was thrown around me, and I was walked in front of the camera. For the first time in my life I realised that I had feet, hands, and a tongue, and I didn't know what on earth to do with them. Where to put my hands and what to do with my feet became a most colossal enigma, and how to repeat a simple sentence became a great problem."

It was not just that she found acting in the film hard; when she saw herself on screen wearing a shawl, playing the part of an older woman, she was, to say the least, most unimpressed, and frankly admitted that it was a blow to her ego. "I was disillusioned almost to the verge of tears."

Still, she need not have been so hard on herself, because while it is plain she was not all that sure of herself in the part, she more than held her own with the other amateur and professional actors – among them, Florrie O'Sullivan, a Killarney man, Eileen Curran, from Cork (Chris Curran's sister) and Cecil Forde of the Gate Theatre in Dublin. For some strange reason, Delia's name in the credits is given as 'Daisy' Murphy!

But while *Islandman* is not one of the most memorable pieces of filming ever done in Ireland, it has left us with at least a few precious minutes featuring Delia in the only piece of film we have of her, talking and singing. All the interior scenes were filmed in a London studio, and in one of them ––the house céilí – she sings, *On the Deck of Paddy Lynch's Boat*, the 1848 translation of *Ar an Loing seo Paidí Loingsigh*, by The Trinity College graduate, George Fox.

One is immediately struck by the contrast between Delia the singer and Delia the actress in the film. When she sings, she is entirely relaxed and natural, just as if she were on stage in a parish hall whereas her acting is marked by a certain stiffness.

But if her experience as an actress was a bit of a trial, the time Delia spent filming on the island was, she said, most enjoyable. "The nights on the Blaskets were something we would never forget. The whole population – or at least the younger generation of them – was about enough to fill one kitchen comfortably, and the film crew thrown in. We sang and danced and talked from sunset till bedtime." Delia was struck by the natural dignity of the islanders in the way they carried themselves. "Even in the way they walked," she said, "they displayed a freedom and ease of movement that had none of the self-consciousness of the city about it. The step was proud and brave, and there was an honesty of purpose in their approach to the camera which didn't bother them one little bit, whereas the rest of us who had been destroyed by years of life in the city became almost like pillars of salt at its approach."

According to businessman, Tadhg 'Kerry' O'Sullivan, brother of Florrie, nothing very much came of *Islandman* at the time, and it did not do well in Ireland. He also said that there had been some friction among those making the film. Part of the explanation for its lack of success, too, might be put down to the outbreak of war the following year. It would appear that Donal O'Cahill, who seems to have been sole owner of the film by the 1950s, attempted to revive interest in *The Islandman* later that decade. Tadhg 'Kerry' O'Sullivan said that O'Cahill also tried to push the film as a documentary, changing the name to *West of Kerry*. It could be that with this film, he had hoped to do for the Blaskets what Robert O'Flaherty had done for the Aran Islands in *Man of Aran* in 1934.

Halfway through a *Cork Examiner* article quoted in a 1960s publicity flyer, the film is referred to as a 'Historical Document', and towards the end of the piece is the statement in bold type: "The Blaskets have their lasting monument here." If the writer had stuck to his or her more modest line at the start of the article where Islandman is described as "a black and white talkie with a pleasant love story and runs for about one hour", perhaps it might have been a lot nearer the mark.

Delia Murphy, in a short time became so well known to the Irish public that she attracted the attention of sculptors and artists, who wanted her to sit for them "Delia had a fine head," the renowned Dublin painter, Harry Kernoff said, and he used her for his oil painting, *The Connemara Turf Girl,* and a woodcut of the same title. "It wasn't just that she was good-looking. She had the classic features of the West," he said. "Great bone structure, including the distinctive high cheek bones, and the liveliest brown eyes you ever saw. She had a fine head of black hair, and beautiful skin."

Sculptor, Helen O'Malley, used her as a subject for one of her pieces, and Andrew O'Connor, too, sculpted a magnificent head of Delia in marble. It is an excellent likeness and it does justice to her fine features. Photographs of Delia during these years reveal a woman who seems carefree and contented with her lot, wearing an expression which is almost always happy and serene.

One of Ireland's most prominent portrait artists of the period, Seán O'Sullivan, also admired the combination of looks and personality, and according to Delia, he paid her the greatest compliment she ever got. "I met him one day on Dublin's O'Connell Street, and he invited me to a men's only meeting in the Metropole. The meeting was to decide about the finances of the widow of the poet, F.R. Higgins who had just died. 'You're the only woman in the world I would walk into this meeting with and not be embarrassed,' he told me. The meeting was wonderful. Every artist offered to paint a picture, and every writer, a story, to raise money for the widow. I decided to do a concert at the Gaiety Theatre, and I raised £1,000 for the widow."

Delia's instinctive generosity was also recalled by the actor Liam Redmond in another instance – again, to do with a young widow. "Delia was visiting some friends and they told her about the plight of a young widow who was ill in a neighbouring house and quite alone. This woman's son was away at boarding school. Delia's reaction was, 'What are you doing about it?' She went over to see for herself how things were with the woman. She found there was no food or fire, because all the money was going to serve the child's needs. Delia stocked her up with food and fuel and moved in to nurse the young widow back to health."

For three years 1938-1941, concerts and recordings were to be Delia's main interest outside of family concerns and her engagements took her all over the country. Seán Ó Síocháin remembers that, typical of the concerts where he and Delia appeared regularly, were those in Arklow and Mullingar in the early 1940s.

"Those performing were a mix of visiting and local artistes, and the purpose was most often for some local charity or fund-raising venture – the GAA, the parish, the Gaelic League, that sort of thing. There'd be a comedian, singers, dancers – these were usually locals – and instrumentalists. Delia, of course, would be the 'star' attraction. Albert Healy was one we regularly performed with, and Pascal Spelman, the Limerick comedian, and the harpist, Máirín Ní Hea, and the singer, Máirín Fenning."

Seán paints a vivid picture of Delia as a performer at this stage of her career: "People were expecting a sophisticated lady to perform and I think it was a great surprise and a pleasure, too, for them to find just one of their own coming on stage. For that reason I think she was a surprise to a lot of people. The way she acted out her songs, too, was a delight, because she really got into the spirit of songs like *The Spinning Wheel* in particular, where she kind of swayed to it – like they do now in rock 'n' roll – but not in an exaggerated way in her case.

She had no inhibitions, and she was totally fearless. I have met many performers – women especially – who became a bit rigid, a bit stiff, and possibly a bit fearful, coming up to their performance. But not Delia. She opened a window, and here she was in her full glory on stage, and she gave full justice to her song."

Seán said that he had heard a few criticisms that she was a bit 'bold' in her appearance, but that these were totally unjustified. "I even heard somebody say that she was a bit 'common'. She was common in the sense that she was at our level. Nothing more, nothing less."

In Dublin, Delia sang at venues like the Father Mathew Hall and the St. Francis Xavier Hall. Others who performed with her on these occasions were Jimmy O'Dea, a very young Maureen Potter, Michael O'Higgins, and Danny Cummins who appeared with Maureen in the Gaiety pantomimes for years right up to the late seventies.

Albert Healy told a hilarious story concerning a Christmas concert in Mountjoy jail. "Delia was in the wings waiting to go on – this young aspiring tenor went out on stage and sang – of all songs – *Bless This House*! There was uproar among the inmates. Well, Delia went out and took control and had them singing along with her in no time in the chorus of *Three Lovely Lassies from Bannion*, and the whole thing was forgotten."

The projectionist at Killarney's Casino cinema for many years, Paddy Kiely, remembers her singing at a concert in the town in 1940, and the place was packed. As far as he could recall, it was organised by either Frank or Harry O'Donovan, and it was broadcast live on Radio Éireann. Paddy often played Delia's records before showing the films, and was of the opinion that her discs would have been played in many other cinemas, as well, because it was common practice to play currently popular music and songs on these occasions. He recalls that *The Spinning Wheel* was probably the most popular.

Thomas Donoghue, Templemichael Glebe, Longford, was in a concert with Delia at The Magnet Ballroom, Strokestown, Co. Roscommon, in 1941 when he was 28. "I think she was forty years too soon." He said he had a céilí band at the time and sang "the usual waltz numbers which included some of her favourites. In concerts then I always sang the ballads favoured by Delia."

Leo Cullen, Delia's nephew, said that she encouraged a hard-drinking image of herself at times. It was her way of thumbing her nose at convention. One of these stories involved Jack Murphy and some of his in-laws who were returning from a funeral in a car driven by Delia.

"Delia's sister, Mary, who was known as 'Baby', was married to Paddy Mellett from the Hollymount area. The whiskey bottle clanked about the car, and that was not the first or last bottle of the day. Suddenly, a door opened and somebody fell out into the side of the ditch. His loss wasn't discovered until they were well home. She encouraged the image, and the way she used to tell it is that she had the car on three wheels coming up the long drive to Mount Jennings. The other wheel was also lost, and like the passenger, the loss went unnoticed! Now, when 'Mac' Kiernan used to hear this, he would always attempt to correct her. 'I don't remember the bit about the wheel,' he would say, whereupon he would be dismissed with a wave of the hand."

When she found the time, Delia liked nothing better than to pay a visit to her family home in Mayo. It was the place she liked the most and where she could relax completely with members of her family and the neighbours. These visits provided her with a whole new batch of amusing and far-fetched stories for her friends on her return to Dublin. Her sister, Angela, had married Leo Cullen (Leo Junior's father), a Tipperary man, and they used to visit Mount Jennings with the children in the summer.

The Murphys' housekeeper, Mary Cassidy, first met Delia on one of her visits home and said she would never forget it. It was in the late thirties, and she was in the job about three months. When Mrs. Murphy told her Delia was coming, she thought it was 'the end'. "She was a real big-shot by then, of course. I well remember the feeling when I first saw her. She came running down the stairs to the kitchen holding a copy of one of her records in her left hand, and she was singing. I can always picture that day. 'I'm going to play this record for you now, Mary,' she said. And it was lovely – it was *If I were a Blackbird*. We had a great debate that evening about everything. You'd think she knew me all her life."

Mary said she never felt she was a stranger at Mount Jennings; more like one of the family. She said Delia would never spend a lot of time upstairs on her own and preferred to be doing something. "She'd sit down at any time and sing songs with you. She was very ordinary, very nice." And Mary being a fine traditional singer herself, of course, was able to pass on new material to Delia.

One of Delia's qualities which she herself identified - a rebellious stubborn streak – was tested one evening at a concert she was giving to a packed house in the Ulster Hall, in Belfast. It was at Céilidhe Mhór na Cásca, Easter Tuesday, 15th April 1941, and German bombers blitzed the docks area of the city. There could have been total panic in the hall, but in her inimitably cool fashion, Delia told the audience to defy the Germans to do their worst, and she kept on singing. The papers were full of it over the next few days. *The Irish News* report is typical:

A DUBLIN HEROINE
The raid revealed many heroes and heroines among quite ordinary people in the city. The bravery of Delia Murphy, wife of Dr. Kiernan, Director of Radio Éireann, Dublin, during the height of the blitz has been the subject of much discussion in Belfast. She was singing at a céilidhe in a large city hall. As bombs rained down, many of the women present became fearful of the consequences. Miss Murphy, however, remained perfectly cool, and kept singing continuously, asking those present to join her. Dr. Gerard McCloskey, a well-known Catholic medical practitioner, who was visiting his home from Portsmouth, was killed by a flying splinter of glass.

It is interesting that the report states that only women became fearful during the bombing. Those were the days when men were men and big boys were not supposed to cry! Mrs. B. Acton, Eastern Road, Kinsale, was a telephonist at the Royal Avenue

Hotel, Belfast, during the war. She said Delia stayed there, and that sometimes her sister, Angela, was also there with her.

"Delia was very popular with Belfast audiences, and always had a packed hall. One night she omitted to bring along some cold cream to remove her makeup, so I gave her mine – just a little from a jar. The following morning she presented me with the largest jar of cold cream available on the market at the time."

Joseph Mooney who owned the hall in Drumshanbo, Co. Leitrim remembers well the publicity Delia got after that Belfast concert. He said she had performed in his hall earlier that same week and was announced in the newspaper advertisement as, *"Delia Murphy, Ireland's Own Traditional Ballad Singer, Supported in a High-Class Programme by..."*, and the performers – all locals – are listed. The MC was Rev. Fr. Fee. Joe Mooney said that she came for 'expenses' because the concert was organised by the LDF (Local Defence Force) and the Red Cross.

The newspaper ad stated that tickets were three shillings and two shillings each (15p and 10p in today's money). "She stayed at Flanagan's Hotel, and I remember that Richard Hayward had been there a short time earlier when he was making the film, *Where the River Shannon Flows*. Their duet recordings were very popular at the time. She was a very gracious person, and no singer of ballads, before or since, could equal her. The Mayo accent added to it all, and as well as songs like *The Spinning Wheel* and *If I were a Blackbird*, she sang, *Coming home from the Wake, I was told by my Aunt, The Girl from Donegal*, and *The Croppy Boy*."

Not satisfied with her two nights performances for which she got no fee, Delia was brought to sing a few songs at the local Convent of Perpetual Adoration, an enclosed order of nuns, on Tuesday morning before she left. "She was seen off at the Drumshanbo station then," said Joseph Mooney, "and she took the narrow-gauge railway line from Drumshanbo to Belturbet, transferring to the Northern Line for Belfast. Belfast was bombed that night. We brought her back again on Ascension Thursday that year, and again she sang for the LDF. Among those in the audience was General Eoin O'Duffy, former Commissioner of the Gardaí."

Children at Gortskehy National School, Hollymount, Claremorris, Co. Mayo, 1910. Delia Murphy is seated in the front row, 5th from the right; her younger brother, Paddy, in the outfit with a 'sailor' type neck – the only boy in the photograph – is 3rd from right, front row.

Photo: The Heaney family.

Delia is standing 3rd from left in the row behind the girls who are seated; photographed in her final year at the Dominican Convent, Eccles Street, Dublin, 1920.

Photo: The Dominican Sisters, Griffith Avenue, Dublin.

Dr. T. J. Kiernan, Delia's husband, in 1930s.

Photo: The Capuchin Annual, 1940.

Delia in the 1920s.

Photo: The Capuchin Annual, 1940.

Delia's younger sister, Angela Murphy (Mrs. Leo Cullen), who also made a few recordings with HMV.

Photo: The Capuchin Annual, 1943.

Woodcut by Dublin artist, Harry Kernoff, RHA, of "Turf Girl", for which Delia was the model.

Photo: The author.

Delia, mother of four, in the 1930s.

Photo: The Capuchin Annual, 1941.

Described in the English publication, *Radio Pictorial,* 29th October, 1937, as "Athlone's (Radio Éireann) three compères"; l. to r. John Burgess; Ian Priestly-Mitchell; and Leslie Thorne, HMV's man in Ireland in the 1930s, who "signed her up" for recording.

Photo: Leslie Thorne.

A Gramophone Co. (HMV) advertisement *circa* 1940, promoting new recordings of duets by Delia and Richard Hayward.

Photo: EMI Ireland.

Front cover of the Waltons' music sheet, *The Spinning Wheel*, one of Delia's most popular songs, which she recorded in July 1939.

His Excellency T. J. Kiernan and Delia receiving a presentation prior to their departure for Rome in October, 1941. In the group are Dr. James Ryan, TD, Minister for Agriculture; Mr. P. J. Little, TD, Minister for Posts and Telegraphs; the Very Rev. Dr. Colman, OFMCap., Minister Provincial; The Hon., Mr. Justice Maguire, President of the High Court; His Excellency Vincenzo Berardis, Italian Minister, and Signora Berardis; Mr. Thomas Collins; Mr. Tadhg O'Neill; two of Delia's children, Colm and Nuala Kiernan; and Fathers Gerald and Senan, OFMCap.

Photo: The Capuchin Annual, 1942.

At Mont Dore, France, l. to r.: V. Rev. Canon Harmon, PP, Ardee, Co. Louth; C. W. Little; Arthur Darley; and his son, Arthur, who arranged a number of Delia's songs and accompanied her on the guitar in several of her recordings.

Photo: The Capuchin Annual, 1945-46.

DELIA MURPHY

IRELAND'S OWN BALLAD SINGER
will be the Guest Artiste at

THE TOSTAL CELEBRITY CONCERT

in

DOHERTY'S HALL, DRUMSHANBO

on

Sunday and Monday Nights Next, 12th & 13th April

Supporting Artistes include JEANETTE QUINN, Champion Step Dancer
NOEL GAFFNEY (Tenor), of "Beginners Please," and JAS. EARDLEY
(Violinist), of Radio Eireann Broadcasting Fame. Instrumental, Singing
and Dancing Items will also be contributed by local talent

TICKETS - - - - - - - - - - - - 3/6 and 2/6 (limited
Doors open 8 p.m.; curtain 8.30 p.m. sharp.
Seats may be booked with Mr. J. M. Mooney, Co.C., or Sergt. M. Joyc
Joint Hon. Secretaries, on or before Sunday afternoon.
Only Booked Seats Guaranteed

MONSTER TOSTAL

MOTOR - CAR RALLY

at

DRUMSHANBO on Wednesday, 15th April

at 2.30 p.m.

Only main road will be used. Cars will not be required to be
used in any way that might cause them damage.

FIRST PRIZE, £5; SECOND PRIZE, £4; THIRD PRIZE, £3;
FOURTH PRIZE, £2; FIFTH PRIZE, £1.
Prizes will be presented at Red Cross Visitors' Re-Union Dance on that
night. No entry fee for car owners; passengers, 2/6 each. Whether you
own an old or new model car, you can enjoy the scenic beauty of Drumshanbo and district by participating in the rally.

A cutting from
The Leitrim Observer,
of an advertisement for
a concert featuring
Delia, April, 1941.

Photo:
Mrs. Eva Mooney.

Left: Fr. Tom Twomey, OSA, photographed during the War in Rome when he was Prior
of St. Patrick's, the house of the Irish Augustinians. He was one of the many Irish priests
who helped people on the run from the Fascist and Nazi regimes. *Right:* German troops
fleeing Rome, June, 1944, photographed by Fr. John "Spike" Buckley, OSA, from the roof
of St. Patrick's. If caught, Fr. Buckley could have been shot.

Photos: Fr. Tom Twomey, OSA.

VII

Rubbing shoulders with 'the warlords' in Rome

"Mistakenly or not, people thought I was on the threshold of sweeping the world with my first ballad recordings when Dr. Kiernan was transferred to Rome as Minister to the Vatican." That is how Delia recalled her situation when it was announced that her husband was to be given the key post of Minister Plenipotentiary to the Holy See on 15th October 1941. She must have had mixed feelings, at least, about having to give up her singing career just when it looked like she was destined for stardom. But however she felt, it seems she didn't hesitate in accepting what she saw as her duties as wife and mother to leave it all and take on the new role of 'Her Excellency' in Rome, even though she knew that in so doing she was bringing her career as a singer to a fullstop, perhaps never again to be re-established.

Delia had had just three short years of a whirlwind success as a performer that was unprecedented in the annals of Irish record publishing and entertainment. When she was interviewed by an *Irish Press* newspaper reporter about it she said that all her plans for the editing and recording of new songs "...were in the lap of the gods. Twelve or fourteen new recordings which I made for the HMV Company are due for release at any moment."

On the eve of her departure for a new life abroad she was suggested as a participant in a proposed BBC Radio variety series early in the war which was aimed at Irish listeners. Other names put forward were John McCormack, Jimmy O'Dea, Barbara Mullen (later of *Dr. Finlay's Casebook* fame on television) and Harry O'Donovan. The programmes would be presented by Joe Linnane who became best known to Irish radio audiences in later years as the chirpy piano-playing question master in *National Question Time*. Delia, forty-year-old mother of four would be in august theatrical company indeed. The aim of the series, to be called *Irish Half Hour*, was to "keep alive among soldiers serving away from home the sense of nationalism in the broadest meaning of the term". These were the words used by the British Cultural and Press Attaché in Dublin, whose job it was to sell the idea to Irish officials. The Attaché was the much-loved English poet – later poet laureate – John Betjemen.

The Radio Éireann authorities were initially cautious, but quickly approved of the idea and were anxious to be as helpful as possible. In his book, *The Most Contrary Region – the BBC in Northern Ireland, 1924-1984,* Rex Cathcart said that the quid pro quo was that British artistes were to be allowed to travel to the Free State for the first time since the war began. Theatrical circles were delighted. But then a rumour began circulating in the BBC that Dr. Kiernan and his wife were pro-German, and the Northern Ireland government at Stormont – which insisted on the right to vet anything Irish on the BBC – was informed. Prime Minister Andrews objected not only to Delia because of her allegedly pro-German sympathies, but also to the producer's plan to use "a few words of Erse" in the programmes. Its use, he said, would be "expressive of separatism" and would be resented in Northern Ireland. He had a number of other objections, as well, and while the *Irish Half Hour* did go ahead, Delia was not one of those invited to participate, nor was the Irish language used. The series proved to be highly popular all through the war and continued for some time afterwards.

Dr. Kiernan's appointment to Rome did not come as a total surprise. Two years earlier he had been chosen as Irish Minister to Germany, but the outbreak of war made it impossible for the Government to ask for King George's signature to his credentials because neutral Ireland was still in External Relations with the British Crown.

By the time Kiernan took up office relations between Ireland and the Vatican were extremely good. However this was not the case in 1932 when Fianna Fáil first came to power. Éamon de

Valera was being portrayed by elements of the national and international press as an extreme revolutionary and nationalist with socialist leanings. The British envoy to the Holy See had been less than flattering in his representations of the leader of Fianna Fáil, and the Irish envoy – who had been appointed by the Cosgrave administration – did not help matters much either by sowing seeds of doubts about Dev. The Papal Nuncio in Dublin, Archbishop Paschal Robinson, tried to calm Vatican fears of an outbreak of anti-clericalism in Ireland, advising a wait-and-see policy. When de Valera ensured that the Eucharistic Congress that same year was the unqualified success his predecessor in office, William T. Cosgrave, had planned it to be, Vatican doubts and fears were somewhat mollified. Following a visit to Rome by de Valera in 1933, and his speech at the League of Nations, where he demanded from the Soviet Union assurances on religious freedom there, the Vatican pronounced itself pleased with the Irish leader. But there were still some lingering doubts, and the Secretary at the Department of External Affairs, Joseph Walshe, was told to send the following instructions to Charles Bewley, the Irish envoy at the Vatican, to stress the Christian basis of de Valera's philosophy:

> The President believes that poverty can be eliminated to a very large extent by governing the State according to the Christian principles laid down in the *Rerum Novarum* and other Papal encyclicals. He holds that, by governing the State with the betterment of the poorer classes always in view, he can raise their standard of living in a very short time to such an extent that they will be able to enjoy all the advantages for human development hitherto confined to the rich.

The Irish envoy to the Vatican from 1934 to 1940, was William Macauley, an extremely able diplomat who was so successful in his dealings with the Cardinal Secretary of State, Eugene Pacelli – who became Pope Pius XII in 1939 – that within a matter of months Walshe wrote to him saying that de Valera was very pleased with his work and if there were any prejudices he had succeeded in removing them completely.

In his fascinating work on Irish/Vatican relations, Professor Dermot Keogh says that successive Irish governments always regarded the Holy See as a diplomatic post of great significance, and now that the war was on, it had developed an even greater significance. However, Macauley retired from the diplomatic service in the summer of 1940, and his departure was a serious setback for Irish diplomacy at the Holy See. The Department of External Affairs paid a great deal of attention to cables and reports from Rome.

The government had the worry of finding a suitable replacement because there was no one of senior rank they could really spare at the time. Dr. Kiernan was just forty-four at the time of his appointment. Keogh describes him as a quiet, bookish man, who had gained a solid reputation among his civil service peers. de Valera would not have entrusted him with the task if he had not held him in the highest esteem.

Little did Delia realize what extraordinary events lay ahead of her as she completed the last of her many singing engagements around the country. She and her family were going to Rome, the capital of Fascist Italy which was allied with Nazi Germany, and they would find themselves trapped there for the duration of the war, the only English-speaking diplomatic delegation free to move about the Eternal City. It would lead her into what would become for her yet another challenge, which was, she said, "...a heaven-sent opportunity to joust with life itself..."

In the weeks before the Kiernans' departure, there were farewell parties and concerts to be attended to, and Delia, who was at the pinnacle of her career, was busier than ever. Liam Redmond recalled a farewell concert she gave at the Father Mathew Hall, Church Street, in Dublin.

"Delia wasn't a pietistic woman, but she was deeply religious, and she had a great affection for the Capuchin Fathers. Now, that concert stands out in my mind, because I don't think I ever saw her looking so beautiful, and I don't think she ever sang as well as she did on that occasion. Sitting in the audience, I had a sense that a great change was coming over her life, and in our lives in relation to her; that we would never see the same Delia again. And it was wonderful that she was so brilliant on that night. It was saddening to think that it would be so long before we would see her again, and that inevitably she would have changed. But, of course, she was very gay. Considering the location – a hall named after Ireland's great Apostle of Temperance – it was amusing that she should have sung *The Moonshiner*, the American drinking song. Well, there was an old Capuchin priest there and he had a long beard, I remember. He obviously enjoyed Delia's singing of the song, and he even joined in the chorus: '*I'm a rambler, I'm a gambler, I'm a long way from home, And if you don't like me, then leave me alone, I'll eat when I'm hungry, I'll ...*' "When the old priest was faced with singing the rest of the line, '*...drink when I'm dry, And if moonshine don't kill me, I'll live 'till I die*' – he paused ever so briefly and continued, '*La la la la la...*' He wasn't going to surrender his convictions that much! Afterwards, the Capuchins gave a little party for Delia, and she was going round talking to the priests and saying to the old Capuchin with the long beard, 'You'll have to treat me well tonight, Father, because I saw you singing along in *The Moonshiner*, and I'll tell the Pope on you!' There was a lot of laughter, of course, and it was a marvellous evening."

At the Clarence Hotel in October, Fr. Senan of the Capuchins, made a farewell presentation of a miniature reproduction in solid silver of the Brian Boru Harp to his friends, the Kiernans. The Capuchin Annual for 1942 shows a photo of the foot high miniature, and a group picture, includes Dr. James Ryan, T.D., Minister for Agriculture, Mr. P.J. Little, T.D., Minister for Posts and Telegraphs, The Hon. Mr. Justice Maguire, President of the High Court, the Italian Minister, and two of the Kiernan children, Nuala and Colm.

The Kiernans' eventually reached Rome in October 1941 "after a lot of ups and downs in three different planes", Delia said in a letter she wrote to Kathleen O'Connell, de Valera's secretary, on 14th November, 1941. "Rome is lovely and everyone here is on intimate terms with the Almighty. They stroll around the churches on Sunday – armed with two chairs as a rule – and don't take the least notice of the priest who is trying to preach a sermon. I'd like to see them doing that down in Co. Mayo."

She also said she planned to learn Italian. She must have applied herself with some energy, because by the time the war ended, she had achieved a commendable fluency in the language. However she hadn't a word of Italian when she first met Benito Mussolini shortly after her arrival in Rome.

"I'll never forget it," she said. "I attended a reception in his honour, and I had to walk the length of a room that seemed a mile long, to be received by the high and mighty Benito. I was determined to put him off his majestic stroke and gabbled away to him in English. He had to call on the interpreter," she laughed.

Over the years in Rome, Delia became quite friendly with Mussolini's daughter, Edda, who was, she said, "the most beautiful and best-dressed woman in Rome". It was from her Delia heard what opinion Il Duce had formed of the wife of the Irish Minister. "Edda told me he had described me as a charming person! Strange, isn't it?"

That sentiment is echoed time and time again by people who knew Delia throughout the war years in Rome, and in his account of Irish-Vatican relations during those years, Dermot Keogh said that many in fact regarded her as being "an extraordinary person". Through her efforts the legation at San Martino della Battaglia became a safe haven and refuge for priests, religious, seminarians and lay people.." Delia kept open house at the legation, and loved her new home. "How I wish all Ireland could have seen our Legation in Rome," she said. "A three-storey villa with a roof garden that looked out over the city. The reception room was called, The Green Room, and it had one of the most beautiful Dun Emer hand-loomed carpets I have ever seen. The dining room could seat sixty guests, and there was one of those handy 'dumb waiters' to bring the food up from the basement kitchen where it was cooked by our Italian staff. It was there I was your drawing-room hostess to dignitaries of the Church, Italian generals and leaders, Rommel and Kesselring of the German High Command, and later, General Mark Clarke of the U.S. forces, and Alexander of the British."

The late Bishop of Clonfert, Dr. Tom Ryan – of 'the bishop and the nightie' fame on RTE's *Late Late Show*, 14th February, 1966 - was a young diplomat in the Vatican at the time. He acknowledged the debt owed by the Irish colony in Rome to Delia and her husband. He recalled that when Delia and Dr. Kiernan arrived in Rome in the late autumn of 1941, they were welcomed by the whole Irish colony there as an ideal family.

"She and her husband opened the doors in characteristic Irish hospitality. Later when food conditions worsened in the war years they were most hospitable to the students, especially those Irish lads in foreign institutes, and I would venture to say that there are many priests alive today working for God and the Church who owe their lives to her generosity and kindness. I attended several receptions at the Irish embassy with Dr. Kiernan and Delia, at which were present cardinals, archbishops, bishops and various prelates, and I heard them all express their charm at her warm reception, her natural, unaffected hospitality. When I speak of her naturalness, I'm not speaking of a kind of grá mo chroí type of reception. It was always dignified. And when I say 'naturalness', I mean her capacity to sit back in an armchair, completely relaxed at the coffee stage of a meal or reception, and on the slightest provocation – which incidentally was always forthcoming – she would sing *The Three Lovely Lassies*, or *The Poor Farmer, Dan O'Hara, The Moonshiner*, or *The Spinning Wheel*, and it didn't matter who was present – cardinals, or whoever."

Bishop Ryan became a close friend of the Kiernan family and said that although 'Mac' and 'Murphs' were two very different people, he never noticed any disagreements between them – except perhaps on one occasion.

"Dr. Kiernan had invited the wife of the ambassador from Vietnam to the embassy because there was a plan to send his son and the Vietnam's ambassador's son on holidays together, and Delia was to come back from the English villa near Rome where they were on holidays. I was with them there. And at the legation, there was Kiernan trying to entertain the lady from Vietnam who spoke very little English. But Dr. Kiernan was fluent in French and they were getting along alright conversationally. However, Dr. Kiernan was faced with the job of catering, and when I came in he asked where 'Murphs' was. I said she didn't come because she wanted to stay at the villa with other priests who were there and entertain them. 'My God,' he said. So, between Dr.

Kiernan and his assistant housekeeper and myself we put up tea, but we couldn't find the butter, and we gave the ambassador's wife bread and jam! Some time afterwards in a jocose conversation between Dr. Kiernan and Delia, she said, 'Well, you can't do anything without me, after all.' 'Yes,' he said, 'I entertained the wife of the Vietnamese Ambassador without you.' 'Yes,' she said. 'Bread and jam!' But they were a perfectly suited pair despite their contrasting physical and temperamental and recreational interests. They were completely absorbed in their family."

One priest who was in Rome during the war told Dermot Keogh that not everyone was favourably impressed. "Her spontaneity brought its share of criticism. There were those Irish religious who chided Delia Murphy, thinking that an Irish envoy's wife should be more 'dignified'. Whatever the critics might have said, Delia brought a much-needed flamboyance to the Irish community in Rome during World War 11."

Italy had been at war since 10th June, 1940, after Mussolini had mistakenly assumed that German successes meant that the Nazis were going to be victorious. But the Italian forces were ill-prepared for what lay ahead, and very soon the majority of citizens were in open opposition to Il Duce's policies. When the Allies landed in Sicily on 10th July, 1943, the Fascist government was soon under severe pressure and it was only a matter of time before the regime collapsed. On 3rd September the Italian armed forces surrendered unconditionally, and an Allied administration was established.

All was confusion, with the northern half of the peninsula remaining under German occupation, and the south under the control of the Allies. Rome became an occupied city for the next nine months when the Germans and their Fascist supporters took control. The commander in chief of the German forces in southern Italy was Field Marshal Albert Kesselring, one of Hitler's top defensive strategists. It was Kesselring who had commanded the Luftwaffe bombings of Poland at the outset of the war in September 1940, and during the Battle of Britain the following year. He had shared the direction of the Axis campaign in North Africa with the brilliant "Desert Fox", General Erwin Rommel, before taking over command in southern Italy.

Kesselring's headquarters were at the Hotel Excelsior in Rome, near the Augustinian's international college, St. Monica's. Along with other members of his staff he would become a familiar figure on Rome's diplomatic scene during the Kiernans' time there. While there is no reported conversation between Delia and Kesselring, she did say she met General Rommel at a reception, and she was very impressed with him. And well she might, because "The Desert Fox", commander of the Afrika Korps, had even won the grudging admiration of those opposing him in North Africa for his brilliant and audacious surprise attacks which had the Allied forces on the run for well over a year. In the thirties, Rommel had actually written the textbook on infantry attacks – *Infanterie greift an* – and was appointed commandant of the officers' school at Wiener Neustadt. Delia said he spoke very highly of a young Irish army officer named Michael A. Costello who had one of the best military minds he had ever come across. The young officer would later rise to the rank of General in the Irish Army. Later in civilian life, General Mick Costello, gained a high reputation in industry.

Conditions during the war years in Rome were extremely grim for the Irish, and food was in short supply at times. Many of the religious houses sent most of their seminarians back to Ireland and reduced the number of staff at their respective houses. The principal Irish religious orders were, the Augustinians, Dominicans, Franciscans, Jesuits, Carmelites, the Society of African Missions (SMA), and the Irish Christian Brothers. Among the orders of nuns were, the Little Company of Mary (the 'Blue Nuns'), Poor Servants of the Mother of God, Franciscans, Sisters of Cluny, Sacred Heart, Dominicans, and the Little Sisters of the Poor.

Before his departure in 1940, Macauley had sought to assure the superiors of the various religious congregations that the government would help in any way they could to secure the transfer of funds for the upkeep of their houses. One of those who was asked by his prior to stay on in Rome was Fr. Tom Twomey, a young Augustinian at his order's house, St. Patrick's College. He was from Tralee, Co. Kerry, and came as a student to Rome in

1934. In agreeing to his superior's request, this fervent young monk who was of an academic bent could hardly have anticipated the intrigues and adventures in which he would become involved, nor the resultant unwelcome attentions he would receive from certain sinister elements among Heinrich Himmler's secret police in Rome.

Tom Twomey was ordained in 1939, and became a member of the college staff in 1940. He was awarded his Doctorate in Theology at the end of '41. When the Prior, Fr. Maurice McGrath, died on 1 January, 1944, the young Fr. Twomey was appointed Prior. He described the arrangements St. Patrick's had with the Irish legation: "Food was scarce then but the black market helped. The Kiernans were alright because they were supplied. But it was difficult for the Irish colleges and houses." Like all the Irish in Rome, the Augustinians had little choice but to get involved with the black market if they wanted to keep staff and students supplied with basic necessities.

"The Kiernans were good to us and I was able to get a good exchange for the pound. Dr. Kiernan offered to help out and I'd go to him once a month or so. He'd write out a docket for me, and when the war was over, Dr. Kiernan got back to Ireland and gave the dockets to our provincial. He'd check them against the facsimile dockets I had sent, and then Dr. Kiernan got his money. I'm sure that he did the same for other colleges in Rome, as well."

Fr. Twomey recalled with amusement one of the ways they survived during those difficult times: "There was a chap came in to St. Patrick's College one morning, and he had five thousand eggs. I asked him for some of the eggs – five or six from each group – to see of they'd sink or float. They were okay, so I bought the lot. This was all on the black market, and this man was from the country, and how he found our place I don't know. I rang various others – the Franciscans, etc. – and they took some, and Mrs. Kiernan, too. 'I'd love some,' she said, 'but how will I keep that many – a thousand?' Well, I said, you put them into salt water and leave them there as long as you like. The legation car came and took them away."

When they first came to Rome the Kiernans visited the various

Irish colleges, houses and convents. Right from the start, Dr. Kiernan arranged that the senior representatives of the Irish religious houses would visit his home every Thursday afternoon. Delia made up little parcels of food and drink for them to bring back to their colleagues. Members of the religious orders recall with obvious pleasure and delight the times they spent with the Kiernans at their residence at San Martino della Battaglia. There was much music and laughter.

"Tea, coffee, biscuits, and sandwiches, were served," Fr. Twomey recalled, "and there was whiskey, wine, brandy, sherry, whatever you wanted. A Monsignor Hugh O'Flaherty was there, too, on occasion, but when the Germans took charge following Italy's exit from the war, he launched an escape line for Allied POWs from inside the Vatican, and he was never seen much after that in the city. He was confined to the Vatican. The occasion was largely a social one. Delia would often regale us with a song or two. She had a fund of Irish songs and stories, and it seemed that the old Irish tradition must have been deeply imbedded in her, coming from the West of Ireland.

"She was a regular visitor to St. Patrick's and knew several of the priests very well. One of them was practically a neighbour of hers in Mayo – Fr. John 'Spike' Buckley, and she at the time was very interested in having his voice trained. Her own daughter, Nuala, was having her voice trained in Rome, too. Delia maintained an interest in Spike's singing.

"She liked to go the Augustinian's summer house in San Pio, thirty-two miles south-east of Rome, and spend two or three days there with her children. She might have done that about five or six times in the year. We might be there with her on occasion, and she was full of joy and frivolity. She was like a mother to us all then. The Italians fell for her very much, especially out in the country. She enjoyed going around to the ordinary simple folk in the country. She'd speak in Italian quite well."

One of Delia's favourite stories from her days in Rome concerned an Italian version of *Three Lovely Lassies* which, she claimed, she overheard being sung on the street one day. She said she had translated it herself. "I heard a small boy singing *Sono tre le piu belle di Bannion*. He said it was an old Neapolitan folksong, and I told him it was mine! But perhaps I should have been flattered instead of being annoyed."

Whether this story is true, or whether Delia simply made it up, is hard to say. How did the youngster get the song in the first place, for instance? She did not say. However, Fr. Twomey was not so sure, because he had never heard it sung in Italian.

Delia expanded further on the Italian translation of *Three Lovely Lassies* in an interview she gave to Martin Walton in the 1950s "In the horrible atmosphere of war Irish music became a very parochial affair, and I sang very little when I was in Rome. It was hard to have a song in your heart when you were close up against the tragedy of war. I think those were the loneliest years of my life, but all the same, my songs were going around the world. Nostalgically in the Legation one day, I played my *Three Lovely Lassies*. Softly I sang a few verses. In verse four before I realised it, I'd been singing half in English and half in Italian. It gave me an idea and I sat down and I translated that whole song. It was perfect. I sang it in English and Italian at a small party for some musicians and artistes and then forgot all about it. Until one day I heard a small grubby- faced messenger boy carrolling it outside the Legation. I stopped him and asked him where he had heard that song. He stared at me and answered, 'Everybody knows it lady. It's an old Neapolitan folksong.'"

There is another reference to Delia's association with the Italian version of the song in an unidentified 1950s English newspaper cutting: "Possibly Delia Murphy's most unusual claim to fame is that she presented the Neapolitans with one of their most popular modern folksongs. This celebrated singer of Irish folk songs lived for six years in Italy...and while she was there she took the opportunity to introduce Irish folk music to the Italians. Needless to say, they liked it very much, particularly the lovely old ballad, *There were three lovely lassies from Bannion*, which Delia translated into Italian – *Sono tres piu bella di Bannion* – and you can hear it sung nowadays in almost any tavern or café around Naples. Indeed, many Neapolitans now regard it as their own and one of their best folk songs!"

Although there is no indication of the date of this cutting, one could be forgiven for guessing that it might have been 1st April. But, in fact, the piece was written to inform readers that Delia would be heard singing on a forthcoming St. Patrick's Night programme, on BBC Northern. It is probably from the early fifties, the only period when she had any sort of serious publicity and promotion through her recording company, and was typical of the kind of publicity material artistes had at the time.

In June 1942, the Kiernan family dressed up in their finest, and went to pay a visit to Pope Pius XII at St. Peter's. A photograph taken for the occasion shows that Delia, bowing to the strict dress code of the Vatican had donned a long black dress and covered her head with a black mantilla. Her husband – always a smart dresser – wore a formal dress outfit, the daughters, Orla, Fionnuala and Blon, wore white, and little Colm wore a dark suit. They were accompanied by Mons. Ryan in full Monsignorial robes, and two Swiss Guards. The Pope had two telephones on his desk and Colm was intrigued with one of them which was white with a yellow receiver. Pius XII seemed quite at ease with the youngster.

"I asked him why he had two phones," Colm said, "and he said this one is for all and sundry, and the other one is for calling special friends. And we believed him. He could talk reasonably good English. He was not a formidable person. Very nice. The only thing was that the protocol was formidable. You couldn't turn your back on him and walk out. Women had to be covered to their wrists and in long dresses. But other than that it was alright."

Noticing that Orla, the youngest of the Kiernans' children, was very quiet, the Pope turned to her and said, "You seem to be a very pius little girl," to which Dr. Kiernan replied, "I'm sure Your Holiness is not speaking ex cathedra!"

Delia recalled that Orla was not always so good. "I'll never forget one April Fools' Day, she and a school friend decided to plague the siestas of people with phonecalls. When they'd answer, Orla's little voice piped up, 'Assino d'Aprile!' and then she'd hang up. Then, somehow, she dialled the headquarters of the German High Command – a secret number. And when they traced the call to the Irish Legation, I was left with the difficult task of explaining it all away as a child's prank!"

Dr. Kiernan developed a strong personal feeling, even a reverence, for Pius XII, and in his biography of the pontiff, published in 1958, he described him as "a realist, above nationality, yet understanding of national feeling". According to Dr. Kiernan, the Pope was a European who was "yet equally at home in North America and in South America...and had all the simplicity of greatness".

The Kiernans settled into diplomatic life in Rome with comparative ease, and very quickly developed close friendships with other members of the diplomatic corps, not only at the Vatican, but also with those accredited to Italy. Among them were Sir D'Arcy Godolphin Osborne, British Minister to the Holy See, John May, his butler, Harold Tittmann, a U.S. foreign service officer at the Vatican, and Ernst von Weizäcker, Germany's minister to the Holy See, and Otto Christian Fürst von Bismarck, second in command at Germany's Embassy in Rome. Diplomatic representatives at the Vatican from those countries at war with the Axis forces, were housed in the Papal Hospice of Santa Marta, just inside the Vatican walls and at the rear of the Holy Office and the Collegio Teutonicum, and remained as virtual prisoners there until the Allies took over. Delia, meanwhile, was busy with her duties as a mother, and in addition to running the daily affairs of a legation household, she had to attend to the children's needs as well. To help her she had a number of Italian servants, and although food was scarce in Rome generally, they ate simply but well.

It was Italian cooking mostly, Delia recalled: "For breakfast, the whole family would assemble in the dining room, and we would have café latte – a mixture of hot coffee and milk – rolls and conserva. Then my husband went to work, the children to school, and that left myself to draw up the day's list of guests and activities. For lunch and dinner we started with soup followed by green vegetables and often veal. We had stewed fruit for dessert. We only drank wine at dinner-time and the children added water to theirs."

When food got scarce later in the war, the family had to make do with substitutes for real coffee, and Delia noted: "Long before we left Rome the children – Blon, Nuala, Colm and Orla – were ground barley addicts." Colm recalled how it was: "You could get all your essentials from the Vatican, but you needed meat, as well, and there were certain places where foreign ministers could get fresh meat. And for that you needed your Carta Identita. There were special shops with people queuing outside, saying, 'Can't we have some, too?' But they couldn't. That card was terribly important, and there were an awful lot of control points where you couldn't get through without it. On Delia's German identity card it said, *Sua Eccellenza*, Her Excellency. She knew the value of these cards very well." Colm said that embassies got food direct from the Vatican. "So, for example, others would be eating dreadful bread and I'd have nice white bread. We got good wine, spaghetti, oil, pure coffee – not the fake kind."

Delia saw to it that Sir D'Arcy was not short of the occasional little luxury. She decided that he had been missing a few delicacies inside his prison-like apartments in the Vatican, and at Easter time, 1944, she found her opportunity.

"Each Easter, as is the custom in Rome, a lamb is cooked. I went out into the country and rescued one for D'Arcy, wrapped it in a sheet, and put it in a big suitcase. Well, I could hardly be seen trundling up the steps of the Vatican with a freshly killed lamb over my shoulder! When he opened it back at the Vatican 'prison', he saw the blood-smeared sheet and turned white. I told him, 'It's your abaccio,' and the colour returned to his cheeks. "Strange to see how the other diplomats fussed over the German ambassador when things were going well for the Germans, and how they fussed over D'Arcy when he at last was free. When he eventually emerged from his 'prison', his first greetings were reserved for the Kiernans."

When talking about stories and incidents from those years, Delia shows fierce pride in her Irishness. "I found out that the Irish controlled Argentine politics because they had married into wealth there. They sent over an ambassador called Sweeney, and with a name like that, you won't be surprised to hear that he deemed it his first duty on arrival to visit us at the Irish Legation. He said, 'I thought I would call on you first and then present my credentials later at the Vatican.'"

Delia also took some racial pride in the fact that her two youngest children, Colm and Orla, were confirmed in the Santa Cecilia catacombs by a Polish prelate by the name of O'Rourke! He was Bishop of Danzig who had been a parish priest in St. Petersburg. Dr. Kiernan, who was with him when he died in Rome, said: "He was a Russian Pole, but on his deathbed he was an Irishman and glad to have an Irishman beside him when he breathed his soul to God."

Early in the war the Pope set up an agency to look into the plight of thousands of Allied prisoners of war, refugees, and displaced people generally. Monsignor Bergoncini Duca was put in charge, and Mons. Hugh O'Flaherty acted as his secretary and interpreter. The Irishman proved to be a real dynamo and made sure that families of the Allied prisoners got word of the loved ones and how they were faring. He supplied the British prisoners of war with books and other basic requirements, brushing aside obstacles put in his path by Italian bureaucratic ineptitude. He became such a thorn in the side of bureaucracy that he was forced to step down after representations were made to the Vatican, and he returned to his work at the Holy Office.

But as the war progressed and there were more and more demands for relief from stress, Mons. O'Flaherty found other ways of getting involved. His activities began to take a definite trend that would lead him into a battle of wits with the German SS, the Gestapo, and their Italian Fascist counterparts, when he started helping POWs and people generally on the run from the Axis powers. It would earn him the enmity and loathing of sinister figures like the Italian Gestapo's 'Torturer of Rome', an Austrian named Ludwig Koch, and the chief of the SS in the city, Colonel Herbert Kappler, also known as 'the Butcher of Rome'.

Mons. O'Flaherty became a legend in no time, and would be presented with decorations and awards by various Allied generals and heads of state at the end of the German occupation of Rome. Delia became one of his most valuable helpers, and she took enormous risks in the process.

VIII

'Fr. O'Flaherty's Spies' Parlour'

On 3rd September, 1943, Italy surrendered, and a week later, 74,000 British POWs were released from the camps. Many made their way to Rome. Half a dozen POWs managed to make it into the Vatican and were interned there for the rest of the war. Another group of a dozen or more also tried getting in but failed; the Swiss Guards were under orders to turn them away. An Irish priest at St. Monica's, the Augustinian international college opposite, saw the forlorn group outside the gates of St. Peter's and he brought them inside. He telephoned Hugh O'Flaherty , who came and took them away. Unbelievably, his choice of hiding place was a police barracks where he knew a friendly carabiniere.

Gradually, many of those who had met Hugh when he visited them in their camps, sought him out when they came to Rome. Things began to get more and more desperate as the Germans took charge and the Gestapo instituted a stern regime to take control of what had become a totally chaotic situation.

Hugh then got to work in earnest, setting up an undergound network of friends and colleagues to help escaped POWs. It involved a most unlikely mix of people from harmless-looking, unworldly clerics to sophisticated titled ladies and gentlemen from inside and outside Rome. It was not just the rightness of it all that appealed to the Monsignor and his team of helpers. Many of them, including Delia, quite relished the opportunity of getting involved, but they could hardly have foreseen what extraordinary hair-raising adventures lay ahead.

One of the POWs who sought Mons. O'Flaherty's help was Major Sam Derry, an extremely able officer in the Royal Artillery.

He was asked by Sir D'Arcy Osborne, the British Minister to the Holy See, to stay with him inside Vatican territory and help organise the escape line with the Monsignor and the Minister's butler, John May. May, was a remarkable man with a broad Cockney accent, whom Hugh later described as "indispensable, a genius, the most magnificent scrounger I have ever come across". Through John May the priest helpers also became au fait with the workings of the Black Market, something which was to prove very useful for their own requirements over the nine months the Germans were in control. Fr. Twomey explained how he and his colleagues became involved.

"Monsignor O'Flaherty would send two or three POWs along to St. Patrick's, for instance, ringing beforehand to say when they'd be coming. He gave instructions where they were to be brought, and myself and my colleagues from the community would take them through Rome, having first dressed them up in Augustinian garb. They might be English, or Scots, or Irish, and we warned them not to speak. I was doing it very quietly and discreetly and wanted to keep it that way. After the prisoners were in hiding for about a fortnight or three weeks, I'd check in on them to see that they were alright. I did this quite a few times, but then I said to myself that I'd have to be careful. But the Germans had already spotted me going to this hiding place. I'd go there to bring them the sacraments, Holy Communion, hear confessions, and give them a little talk, perhaps."

When interviewed for the RTE TV documentary in the mid-1980s, Fr. Twomey's appearance brought to mind the Professor in Rupert the Bear. He wore a happy and contented expression, and one would never have suspected that this humble and learned divine could ever have become involved in anything as irregular and as hazardous as "a spies' parlour".

One of those helping Mons. O'Flaherty was a Belgian colleague of Fr. Twomey's who had been captured and tortured by the SS. After managing to escape, he informed his Irish confrere that his captors had told him they could easily identify Fr. Twomey from his distinctive glasses. And even though he was much younger then, and somewhat boyish-looking for a prior, one can see from his photograph album how his round-rimmed spectacles, which gave him an air of unworldly innocence, would make him appear the most unlikely type of person to be involved in a deadly game of cat-and-mouse with the Gestapo and the SS.

How exactly Delia got caught up in the undergound network we cannot be sure, nor how deeply involved she was cannot be easily established. It was because of Hugh of 'the twinkling eyes' she began helping the POWs and others on the run, she said. But because of her husband's career as a diplomat, she refrained from talking about it until after his death in 1967.

"For a time I had wrestled with my conscience and prayed for guidance about what I should do to help Fr. O'Flaherty. A voice inside me said charity was something God intended for all humanity, in war and peace. And I remembered the words of St. Paul: 'Now abideth faith, hope, and charity, these three; but the greatest of these is charity.' What else could it be but charity to help those in trouble with the Nazis? Around the city during their nine month occupation of Rome, the Germans had splashed posters warning that anyone found sheltering an Allied prisoner of war would be shot. I doubt if they would have shot the wife of the Irish Minister, but they might not have hesitated with others in our group; those others who knew hiding only one Allied soldier meant the firing squad.

"But I was in the thick of it, and determined to save the hides of others and not get caught. I made sure none of the high-ranking German warlords, who invited the Kiernans to their feasts, ever suspected what an Irishwoman in Rome was doing in her spare time! All of it was a challenge, from the scarlet robes of the cardinals to the glittering decorations of the generals. Poking my nose in, call it what you like, but I risked my neck and Her Excellency's immunity because a voice inside of me said it was my duty to help. It was the same when I was child; always the odd one out; always in trouble of one kind or another. What's more, it didn't take me long to find out charwomen were as much a part of life as cardinals; dock labourers were as interesting as diplomats. So, I kept the doors of our embassy, wherever it was, open to anyone I could help. I loved people whether they had everything or nothing."

She said that St. Peter's Square became O'Flaherty's spies' parlour. "He always reminded me of those words on the old walls of Galway city – the words the citizens there used to tack on to the end of their prayers: 'From the ferocious O'Flahertys, O Lord, deliver us!' In Rome his name had been a password to a helping hand while officially he was a member of the Sacred Congregation of the Holy Office. Priests used to shuffle into his Vatican Office and leave with home-made identity cards and forged documents tucked inside their breviaries. When I received a call from 'Golf', it meant Fr. O'Flaherty wanted my help. His code word for escaped POWs was 'golf clubs', and when he said 'breviary', it meant he had an Allied soldier in need of medical care."

In his biography of Mons. O'Flaherty, *The Scarlet and the Black*, J.P. Gallagher describes a meeting between Delia's daughter, Blon, and Sam Derry, in which he makes clear how involved Delia (and indeed, Blon) had become in the Monsignor's organisation: "Derry was gazing pensively out of the window into the gathering gloom and did not hear the door open. He was consequently thoroughly surprised to hear in the Monsignor's rich brogue, 'Blon, I thought you would like to meet this British major.' Blon' turned out to be the extremely beautiful, 19-year-old daughter of the Irish Minister to the Holy See, Dr. Thomas Kiernan, a neutral to beat all neutrals ... and a man who was to be deliciously deluded by both his daughter and his wife ... Delia Murphy..."

One of her earliest exploits in helping the POWs, and perhaps one of the most daring, was the 'removal' of boots from the Wehrmacht shoe repair depot, and it took place right under the noses of the Germans. John May's concern at that particular time was for the increasing numbers of POWs who were on the move inside and outside of Rome and were badly off for shoes. May needed a great many pairs. Delia said when she got the word from Hugh she immediately approached the Italian shoemaker at the depot and persuaded him to part with several pairs. "It was decided I could have as many pairs as I could take away," she said. According to herself there were two hundred pairs altogether. P.J. Gallagher merely mentions 'quantities', while one of those who knew Delia well in Rome, the remarkable Fr. Michael Lee (formerly better known under his religious name, Brother Humilis), a Franciscan monk at St. Isidore's, said it was nine hundred pairs.

Anyway, Delia describes how she carried it off: "While my driver transferred the 'booty' into the back of the diplomatic car, I engaged the German office staff opposite in idle conversation, making sure they looked anywhere but out of their window." The whole thing would have been outrageously bold if carried out in the dead of night; but in broad daylight while diverting the attention of the Wehrmacht?! And just how often was this done?

J.P. Gallagher's account is possibly a bit more credible, although, with Delia, as with Hugh O'Flaherty, one could never tell. "Exactly how it was done," Gallagher wrote, "they have never disclosed, but the boot depot was closed and unguarded at night – the thought of putting guards on a repair centre of that kind never occurred to the Germans – and regularly for some weeks someone in the Irish Legation took quantities of boots from the depot, never too many at a time so that they would be missed...and hurled them over the Vatican wall into a secluded part of the gardens, where they were collected. Exactly what would have happened in Ireland if this exploit, and others yet to come, had become known to the Germans is a very open question." So, perhaps Delia's version of what happened was to help avoid implicating her husband too deeply. He must have known something was going on.

But it was not just downed American fliers, or Free French soldiers, or escaped British POWs Delia helped. "One day, I remember, an Italian brought us a German soldier he said he had found slumped across the Tiber bridge. The soldier was exhausted. He told us he hadn't eaten for days, and explained that he was fasting in the hope that he would be able to say Mass when he found someone to help him. Yes, this German soldier was a priest. At first we suspected him; that perhaps he was a spy, and it didn't help that he was brought to us by an Italian we hardly knew. But soon he satisfied Fr. O'Flaherty and the others that he was telling the truth, and we took him to the sacristy of a nearby church. There he shed his battledress and donned the vestments of Pentecost. And as I watched him slowly mount the steps to God's altar, I wondered about the foolishness of war and its sacrifices of life. Say what you like. I'm sure if women were allowed to rule the world there would be no more wars."

Br. Humilis, who was also one of the Monsignor's helpers, was a most unlikely looking secret agent. In complete contrast to the towering O'Flaherty, he is quite a small man and very soft-spoken. Indeed, he is totally self-effacing and is happiest when he is engaged in prayer or working in the service of others, as he does right to this day in his monastery in Cork City. He most certainly did not look like he would be engaged in anything more dangerous than leading the congregation in a decade of the Rosary.

The Monsignor picked his people carefully, and to Br. Humilis he entrusted two million lire to buy food and other necessities for the escapees. Like everyone else, this humble Franciscan monk saw it as his duty as a Christian to help those in distress, and took huge risks with his own life to do so. Br. Humilis was the bursar at St. Isidore's, and he became an expert in the workings of the black market. As part of his regular work in feeding his POWs, he had his provisions of Olive oil delivered in a Volkswagen beetle, hidden in a pigskin under the back seat. His work as bursar for the Franciscans was an excellent cover for frequent visits to the Vatican as he went about his other regular work on the escape line. He often went up and down in the lift in the company of Monsignor Montini (the future Pope Paul VI) who must have thrown the odd curious glance at the diminutive monk and wondered what on earth he was up to.

Dermot Keogh says that Montini must have had some idea of what Mons. O'Flaherty and his helpers were doing. Certainly he called in the Monsignor a few times for a dressing down. But he may have resolved to know as little as possible of what was happening.

Br. Humilis knew of Delia's work with Mons. O'Flaherty. "She did help him a lot that time. Besides getting them German boots and supplying them to the Allied soldiers, she got them food, too. I don't know where she got it, but she did. It was risky and highly dangerous as an ambassador's wife to have herself implicated in anything like that. She could have got into serious trouble."

He also knew Delia was very friendly with Sir D'Arcy Osborne, and with John May, and he recalled Delia telling him what she would say to the distinguished and gentlemanly envoy when he expressed concern about his country:

"What are you worryin' about? The British Empire's comin' apart at the seams, and your worryin' and my worryin' is not goin' to save it." Br. Humilis said, "Sir D'Arcy really enjoyed her. He really loved her. She did it for humane reasons to save lives. That was my thinking too, because it made no difference to me if they were Germans or English. I did it to save lives."

Delia certainly seems to have had a great relationship with Sir D'Arcy, an old-style British diplomat, a reserved, and gentleman bachelor. He gave Delia one of her favourite stories. "Edward V11 was a very sick and delicate man, y'see, and he needed a blood transfusion urgently. Well, it happened that an Irish policeman had the right kind of blood and gave some to the King. Next morning, the King was as bright as a button. When the doctor said, 'Good morning, Your Majesty,' and asked him how he was, the King said, 'Your Majesty be damned – up the Republic!"

During the war years, Sir D'Arcy was confined to the Vatican. He relished visits from friends like the Kiernans. Colm Kiernan said that he thoroughly enjoyed the company of Sir D'Arcy. "He seemed to be able to relax very much with young people," he said, "and he was very kind to me. I liked him. He was very friendly with our family. He was indeed a very close friend. I used to go there and have dinners and lunches, and he'd talk to me. He was a bachelor, and had a dog. He'd show me eagles, pools the dog would bath in, some fountains. How lonely he was, and apparently he had been in love with the Queen Mother. He wasn't homosexual. He was an aesthetic, and he lived a beautiful lifestyle, so that you could be attracted to beautiful dinners and lunches there, even during the war, because embassies got special food."

Br. Humilis himself obviously had great affection for Delia and the Kiernan family, and remembers with gratitude the work they did for the Irish community in Rome. "I first met Delia at St. Isidore's, during the war. She and her husband used to go there for Christmas Eve Mass. They had their family with them and were entertained by the community afterwards. Delia sang *The Three Lovely Lassies from Bannion*, and Blon accompanied her on the piano accordion. I met her several times after that, usually on Thursdays, when the Kiernans entertained the Irish from the colleges in Rome at their home. They'd give them a meal which was much appreciated at that time."

He also recalled an incident that made him smile. "Cardinal Pizzardo was in the Congregation of Religious, and I used to go back and forward to visit there with messages for our own superior. One morning myself and Br. Conrad and the Cardinal called at the embassy about ten o'clock and Delia was there. She was delighted to see us come in. The Irish were always welcomed by Delia. There was never a closed door. She brought down boiled eggs and red wine. We weren't used to drinking wine at that hour of the morning and when her back was turned we dumped the wine in a palm plant."

Although it had been hoped that Rome itself, the Holy City, would be spared from Allied bombings, it was decided after much discussion between the British and Americans that military objectives such as railway yards and facilities in the city should be attacked. This decision was reached in anticipation of the invasion of Sicily, in July 1943 in order to damage the transportation system and to interfere with the passage of troops and supplies to the south. The Pope appealed to the British not to bomb the city, and Dr. Kiernan reported by cable to Dublin that if anything happened, His Holiness would make a protest, pointing out influence of such protest on the Catholic World. The British government was irritated by these protests in view of the Vatican's silence on Jewish persecution.

On 19th July five hundred American aircraft bombed the railway yards and the central railway station in Rome. Dr. Kiernan reported that while the operation was a military success, 1,500 people in the heavily populated area of the central station were killed. He and his family stayed on the first floor of the legation during the attack because they had no air-raid shelter. Some of the bombs landed quite close to the Legation, and although Delia said that a window in the house was blown in, her husband made no mention of it in his report. While the bombing was in progress Dr. Kiernan received a telephone call from Dr. Hoffmann, head of the Vatican division at the German Foreign Office in Berlin who was on a few days' visit to Rome. This was strange since it was forbidden to phone during an air-raid. Dr. Kiernan reported to Dublin that the official came about noon, while the bombs were dropping near by, and chatted for almost an hour about nothing in particular.

How Delia and the children fared during all of this we do not know. No doubt she was as cool and calm as she was in the Belfast air-raid two years earlier. Later that same day Dr. Kiernan visited the scene of the bombing and was struck by the calm and quietness of the people. Bodies were being dug out of the ruins, but he wondered that there were no priests or nuns around to console them. He noticed a car at one stage hemmed in by the crowd and was surprised to see Pius XII in the back seat handing out 1,000 lire notes to the people. He said that as much as 60,000 lire were distributed, but that unfortunately those who got them were mainly 'toughs'.The King got mild cheers but the Fascist Secretary General was hissed by the crowd. None of the Irish houses was damaged. An estimated 450,000 children were subsequently evacuated from Rome.

With the onset of winter, conditions in Rome were deteriorating and the ration entitlements for November, December, and January had not been given out. There was no water for days at a time, and electricity was cut regularly. Feeding the POWs in hiding was becoming more and more difficult. By Christmas conditions in Rome had become desperate and the population had risen to over two million, swollen by three quarters of a million refugees, who had no rations except bread. The Germans imposed the death penalty on food hoarders, and Dr. Kiernan reported that the "black market is the only market", and that the Irish communities were fine and were well enough stocked.

Obviously the Irish priests were becoming more and more knowledgeable about things, in spite of the dreadful risks involved. Dr. Keogh gives the following amusing quote from

Kiernan's report to Dublin: "The nuns pray to St.Joseph to discover black market 'bargains' for them and they say he answers their prayers. I don't know how this fits in with moral theology!"

Meanwhile, the Kiernan family had to survive too, and they managed to acquire a pig for forty-five pounds. The nuns at the Irish College cleaned and cured it for them. Then the fridge gave out and gas was cut, and Dr. Kiernan had to buy a wood stove for 17,000 lire. He anticipated screams of anger from "the Department concerned.... We must live, anyway."

It is quite a comment on the contrast between the personalities of Delia and her husband to compare her cloak and dagger activities at this time with his almost detached account of things in a report to Joseph Walshe on 19th December 1943:

"Since the occupation of Rome there has been great normality – all kinds of rumours and counter–rumours and apprehensions but beyond the mass-arrest of Jews and the taking of some escaped prisoners of war...there hasn't been much out of the ordinary. The Vatican functions as usual, and the German Ambassador is a first-rate smoother of difficulties and exceedingly friendly with us. Some time ago he asked me if I could help him in getting certain supplies and in return he got me a permit for tyres for the car. A few days later the British Minister, who is also very friendly, asked me to help him with some things he was short of, though his request to help him to get a couple of bottles of Scotch whiskey had to meet with a decided negative. Our policy of neutrality in this war has certainly put our flag up and made great respect for us ...... Delia is in good form and keeps the Irish community cheerful – and sends you all the best of good wishes".

Although Dermot Keogh failed to locate any information in the archives of the Department of Foreign Affairs that would indicate Dr. Kiernan's personal involvement in the Vatican 'escape line', all was not as it may have seemed. Delia did say that one of those who was given refuge in the Legation was the daughter of Lord Granard, and wife of the anti-Fascist, Count Rossi, who was on the run. She merely mentioned her in passing when talking about the food shortages in Rome in late '43, early '44:

"Some days it was difficult to know what to cook up for the

constant flow of hungry guests at the Legation. Certainly all the family cats disappeared! Among them my favourite Persian, 'Mayo'. And Moira Forbes, an Irish citizen, who was one of my refugee guests remarked, 'If it was your cat, Delia, it tasted good!' We never knew. But I must admit the meat, when we did get it, looked unusual. I knew only too well, my Italian cook was an expert at sauces, and in turn, she knew hunger was the best sauce of all."

Once again, one never knows for sure if Delia is pulling one's leg. It seems, too, that Moira Forbes shared a room with a 'mysterious' Natalie, the wife of a senior Italian civil servant in Foreign Affairs who was on the run from the Fascists. It was thought that Natalie's husband was in the Italian Foreign Service in the United States.

Dr. Kiernan was noted for his discretion and his quietly effective methods in diplomacy, and if ever Dublin suspected anything of his decidedly un-neutral activities in Rome, they were not saying. It could not have been easy for him, an intense and extremely discreet man in every way, to allow his Legation to be used for sheltering those on the run from the Fascists and the Gestapo, but it seems he did. And by maintaining excellent relations with the diplomatic representatives of the Allied and Axis powers, he ensured his charges – family and guests – would be safe and well protected throughout the most dangerous and trying times in Rome. When the occupation eventually ended and the Allied soldiers entered Rome, according to Delia, the Legation 'was full of prisoners'.

But throughout it all Dr. Kiernan had to try and maintain a semblance of normality in fulfilling his role as neutral Ireland's Minister to the neutral Holy See. This involved entertaining distinguished guests of Church, State, and the Military. According to Delia: "If a cardinal came to visit the embassy we gave him the red carpet treatment. This was Vatican protocol. Women can't wear cosmetics, smoke, or drink, and they have to enter the room after the cardinal has been in it for some time talking only to the men. Before he came, I had everything ready for him – the two lighted candles and the red carpet. I was in the back room away from it all, busy fixing my suspenders, when who walks in only himself, this cardinal! He walked straight in without knowing I was there, and he saw me. 'Whoo!' I yelled, but he took no notice; just grabbed me by the hand and led me out into the other room dispensing with all the red tape. Well, anyway, I was having a great chat with him, y'see, and didn't I spill some of my sherry down the front of his red robes, and in the rush to wipe it off, ashes from my cigarette spilled on to the lot as I was rubbing away. It was a mess! But it didn't seem to bother him."

Among the many other visitors to the Legation Delia would talk about in later life was Bishop Gerald Patrick O'Hara of Savannah-Atlanta, Georgia, who in 1952 would be appointed Papal Nuncio to Ireland. "One day sitting in the Irish embassy, I heard a knock on the door. In came Bishop O'Hara from Atlanta, clanking with a gold chain and cross, and bubbling with good humour. He told me a wonderful story about the novel, *Gone with the Wind*, by Margaret Mitchell. He said that Margaret Mitchell hired an attorney to research all of Atlanta to make sure there was not another Gerald O'Hara (that was the name of Scarlett's father in her novel). 'And dammit,' he said, 'she had to find there was one – and a bishop at that!'"

On St. Stephen's Day (Boxing Day), 1943, the Kiernans themselves were guests of Mons. O'Flaherty at the Collegio Teutonicum. Major Derry and Sir D'Arcy Osborne were there, as well as priests of half a dozen nationalities. One of the priests, the Augustinian, Fr. Spike Buckley, was a special kind of 'bag man' for the escape organisation in that he had the job of taking care of sick and injured POWs. He used to have his cassock pockets filled with medications and he carried a battered old suitcase filled with bandages, insulin and ointments.

Delia sang *The Spinning Wheel,* and Spike sang *Mother Machree.* But the season of peace and joy had little meaning for the SS, and next day Colonel Herbert Kappler of the Gestapo increased the pressure on the organisation's escape work by imposing a 7 p.m. curfew which meant that POWs had to be moved about in broad daylight. A gate at the Holy Office was closed and men had to be brought in through the more heavily guarded entrance at the Arco delle Campane. Kappler was certain that Hugh was the moving force behind the escape organisation and spoke with Baron Von Weizäcker and von Bismarck. The German Rector at the Collegio Teutonicum then spoke with Hugh. He told him he sympathised but that Derry had to go, and he did. The major moved into Sir D'Arcy's suite in the Santa Marta Hospice where he was to remain a virtual prisoner for five months. Hugh himself was called to the Vatican Secretariat which had heard from Von Weizäcker, and he was given a severe dressing down. But he continued with his work, although he was more cautious and did not move about the city as much as before.

One of those who looked after twenty POWs in a country area, Concetta Piazza, a district nurse, was arrested by the Germans. She guessed they had little information on her activities and from her cell in the Regina Coeli Prison, wrote a note on toilet paper to Field Marshal Kesselring, the German Commander-in-Chief. She complained that she had looked after everybody, Germans included, and should not be held merely on suspicion. The note reached O'Flaherty and it was decided to have it properly typed up in a way fit for a Field Marshal's eyes. The problem about getting it to him was solved by Blon who happened to be on one of her regular visits to Hugh. "I'll get my father to do it," she volunteered. Dr. Kiernan did as he was asked, and wrote on the envelope, "For the personal attention of Field Marshal Kesselring." Concetta Piazza was released in a couple of days.

Delia and her husband both got involved in the case of another prisoner in the Regina Coeli Prison. The man in question was an Irish priest, an Augustinian, and confrere of Fr. Tom Twomey's. He recalls what happened. "From September '43 until the Allies came into Rome in June, the Germans were completely in charge. The Italians counted for nothing. In the earlier years of the war the German military would pass through Rome on their way south and on to North Africa. But in the months leading up to the Allies taking over, Italian soldiers never appeared. The carabinieri played second fiddle.

"I remember, one of our students, Fr. Ambrose Roche, from Clara in Offaly, offered a cigarette to one of a group of three thousand Allied prisoners as they were being marched through Rome on 3rd February, 1944. Roche was returning from class in the morning, and he was standing in front of the Capuchin Church with many onlookers around. One of the American prisoners asked him for a cigarette, so Fr. Roche threw him a packet. The next thing was, a hand grabbed him by the shoulder from behind and he was taken away. He was brought by car to the German High Commission. The Germans said to let him go free, but the Italian Fascists who had arrested him didn't want to do so and he was taken to Regina Coeli jail. We had our lunch at about half past twelve and this man didn't appear at all, not at half past one, nor later, and at six when everyone had to be off the streets, he still hadn't appeared. I began to get worried, and started to ring the police stations around the area. After calling about five or six of them I was referred back to the first one again. I then rang Dr. Kiernan about a quarter to seven and told him what the situation was. Dr. Kiernan said there wasn't much he could do right then and that they would see what could be done in the morning.

"I wondered if Fr. Roche was at the bottom of the Tiber, had been shot, maybe. At about five-thirty the following morning I got the first bus to the Hospital di Sancto Spirito near St. Peter's. I inquired for Fr. Roche there and described him – six foot tall, dark hair. No luck. They suggested that I should go to a police station in the centre of the city, and I told them my story. They asked me where I was living and I told them – Via Piedmonte 60. They then gave me the name of the station I should go to off the Via Genera.

"I went there at about a quarter to eight and explained my story. They said they had him. They couldn't tell me why he was being held or where. Thinking very quickly I thought of Dr. Kiernan again and went to see him. He was having his breakfast with Delia when I arrived and I had a cup of coffee with him. So Dr. Kiernan put on his best outfit, trilby type hat, and off we went in the embassy car with the tricolour flying. He was brought in to the head man, but I wasn't allowed in. Dr. Kiernan found out Fr. Roche was in Regina Coeli jail. The ambassador was permitted to visit him, but no one else. He made arrangements to visit him the next evening, and told me to prepare foodstuffs, fruit and so on. Dr.

Kiernan met him and Fr. Roche was in good form. This was on Thursday afternoon. He had a good beard by this time.

"Dr. Kiernan was quite a good friend of Von Bismarck's in Rome. I had met him and a friend of Von Bismarck's in Dr. Kiernan's house one time – Scheibert, a senior man in the SS in Rome at the time. So, Dr. Kiernan went to von Bismarck and told him the story. The following morning von Bismarck appeared in full regalia at the jail, asked for Fr. Roche and he was brought out. 'You are from St. Patrick's College in Rome?' 'Yes.' So he told him to come with him, and he took him home. The extraordinary thing was that Roche was a fluent German speaker, and like all the Irish got on well with von Bismarck, and of course, they spoke in German all the time."

That is how Fr. Twomey remembered the story. But to listen to Delia's account of what happened, one would think that she sorted the whole thing out single-handed. Fr. Twomey was Master of Students at the time, and obviously his account of what occurred is precise in every detail because it was his job to locate the missing student priest. But Delia does not mention him or her own husband in her account. Nevertheless, while she was aware of what was going on, and may even have played some part in the affair, it is worth hearing her brief summing up of what she says was her involvement, because it helps us to understand her attitude of mind and her thinking in this and many other stories.

"We had to decide how to free Fr. Roche before he was shot. It was decided that I should contact one of the German big-wigs, a high-ranking warlord, who was among that collection that were doing their best to gatecrash Roman Society." It did not seem to dawn on her how hilarious it sounded when she, a 'country girl' from Co. Mayo, described the noble Prince von Bismarck – a diplomat, and hardly a 'warlord' – as 'gatecrashing' High Society in Rome.

She continues: "I had met von Bismarck at informal parties, and I located him at his home in the hills at Frascati. He was young – in his twenties – handsome and intellectual. I told him that by going ahead and putting that priest in prison, the Fascist police would overrule the German SS. If the Fascists were allowed to get away with that sort of insubordination, all Rome would be talking about it and the German HQ would look silly – in fact, would become a laughing stock! He agreed, and the priest was released."

Delia's account of her involvement in another one of her rescues of a POW is corroborated by J.P. Gallagher in his book. Whereas her account starts at the point where she was called in, Gallagher's begins when Mons. O'Flaherty went to Major Derry to tell him that a Scottish soldier in the Subiaco Hills outside Rome was in a bad way with what looked like appendicitis. Derry decided that the only thing to do was to bring him into the city and leave him outside the German Embassy and tip off von Bismarck. He would lose his freedom, of course, but he would be looked after. However, the young private, Norman Anderson of the Cameron Highlanders, would have none of it. At that point the Monsignor took over, and called Spike Buckley and Delia. She takes up her version of the story.

"We collected him on the Via Venetto. Another POW we had also rescued was a doctor, so he examined the Scot, and diagnosed peritonitis. So we needed a surgeon and an operating room. The only one available was in a convent hospital that the Nazis were using for their sick and wounded. So, as soon as the patient had come out of his anaesthetic after the operation, he would have to be removed. I called for Fr. Spike in what must have been one of the fanciest ambulances in Rome – my roomy limousine with diplomatic licence plates, and the tricolour of Ireland fluttering from the fender. The sick man weighed close to 150 lbs., 15 lbs. less than Spike. But Spike's muscles were hard and strong, and he picked up the young soldier like a baby and carried him into the operating room, and covered him with a priest's cassock. We drove round the neighbourhood for a couple of hours while they operated, and then Spike went in for him again.

"O'Flaherty's instructions were to take the soldier to the house of a Mrs. 'M'. The SS stopped us at a set of traffic lights and asked us who was it lying in the back seat. Spike explained that he was an Irish priest, and that we were taking him to hospital. The Scottish soldier looked pretty awful, and it was enough to convince the Germans, and they let us drive on. We left him at the home of Mrs. Henrietta Chevalier, a Maltese woman (Mrs. 'M')."

Delia and her husband boarding an Aer Lingus flight at Dublin Airport on their way to London , 6th October, 1945.

Photo: The Capuchin Annual, 1945-46.

"Best wishes from Delia Murphy, 5th June, 1950". A copy of the concert programme which Delia signed for Fr. Jarlath Waldron, who helped organise her first concert after she returned from Australia.

Photo: Fr. Jarlath Waldron

St. COLMAN'S COLLEGE,
: Claremorris.

Welcome You To Their Celebrity

CONCERT

In The

CENTRAL CINEMA,
CLAREMORRIS.

ON MONDAY NIGHT, 5th JUNE 1950.

Master of Ceremonies: PADDY McELLIN, Solr.
Accompanist: Mrs. SINCLAIR, Claremorris.

Programmes - 3d each.

Kilcolman Press, Claremorris.

1.—OPENING CHORUS. "Count Your Blessings One By One" St Colman's Choir.	13.—QUARTET. "Come Where My Love Lies Dreaming" Foxford.
2—SONG. An Irish Emigrant. Wm. Kealy, Tuam.	14.—RECITATION. "Jimmy From Cork" P. Tolan, Foxford.
3.—RECITATION. Selected. Jack Cunningham, Ballina.	15.—SONGS. Selection. Delia Murphy
4.—TRUMPET. Selection Paul Karol.	16.—VIOLIN. "Souvenirs" Charlie Reynolds.
5.—SONG. "Birds Song At Eventide. Peggy Dolan, Milltown.	17. SONG. "Trotting To The Fair" J. Walsh. Ballina.
6.—QUARTET. "Oft In The Stilly Night" Foxford.	18.—DANCE. "The Blackbird" Bridie Quinn.
7. VIOLIN. Sel. Gilbert and Sullivan. Charlie Reynolds, Ballina.	19—SONG. "Killarney" Mrs. O'Sullivan.
8.—SONG. Selection. Delia Murphy.	20. THREE VIOLINS IN HARMONY. "Bolero" Ballina.
9. RECITATION. Andy McTigue, Castlebar.	21.—SONG. "Song In Our Heart" Peggy Curran. Ballina.
10.—SONG. "It's A Great Day For The Irish" Tom Eagleton, Tuam.	22. SAXOPHONE. "My Own Lovely Lee" Phyllis Ruane.
11.—SAXOPHONE. "River Shannon" Phyllis Ruane, Ballina.	23.—RECITATION Andy McTigue.
12.—SONG. "The Trumpeter" B. O'Donnell, Enniscrone.	24.—GRAND FINALE. Selection. Jack Ruane's Orchestra, Ballina.

Left: Delia's friend, the world–renowned Irish tenor, John Count McCormack, September, 1936. *Right:* Most Rev. Dr. Daniel Mannix, Archbishop of Melbourne.

Photos: The Capuchin Annual, 1940.

Donagh MacDonagh, presenter of folk-song programmes on Radio Éireann in 1930s.

Photo: The Capuchin Annual, 1942.

Éamon De Valera, photographed during the War when he was Taoiseach, with Fr. Senan, OFMCap, and Dr. McNeeley, Bishop of Raphoe.

Photo: The Capuchin Annual, 1941.

Top: Taoiseach Éamon De Valera during World War II; behind him, first left, a future Taoiseach, Seán Lemass. *Centre:* Delia and her husband having dinner with friends, including, far left, Fr. Senan OFMCap, and in the centre, Dr. McNeeley, Bishop of Raphoe. *Bottom:* Delia, 3rd from left, with a group of friends at a function in Dublin in mid–1940s.

Photos: The Capuchin Annuals, 1943 & 1945-46.

Leo Maguire (pen-name 'Sylvester Gaffney'), host of the popular Walton Programme on RTE radio for many years.

Photo: The Capuchin Annual, 1945-46.

Photograph taken in August 1968, on the day the author and Delia first met, outside her house at Jasper, Smiths Falls, Ontario, Canada; seated l. to r.: Delia, the author with his infant daughter, Kathleen; standing behind is an elderly neighbour who occasionally helped Delia on the farm.

Photo: The author.

Seán Ó Cillín, a friend of the author's, and Delia, at the back door of her farmhouse, in Ontario, winter of 1968-69.

Photo: The author.

Delia's farmhouse in Ontario, winter of 1968-69. The house was built by Scottish stonemasons in the last century.

Photo: The author.

Studio recording for a Canadian Broadcasting Corporation radio programme, Ottawa, Ontario, Canada, May, 1969. l. to r.: Joyce O'Hara, wife of the author; the author; Delia; Sandy Carson; Tom Kines; and standing at back, bass player, Ron McGee.

Photo: The author.

Delia on stage at Camp Fortune, Gatineau Hills, Quebec, Canada, July, 1969, on the occasion of her last major concert, which was broadcast on radio by the Canadian Broadcasting Corporation.

Photo: The author.

This middle-aged widow played an extraordinary part in the Monsignor's rescue operation for POWs, and risked her life, and that of her children in the process. She had several incredibly lucky escapes from the SS and the Gestapo, but survived the war.

There are a few minor differences and one major one in Gallagher's version of this story, however. The principal difference is that Spike Buckley 'borrowed' the car from Delia, and drove it, and his companion was a De la Salle brother named Bob Pace.

From what Fr. Tom Twomey, OSA, says, it is just possible that Dr. Kiernan's influence with key German diplomatic and military figures helped, and it could explain to some extent why none of the Irish priests in the rescue work were caught or suffered any physical injury during the German occupation of the Eternal City.

Fr. Twomey says that it was not generally known that the Irish Legation was engaged in helping O'Flaherty. He remembers what happened to one of his own colleagues, a Belgian Augustinian who was involved in the rescue operation. (In his book, Gallagher says he was Dutch, and named him as Fr. Anselmo Musters, whose code name in the operation was 'Dutchpa'.)

"I remember one time during the occupation by the Germans – early March 1944 – the SS were looking for certain people who were helping escaped Allied prisoners. One of our own priests, a Belgian, who was deeply involved with O'Flaherty, got on board a bus one day in St. Peter's Square. Two Germans boarded at the same time, but he spotted them. He got off near the Coliseum, and they got off, too. He got on board another bus, and so did they. When he got to St. Mary Majors, he got off and ran up the steps followed by the two Germans. Just as he reached the door of the basilica, they grabbed him. Within minutes there were about two hundred German soldiers swarming about the place. He was taken away in a car to the Via Tasso in Rome. This was the place where a lot of people were executed – like Auschwitz."

It was the one thing that Mons. O'Flaherty and Major Derry had feared, because they knew that Kappler would stop at nothing to break up the operation. The Germans thought they had captured a British officer, Derry himself, possibly, and they tortured Fr. Musters unmercifully. He never talked.

"He was there for three months," Fr. Twomey continued, "and around the time the Germans moved north in early June, he was taken away. Somewhere north of Florence at around midnight, the car stopped in the wilds, and he escaped into a wood. He managed to make his way back to Florence and made his way to an Augustinian priory. He stayed there for a few days before heading back to Rome. By then the capital had been freed."

He headed for St. Monica's, the Augustinian international college, and rang Fr. Twomey at St. Patrick's and asked for a meeting. He told him that during his time in the Via Tasso, his clothes were taken from him each day, he was whipped and beaten, everything one can imagine was done to him. "They asked me regularly about you," Fr. Musters said. "They knew all about you. That you wore glasses of a particular type, your height, that you had white hair, everything. But the extraordinary thing is that you were never taken. They knew your name, that you were Prior of St. Patrick's. But I think what saved you was that your ambassador was very friendly with von Bismarck and Scheibert."

Cardinal Knox, later Archbishop of Melbourne, was studying in Rome at this time, and had become involved in helping O'Flaherty. So had Fr. Sneddon of New Zealand, who also became a bishop. Fr. Twomey said he knew of roughly twenty priests in Rome at the time who helped in the rescue effort. Among them, Frs. Claffey, Treacy, and Buckley. "Claffey and Treacy from the west of Ireland, were members of the congregation of Our Lady in Rome. They were both close to O'Flaherty and they helped thousands."

While Fr. Twomey was always willing to help, he exercised his own judgement about the methods he would use, even if that meant having to say no. Someone once told him that he had "better get two priests out of here fast" and into St. Monica's (which is in Vatican territory). He refused. "But," this person protested, "I have information that the Germans might visit here." Fr. Twomey said he did not believe the Germans would ever visit St. Patrick's. "The only time they did come was when the famous Kesselring, head of the German Army, came to live in the Excelsior Hotel not far away. Two German officers who spoke English very well came to see me one day, and they said they'd be very happy if six of their soldiers could come in to St. Patrick's every day, one from 6 to 12, another from 12 to 6 in the evening, and another from 12 midnight. I said no, that it is a house of studies, and it would completely interfere with the routine of the college. They were very nice, kind, and they left, and that was that."

The fact that O'Flaherty's operation managed to house and shelter about four thousand POWs and thousands of others on the run is testament enough to the Monsignor, his team of helpers, and the citizens of Rome generally; but that they so successfully managed to avoid detection and lost so few of those in their care, is nothing short of miraculous. The great majority of them have remained anonymous and unrecognised for their humanitarian efforts.

The Irish priests, for example, did not seek reward or recompense, nor did they expect it. Indeed, most of them are quite reluctant to talk about it even to this very day, and those who did, agreed only because it was to help tell Delia's story. Br. Humilis emphasised that Mons. O'Flaherty made sure that those involved with him were well protected from detection. To do so, he made extensive use of the Vatican's neutral position as an independent sovereign statelet, and provided official documents and passes for priests and others that would ensure their easy passage around Rome. "I never knew who the others were," said Br. Humilis. "So if anyone was caught they could never squeal. We never lost any of the soldiers." And it was not just POWs who were helped.

"When the war was over, I recall going into a Jewish shop to say good-bye. This Jewish gentleman came over to me and said, 'You don't know me any more?' I said I didn't. He took a photograph out of his pocket which showed him dressed in my habit and he pointed out his wife dressed as a nun. Then I recalled both cases and I remembered where I'd kept them. They came out alive, too."

And so did over 10,000 other Roman Jews who came safely through the war, although a figure of less than 2,000 is quoted for the number arrested during the German occupation. All of those 10,000 owed their escape from transportation to people in Rome, and they included priests and nuns at the many monasteries and colleges of the religious orders in the city, among them, of course, the Irish.

IX

The Allies take Rome

In early January 1944 the Allied Fifth Army opened its main offensive in the south, and the V1 Corps landed on the Anzio beaches later that month. Then Hugh O'Flaherty brought information to Major Derry that he felt might be useful, considering how important it was for the Allies to have a regular and uninterrupted flow of supplies. A priest friend of Hugh's told him that there were a lot of German E-boats tied up at the mouth of the Tiber River, and he knew that they might be used against the Allies. The boats were bombed almost immediately by the RAF, and supplies continued to flow. J.P. Gallagher says that Irish female charm in the person of Delia's daughter, Blon, was also brought to bear on the civilised and gentlemanly von Bismarck, and he explained how it worked.

"Understandably it was when activities of a non-neutral nature became known to, or at least suspected by, the Vatican authorities, that O'Flaherty, despite the indulgent attitude of Cardinal Ottaviani, was in deep disgrace. It is well that none of his superiors could ever have learned of his next adventure into the field of anti-Nazi espionage. For this deeply involved Delia and Blon Kiernan at the Irish Legation, who probably were quite unconscious of the fact that through the Monsignor they were being used by Derry's intelligence service in the Allied cause."

Aware of von Bismarck's friendship with O'Flaherty and the Kiernans, Major Derry, who wanted some vital information out of the Germans' own mouths, so to speak, saw an obvious way to get it. The key question was whether the Germans would in the last resort defend Rome or declare it an open city. Mons. O'Flaherty contrived an invitation for Blon to have tea at the

German Embassy, and on her return to O'Flaherty at the Collegio Teutonicum she reported that von Bismarck was quite convinced that the Wehrmacht would have to withdraw, not fight for Rome.

Derry was informed and he passed on the information to Allied Intelligence. But it seemed that people were being too optimistic. "Far from preparing to pull out," Gallagher wrote, "the Germans were packing Rome with troops from the north, and Derry's radio operators were kept busy reporting these movements – and more tea-table chatter from Blon about top-level German reactions. In the longer term her reports proved very accurate."

Dr. Kiernan meanwhile was busy with reports and correspondence on the subject of Rome's 'open city' status, and sought to further the Irish government's campaign to have the belligerents respect the Eternal City's unique cultural heritage, and the Holy City's 'inviolability'.

Censorship in the Irish Free State during the war years – or 'the Emergency', as this period was called – was very strict, in adherence with de Valera's policy of neutrality. But in early spring 1944, the heavy curtain of censorship lifted briefly and the Irish people were informed by the press of the peril in which Rome stood. Mr. de Valera made an eloquent appeal to the belligerent powers on 19th March asking them to spare Rome from destruction. Dr. Kiernan reported to Dublin that the Pope had 'expressed personal gratitude', and when the Germans left Rome and the Allies arrived without having had to fight their way in, there was general relief, and prayers of thanksgiving were said.

Fr. Twomey recalled the day the Allies entered Rome: "On Sunday, 4th June, 1944, the Allied soldiers came in at about five-thirty in the evening. The following morning we went out and about and met many Americans. That day on my way back to St. Patrick's with another priest, right in the centre of Rome in the Via Tretonne, I saw a man being dismembered. He apparently had been giving information to the Germans. 'The lads' went into his house and brought him out on to the street and they killed him. Word came from Hitler, apparently, that the Germans were to leave Rome quietly. We knew some Germans in Rome – they were Catholics – and they asked if they could come to St. Patrick's for Mass, and I said yes."

All during the nine months the Germans had been in occupation, men like Fr. Twomey and Br. Humilis had exercised the utmost discretion. But then, with the Allies in control of Rome, and perhaps feeling there was less need for secrecy in the more relaxed environment, Fr. Twomey let his caution slip just a little. It could have cost him his life, he said. His story also gives us an insight into how the contacts between German diplomats and Dr. Kiernan operated to the benefit of the Irish community in Rome.

"I saw to it that my name never came up – unlike O'Flaherty whose name was well known. But I'll tell about one time I was almost caught out. A number of people came to St. Patrick's one evening, and there were two or three press reporters with them. Now, we had a place in the country called Genezzanno where Delia used to go from time to time. I had been there, you see, and the man there said that all their wine had been taken by the Germans in the very early days of June, 1944. They had been there for about six weeks before moving away. I was annoyed, but glad they hadn't destroyed the place. Anyway, back to the visitors to St. Patrick's.

"We were talking about this and that, and I just happened to say that I'd been out in our country place, and that the Germans had stolen all the wine. I didn't realise these fellows were reporters, and the very next day – there were two papers, *The Stars and Stripes* was one, and the British had another, *The Union Jack* – and both papers had the story. I thought, God, I hope the Germans never come back or I'll be sure to be shot and no more about it. Anyway, the extraordinary thing was that the Germans got new reserves from Germany and they beat the Allies back towards Rome about twenty miles. Weizäcker, the German Ambassador to the Holy See, rang Dr. Kiernan protesting about me, saying that he should speak to me and tell me to be more discreet. Dr. Kiernan rang me up alright, but the Germans never came back anyway."

It is quite extraordinary how the Germans would be so touchy about their soldiers being accused of stealing wine, considering their brutality in dealing with Jews and hostages in Italy and elsewhere throughout the war. When Italy surrendered in September 1944, and then declared war on Germany in October, the German military went on an orgy of looting, stealing Old Masters, priceless manuscripts and art treasures. But one of their most horrific acts of atrocities, the revenge killing of over three hundred civilians just three months earlier, took place at the Ardeantine Caves outside Rome.

Thirty-two German soldiers were killed on 22nd March when a time bomb went off as they marched down a Rome street on their way to a bath-house. Hitler ordered the massacre as an exmplary reprisal killing, so Kappler decided that ten civilians would die for every soldier killed. He randomly selected people from prisons all over Rome for the slaughter. They included political prisoners, prostitutes, petty thieves, and recaptured escapers.

When the Allied soldiers arrived in Rome, Delia, too, wanted to see 'a bit of the action', and decided to wander outside to see what was going on. She had her youngest child, 11-year-old, Orla, with her. For years afterwards she loved to tell the story of how she met her first American soldier, and always hooted with laughter as she recalled the event. One of the first who heard Delia's account of what happened was the Irish playwright, Denis Johnston, who was a BBC correspondent during the war, and entered the city with the Allied soldiers. He relates her story in his excellent work, *Nine Rivers from Jordan*, one of the most highly acclaimed books written about the Second World War:

"On the neutral territory of the Irish Legation a small party of un-neutral Hibernians gathered to greet the Minister and his handsome, Rabelaisian wife. Out in the yard, somebody obligingly filled the tank of his car with Allied petrol.

– What was the first sign you had that we'd arrived? I asked of Delia. She tossed her head of black curls, and smiled the smile that must have baffled many an Axis official.

– They call me Your Excellency here. It's the way they have in the Diplomatic, d'ye know. Well, I was out taking a walk in the morning to see what was going on. And there was a lot of lads in uniform lying on the pavement in front of the railway station, taking a rest, d'ye know. And I thought they were Germans, until suddenly one of them sat up and said, 'Say, sister. Come and park your arse beside me.' So then I knew I was liberated.

Johnston's account of his entry into Rome makes for hilarious reading as he and other correspondents raced each other to be the first to get there. In his first attempt to get into Rome before anybody else, he was nearly killed when his jeep almost ran into a German tank. For a few seconds the two vehicles just sat there, their occupants not knowing what to think. Then, as if they were responding to a command, each quickly reversed and hightailed it back the way they came. Johnston and his colleagues in the jeep eventually pulled in to the side of the road, and as he waited around for the tanks and armoured cars to catch up, a dispatch rider on a motorcycle handed him a document from the Police HQ of the 5th Army that permitted him 'to enter the city...and circulate therein in connection with his official duties'.

Now that the Germans were gone, the shoe was on the other foot as far as the Axis diplomats were concerned. The Japanese Ambassador was under siege and had his electricity and water cut off by the Americans. Johnston wrote: "By a devious route, the German Minister to Italy was smuggled into neutral territory by Kiernan, the Irish Minister to the Holy See, who previously had been doing the same sort of thing for Allied personnel, to the annoyance of the German Minister. Ireland was sticking to its traditional policy of being on the side of the hunted rather than that of the hunter – whoever the hunter might be."

A short time before the Allied forces reached Rome, Monsignor O'Flaherty was at work in the Holy Office when a visitor was announced. He was a Roman nobleman, and he had come with a most unusual request for help. He said that one of the Monsignor's mortal enemies, the Torturer Ludwig Koch, wanted him to take care of his wife and children because he was afraid what might happen when the Allied army arrived. In return, Koch promised that certain prisoners in his care would be safe, and he would make his way to the North of Italy when the Germans left. The Monsignor agreed, and Koch kept his word.

After that, Hugh O'Flaherty began to work in helping distressed Germans and Italians, and was busier than ever supplying information to families whose sons had been in Allied prisoner of war camps. When General Alexander, Commander-in-Chief of

Allied Armies in Italy, arrived in Rome, he was immediately informed by Major Derry about the work of the Monsignor and his helpers. Alexander, himself an Irish Guardsman, was suitably impressed, and said the Monsignor was to have any assistance he needed in is new work. Right away, O'Flaherty received every help and cooperation from the Allies who even supplied him with a plane at one stage to take him to South Africa where Italian soldiers were imprisoned. An Allied Screening Commission was set up and issued seventy-five thousand certificates of thanks, and refunded £1,000,000 to those who had loaned money to Monsignor O'Flaherty and others who helped the Allied cause.

In further recognition of his gallant work, the British awarded the Monsignor with a CBE. He sent the medal and other decorations he had received from the governments of the U.S., Haiti and San Domingo, Canada, Australia, and Italy, to his sister in Co. Kerry. She put them in a drawer, and he never looked at them again. Others were awarded MBEs, and the Irish priests, Buckley, Claffey, and Treacy, were 'specially commended' by George VI. It is interesting that none of them – including Br. Humilis who did not even get a 'specially commended' – received a decoration. Perhaps it was because as Irish citizens they did not wish to accept any decorations, since many people in Ireland might not have approved.

Sir D'Arcy Osborne was most anxious to see that the Kiernans, too, received proper recognition for their invaluable assistance. In his letter to the British Foreign office praising them for all they had done, he said:

"In fact, Mrs. Kiernan's name was suggested by the War Office for a decoration, but before proceeding with the proposal I was asked to ascertain whether this would be acceptable or, alternatively, might be in any way embarrassing. Dr. Kiernan reluctantly decided that the conferring of a decoration upon his wife for what were in fact un-neutral activities might be frowned upon at Dublin, so the question of a decoration was dropped. I was led to suppose on Dr. Kiernan's arrival that he was anti-British but have never seen any sign of it, and the above mentioned assistance to our prisoners should dispose of any such charge.

Delia told how Sir D'Arcy approached her one day about

rewarding her in some way. After expressing his regret that she could not be decorated, he asked her if there was anything she would like. "Yes, I told him, I'd love diamonds! Anyway,, "he arrived one day with a box, and inside was a beautiful vase. 'It's full of diamonds,' says I to him. And he said, 'No, it isn't, but it is very valuable. It's a Chinese Ming vase.' I asked him how much it was worth, and he said, 'Well, I can tell you that its value is not more than a thousand pounds, and not less than five hundred.'"

Dr. Don Carr, a young Supply Officer with the British Army in Italy in 1944 was one of the many Irish in the Allied Armies, who were warmly received by Delia at the Irish Legation on San Martino della Bataglia. He had met her in 1937 at the P.E.N. Club meeting in Jurys Hotel. He knew that Delia was in Rome, and since it was everyone's ambition to get to Rome, he applied for leave, and the following month he arrived in the city.

"As soon as I got to the Legation, you'd have thought we were childhood chums. She treated me royally. Brought me everywhere and introduced me to Mons. O'Flaherty. An awful lot of chaps had been captured in the desert or in Italy itself and the Monsignor's efforts on their behalf was greatly appreciated. And Delia Murphy, of course, played a very big part in that organisation – she and all the Irish priests who were there. "Take Fr. 'Spike' Buckley – he was one; a Rosminian priest, Ben Forsythe, from Fermoy, and Fr. Dowdall, the Rector of San Clemente, both played an active part in rescuing POWs.

"When our troops entered Rome, Field Marshall Alexander offered an OBE to Delia. But, of course, in view of her position as wife of the Ambassador to the Holy See, and Ireland's neutrality, she had to obviously turn that one down. So he then asked her if he could he do anyt favour for her. She said yes, 'Get me a pass that will let me go anywhere in Italy.'"

Alexander was as good as his word, and Dr. Carr saw the pass he gave her which required every soldier to give her every assistance she needed. And she used it. She even went up to the Front Line, Don Carr said. He also said that during the German occupation, there were so many POWs in Rome that it became a problem, and Major Sam Derry was always trying to get them to stop in the countryside rather than come into the city. "I remember in one place, the Osteria del Orso – a restaurant cum nightclub – the barman there told me that they frequently had German soldiers and officers upstairs, and all British officers downstairs. Now this might have been a bit of Italian exaggeration, but I think I believed it alright."

After his leave was over, Don invited Delia down to his station in Bari in the south of Italy. "I put her up there in the YWCA and fed her in my mess which was very small. To entertain her I thought I'd bring her to the opera one night. So I went to the opera house in the morning and I brought Delia's credential – this famous pass from Alexander – and I said to the officer commanding the opera house that we'd be coming there that night, but in case there was any difficulty, I said the civilian with us is entitled to be here – this is her pass, she's the wife of the Irish Ambassador to the Holy See. So he took the pass and he looked at it and he read it, and he said, 'The royal box.' That's just the job said I. That'll do.

"That night I got ready and we drove down in the jeep. But when we got near the opera house, I pulled up and I said, 'Look, we're in trouble here, because one of the top brass must be going to the opera, because even at a distance we could see there were hundreds of people all around the opera house, and there was a guard of honour and a red carpet laid down, and so on. So, obviously it was the Pope, or the general officer commanding, but not for us. So I said we would wait until the mainstream had gone past and then we'd go in. So we waited, and then in a little meek voice Delia said, 'Don, do you think it could be for me?' And then I said, 'Oh my God. Yes.'

"And sure enough, when the officer saw who it was, we had to drive up in a jeep, and get out, and there I was, a lieutenant, having to march through a guard of honour, salutes and all the rest of it. I never want to have that again. Up the red carpet, and Delia, of course, carried it off with the greatest aplomb. And there at the top of the steps were the brass of the opera house, and we were brought to the royal box and sat down. I never felt so small in all my life. It's not an experience I'd want to repeat in all my life again.

"When my leave was over, I asked for, and got, an extension, but as time was up in the Leave hotel where I had been staying, Delia accommodated me in the embassy where I slept on the sofa in one of the reception rooms. The war in Europe had finished and it continued against Japan. So I volunteered to be part of that, and I was sent up to a little company at a place called Casabrucciatte on the Adriatic Coast.

"I was there for about six weeks with a supply depot, but with nobody to supply. And eventually we got our marching orders to sail from Naples. We set off, and we were to abandon all our supplies in this little village. And I thought, blow me, I can do better than that, and I got a three ton truck, and I loaded it with supplies, knowing there was the Irish Legation, the Irish College, the Dominicans, and all my Irish friends in Rome, and that they could use it. So we set off in a convoy to Naples, passing through Rome."

However, when he arrived in Rome he was disappointed to find that the Kiernans had returned to Ireland. There was nothing for it but to dump the three tons of 'pinched stuff', and somewhere in the mountains between Rome and Naples, the truck with its supplies was driven over a cliff.

Delia appears to have kept it very quiet that during her time in Rome she herself took voice training with a prominent Italian instructor. Dr. Carr said he accompanied her to one of these sessions. "I remember she sang a duet with an Irish priest, Fr. Butler, who was a chaplain in the South African Army. They sang, *Parigi, o cara, noi lasciaremo*, and her teacher was very critical, interrupting every now and then to stress some point in her breathing, or expression, or what have you. I remember this particularly, because Delia was normally a rather forceful character who was more inclined to give orders than to take them. And yet, before this Italian music master, she was as meek as a mouse, and took all his reprimands and criticisms rather like a naughty child being told off by a schoolmaster."

In September 1945 the Kiernan family returned to Dublin for a few weeks holiday, their first since coming to Rome four years earlier. Delia took part in the *Aith Seadh* revue that was playing at the Olympia Theatre. After the performances she would often be presented with a box of chocolates. "I hadn't seen the likes of them during all those years in Rome, and if anyone ever got a sweet at that time, we would make six parts of it. That's how we did everything during the war. We shared and we stuck together. In particular, the Irish."

On 17th September, *The Irish Press* journalist, Anna Kelly, did a write-up on Delia and headed the item, "Chocolates for the Three Lovely Lasses from Bannion". The Press photographer took a picture of Delia signing autographs with the piece of paper resting on the box of chocolates. She said she was delighted the people of Dublin had not forgotten her, and added, "This is great fun." Anna Kelly noted that the Kiernan family was now some-what depleted, with Orla having just been enrolled at the Dominican Convent School, Cabra; Colm was in Castleknock College; and Nuala was studying singing.

The Kiernans returned to Rome on 22nd October. On her way through London, Delia had to obtain an Allied Forces Permit from the Military Permit Office, which stated that, "The bearer of this permit has the permission of the Commanding General Allied Forces to enter the Zone of the Allied Forces in Italy." It was valid for three months. Under the heading, 'Ministry or Dept. support-ing journey', it states, "High Commissioner for Ireland." This was John Dulanty, and the Free State was still a member of the Commonwealth. It is worth noting that he is described as, 'High Commissioner for Ireland', not for 'the Irish Free State'. No doubt, if anyone from the Stormont Government had a look at it, there would have been loud objections.

On 1st March 1946, Dr. Kiernan was made first Irish envoy to Australia. He and the family stayed on in Rome until May when the new ambassador, Joseph Walshe, arrived. In a letter to Frederick Boland, Secretary at the Department, the new Minister had generous words of praise for the Kiernans: "You can tell the Taoiseach (the Prime Minister) that they have done wonderful work in Rome. I have met all the heads of the Irish houses, and most of the inhabitants...and their praise for Dr. and Mrs. Kiernan is beyond all description." He went on to say that the Kiernans had done marvellous work for the Irish community in Rome, and that Delia was regarded "as the finest character of an Irish woman they have ever met" and that she had won the "affection and esteem of all". Dr. Kiernan received a Papal decoration, and Delia was made a Dame of the Holy Sepulchre.

Before the Kiernans left Rome, their oldest daughter, 21-year-old Blon, married a young South African officer named Anthony Hodgson. He was a captain and was in charge of the car fleet of the army during the Allied advance into Italy. Colm Kiernan said that Tony swept Blon off her feet, but that his father "was opposed to that and all the marriages. He thought he had a trump card, and he said to Blon that Tony had been married before, and she said that she knew that, but that he hadn't been married in the Catholic Church. According to Tony, the first marriage wasn't consummated, and it was dissolved."

X

'Far away in Australia'

Before the Kiernans left for Australia, Delia's mother died on 11 June 1946. The High Mass in Roundfort church was celebrated by Rev. E. P. O'Donoghue, assisted by three other priests. There were six priests in the choir. Some years before her death Mrs Murhpy had become reconciled with her family – the Fannings. According to Mary Cassidy, the Mout Jennings housekeeper, the Fannings had been very annoyed with Mrs Murphy for marrying so young and they had never visited her all the time she had been in Hollymount – about thirty-six years. " They used to come often then, after the reconciliation," Mary said. "The Fannings used to come and also a first cousin of hers called Andy Houlihan."

Two months after Mrs Murphy's death the Kiernan's set sail for Australia. According to Delia, "It was during our days Down - Under that I quickly made a mark for myself. It seemed the gossip columnists delighted in reporting what Mrs. Kiernan was doing, wearing or saying, and I was forever in the public eye." Judging from the many newspaper cuttings and photographs she kept of her years in Australia, Delia certainly got plenty of press coverage. And in contrast with the war years in Rome, where she had been relatively confined, the great expanse of the island continent offered her endless opportunities of travel and exploration.

It is clear from what Delia herself had to say about her time there, and the comments of members of her family, that she had a love-hate relationship with Australia. Part of it had to do with the fact that, as Ireland's first representative to the country, Dr. Kiernan – who was Irish High Commissioner to Canberra, with the personal rank of Minister – was obliged to pay his respects to members of Australia's substantial Irish community in every major town and city from coast to coast, and a lot of smaller ones in between, as well. An estimated twenty per cent of the continent's population was of Irish descent, and some 20,000 were Irish-born. And a hot dry continent it was – too hot for Delia's liking. Also, the federal capital, Canberra, which was small and out of the way, had been purpose built as such only as recently as 1927. Canberra is located in the Australian Capital Territory, and lies on a plain at the foot of the 6,200ft. spurs of the Australian Alps.

But perhaps the main reason for Delia's ambivalence about life Down-Under had more to do with frustrated hopes and ambitions concerning her singing career. Following her lengthy posting in war-time Rome, the short spell on stage at Dublin's Olympia had merely re-awoken her long-suppressed desire for the world of showbiz, and her appetite was whetted. All these factors, and the knowledge that she was not getting any younger, did not help Delia in fighting the conflicting emotions she experienced.

In a way, this conflict of who she was, and what she wanted to be, is reflected in how her academic qualifications are recorded in portraits and articles in newspapers and magazines. When interviewed in Ontario, Canada in 1968, she would say something like, "Ah sure, I'm only an M.A. from Galway," the 'A' being pro-nounced exaggeratedly with a broad 'Ah'. In some articles she is said to be a graduate in Commerce and Arts, with a B.A. and a B.Comm. Elsewhere, as in a newspaper report of her performance for the Sydney Women Graduates' Association, the readers are informed that, "Mrs. Kiernan graduated as Bachelor of Economics at the National University of Ireland." But in one of the very first newspaper articles, published on their arrival in Western Australia, in the caption to a photograph of her and Dr. Kiernan, she is credited with an M.A. and a B.Comm.

On Saturday, 14th September, 1946, following a long and tiring voyage, Delia, her husband, and two youngest children, Orla and Colm arrived at Perth in Western Australia, on the liner *Sarpedon*. Blon and her husband, Tony Hodgson, were in South Africa, and Nuala was in Ireland. The Catholic paper, *The Record*, announced, *West Welcomes First Irish Minister to Australia; Catholic Community Greets Dr. Kiernan; Charming and Talented Couple as Eire's Ambassadors.*

On Sunday night they were entertained at an informal reception at the Cathedral Hall by the Celtic Club and representatives of the Irish National Foresters and the Hibernian Society. A Dr. McMahon made a brief speech of welcome. In his reply, Dr. Kiernan echoed Eamon de Valera's thinking from 1943 when the Taoiseach spoke about Ireland being a land of 'cosy cottages' where people were 'satisfied with frugal comforts'. "Ireland today was not over self-conscious in putting forward her national claims," the new Minister said. "She had achieved everything she had hoped for except the ending of the present unfortunate Partition. ... she also had a freedom which was typically Irish – a freedom from materialism. Irishmen tried to make careers for themselves, they tried to get on, but there was always some kind of spiritual background which was more important to them than the material results."

It was a strangely metaphysical line for an economist to take, and could possibly be ascribed to Dr. Kiernan's Roman sojourn among the Princes of the Church, and particularly, the influence of the saintly and austere Pope Pius XII.

When the Kiernans arrived in Canberra and had a look at the place, they might have been forgiven for using the line frequently attributed to Brendan Behan, and said to have been used by him in Canada when asked by Torontonians what he thought of their city: "It'll be a great place when it's finished." Houses were scarce after World War II, and there was no suitable living accommodation to be found, and so they had to make do with modest hotel accommodation. They had hoped it would be merely temporary, but in fact they were stuck there for the best part of two years. That factor could probably be added to the list above as another reason why Delia did not totally enjoy her time in Australia.

In the thirteenth of a series on "Ireland's Diplomatic Establishments" in March 1953 edition of *The Irish Tatler and Sketch*, Kees Van Hoek wrote about Ireland's Embassy (as it had been since 1950) in Canberra, and described the city: "Entirely created as a capital, it is the most original city of its type. No chimney stacks in view, no unsightly corner shop spoils a residential quarter, no petrol pump, a lovely avenue. Canberra has its distinct shopping centre and business district, governmental centre and residential environments. Not that all is still rosy in the planned garden. Through the very nature of its artificial development, Canberra knows many frustrations. A special township with no competition, monopoly prices are higher than anywhere else in Australia, the service take-it-or-leave-it ....The two hotels look more country than town. Altogether the capital has remained a small town with its 25,000 population. It has no theatre or concert hall, only two cinemas, and as public houses close at 6 p.m., entertainment is very much a private matter.".

When they had eventually settled in, making the most of their rented quarters, the Kiernans were ready for a long series of visits to towns and cities where the Irish immigrants and descendants of the Irish were anxious to extend them a hearty Australian welcome. Councillor Connelly was the Lord Mayor of Melbourne when they arrived there for a civic reception for Dr. Kiernan at the Melbourne Town Hall on 10th October, 1946. "This reception was the official one," Colm Kiernan recalled, "a lunchtime meeting. Archbishop Mannix had an unofficial one in the Town Hall Theatre, his own doing, on 21st November."

Eire Minister's Wife Steals The Show" was the banner headline the following day in a Melbourne newspaper. It reported:

> "This is surely a great night for the Irish," said Archbishop Mannix last night at Melbourne Town Hall, when first Minister Plenipotentiary for Eire to Australia (Dr. T.J. Kiernan) was welcomed by a crowded audience. However, it was not the Minister himself, with the brilliant red and blue ribbon of a papal order across his chest, nor the purple and black robed members of the hierarchy, nor the Irish pipers in shamrock-embroidered kilts, nor even the kilted Irish colleens who danced the jig and the sixsome reel, who received the greatest ovation. Surprise and delight of the evening was the impromptu recital of Irish songs with which Mrs. Kiernan thanked the audience for the welcome.

One of the happy outcomes of that evening is that we have the first ever live recording of Delia in concert, thanks to ABC Productions of Melbourne. This was in the days before audio tape came into widespread use, so they recorded the whole evening's proceedings on two extremely long Long Play discs, each approximately 16 inches in diameter. The speed is 33.3 ips, and the stylus is played, not from the outer edge into the centre, but from the centre out. The evening was hosted by Dr. Percy Jones, organist at St. Patrick's Cathedral in the city, and he introduced Archbishop Daniel Mannix.

This extraordinary prelate was born in Charleville, Co. Cork in 1864, and ran foul of the British authorities in Ireland because of his vigorous support for Irish independence. Following a highly successful trip to the U.S. in 1920, where he spoke in city after city on the campaign for independence, he returned to Ireland, but the British refused him permission to land. He was made Archbishop of Melbourne in 1917, and was forthright in his demands for state aid for Catholic schools. Dr. Mannix was also a fierce opponent of Communism. A brilliant public speaker, he hardly ever used notes and never failed to impress his hearers as he delivered his message in a calm and measured way.

The visit of the first Irish Minister afforded Dr. Mannix an opportunity of addressing his favourite themes before an audience he knew would understand his every nuance and subtle reference. The Archbishop was at his most brilliant as a speaker that evening in Melbourne, and as an effective piece of public speaking – in its construction, pace, delivery, and use of humour - his talk could well serve as a prime example of how it should be done. It was delivered in the familiar Churchillian style of the old school, with every key word and phrase receiving its full value.

"…It is a great occasion, because we're not merely exchanging diplomats between Australia and Ireland – even that would be something notable. But our demonstration is something greater than that. It means that we are here celebrating, as it were, the rebirth – perhaps I should say, the re-awakening – of a nation that too long was kept in thralldom. (applause) For myself, I never despaired of the resurrection or resurgence of Ireland. I always thought that God – if I might humbly say so – owed so much to Ireland, that he couldn't leave her always in serfdom. (applause) But what I did feel was – and I had reason – that I myself might not live to see the dawn of freedom in Ireland. (applause) However, history moved rapidly and I tarried long. (applause) And so, I have lasted to join with you in celebrating Ireland's resurgence, as well as the coming of her representative to Australia. (prolonged applause)

"There was a time, of course, – but it is long ago – when Ireland had powerful friends. She could look for help from France, and from Spain, and from Rome. But as time went on, everyone of them fell away. They still continued, of course, to give their sympathy, but it was sympathy without much help. The time therefore came when Ireland, little Ireland, had to face her powerful neighbour – and I'm on my good behaviour tonight. (laughter and applause) I followed the example of Mr. de Valera on a historic occasion when he gave a historic answer to Mr. Churchill. (applause) That Ireland alone had to face one of the most powerful empires that the world ever saw. And Ireland trod alone the hard, dark, lonely road. But in the darkest hour she never lost her way." (applause)

Referring to Dr. Kiernan, he concluded: "He comes to us with a great record. He's a man of rare culture and ripe experience. And therefore, to him, we extend a most cordial welcome. And not merely to him, but also to another, because there is something more exquisite still. (applause and laughter, including that of Delia's, which is easily recognisable nearby) I will welcome the Minister Plenipotentiary, and extend the same welcome, to his accomplished helpmate who has been with him in all his journeyings, and helped him wherever he went. (applause) I think the most discriminating people in Sydney have already realised that Mrs. Kiernan wins where she wanders. (applause and Delia's laugh can be heard again) At all events, to them both, a hundred thousand welcomes. I hope that their stay in Australia will be long. And if they go, and when they go, I hope they will take with them, and leave behind them, pleasant memories, and a record also of good work done for Ireland and for Australia." (long applause)

In his speech Dr. Kiernan referred to the problem of Partition, which representatives of the Irish Government at the time were encouraged to mention at every opportunity. He also told his listeners that everything was now rosey in Ireland, and that emigration, the curse of generations, was no longer a problem!

"Our nearest neighbour geographically is an island to which we are bound right from the dawn of history, by ties of kinship, of intermarriage, of work together. We have the same ideals as the English, the Scottish, and the Welsh in matters of democratic government. We have contributed a great deal to the British system of democratic government which originated with the Brehon Laws, which was broken in Ireland by imperialistic expansion and which survives now. We have contributed a great deal to British culture in its literature and in its music. And we were born side by side, we Irish and English and Scotch and Welsh, to be friends, natural friends, so long as each respects the other's national personality, national responsibility, national individuality.

"A hundred years ago this year when we were in the grip of the Great Famine, and when a quarter of a million people died from starvation, we had, following those deaths, the evictions, because the people who had no money and no food, could not pay their rents, and two millions of them were evicted from their homes, and their homes were burned over their heads. And they emigrated. A great deal of the Irish spiritual empire began then, and of the spread of the Irish tradition abroad."

Dr. Jones then introduced Delia. "And now I would like to present to you something that is not on the programme. At the request of his Grace, we are to be privileged to hear a reply to this grand welcome from Mrs. Kiernan herself."

It is obvious from the instant applause that many in the audience knew of her fame as a singer. Delia introduced the song, using the same words she always used: "This song is called *The Spinning Song*, and if I sing it properly, you ought to be able to hear the wheel spinning. I suppose you all know what a spinning wheel is? (laughter) The newspaper report said, "Flashing a smile at the Archbishop, she waved the musical director at St. Patrick's Cathedral to the piano....Softly he strummed the opening chords of an Irish spinning song. Taking the cue from Dr. Mannix, tapping the time on the arm of his chair, the audience were tapping its feet in time before the end of the first chorus."

When she had finished there was long and enthusiastic applause. The newspaper reporter continued: "The demand for an encore could not be disregarded and after a quick consultation with the accompanist, Mrs. Kiernan began ... And now I'll sing you an Irish boat song, *The Queen of Connemara*." (applause)

When she had sung the song, there was thunderous applause and even cheers from the audience. Then she said "And now I'll sing you an Irish lullaby, *The Castle of Dromore*." Even before she finished off giving the title, the audience applauded as though they recognised what was coming. When she finished there is even louder applause and even more cheering. Then she introduced her last song. "I'm sorry to say that it's time to go home now. (laughter) And I'll sing you a drinking song and I hope you'll join in the chorus." (laughter) She sang *The Moonshiner*. The audience laughed at the humorous lines all the way through. Eventually they began to join in the chorus as they became familiar with it. Then they burst into long and loud applause, stomping the floor with their feet for more.

Finally, Percy Jones invited all to stand for *God Save Ireland* which was played by a pipe band. The audience can just about be heard singing along over the sound of the pipes.

It is obvious from Dr. Jones' accompaniment that he was either reading the music from sheets supplied by Delia, or they had had a practice together beforehand. Certainly, he is an accomplished musician, and there was no hesitation with choosing the key or in the playing. So while Percy says that Delia's contribution was not on the programme, it seems that somewhere along the way, preparations had been made for an 'impromptu' performance by her.

Following on her extraordinary reception at the Melbourne Town Hall, Delia sang at many functions and concerts around Australia over the next few years. Most of them were small affairs, but she certainly seems to have made the most of the opportunities afforded through her husband's engagements. There are no figures available for the attendance at the Melbourne 'demonstration', but just over two months later, on Monday, 3rd February, 1947, an estimated 2,500 people gathered for what was called 'a demonstration of welcome' for the Irish Minister at Sydney Town Hall.

A leading part in the welcome was played by His Excellency Cardinal Gilroy who was presented with a watercolour of his titular church in Rome by Dr. Kiernan. There were seven other Catholic bishops there as well, and His Honour Mr. Justice McTiernan, P.C., presided. A Catholic newspaper reported: "Enthusiasm of the audience in welcoming Ireland's official representative was fully displayed towards the end of the evening, when at the request of a man in the audience, Mrs. Kiernan sang a group of Irish songs. ... 'Come on, Mrs. Kiernan, give us a song,' the man called out." Dr. Kiernan must have been relieved that Delia did not steal the headlines again on this occasion. After all, newspaper cuttings were regularly sent back to the department in Dublin, and to have had the Minister upstaged by his wife on every occasion would have been a cause of some annoyance for him and Dublin.

Having seen how successful she had been at the Melbourne Town Hall gathering in November, someone, it seems, saw an opportunity of exploiting Delia's obvious appeal as a performer, and on 27th March following, she returned to the same venue and for a much publicised 'Recital'. An advertisement announced:

> In the presence of his Grace the Archbishop, Recital by Ireland's Queen of Balladry, Delia Murphy (Mrs. T.J. Kiernan, wife of Ireland's Minister to Australia), assisted by Patricia Howard, soprano, and Basil Jones, Violinist. Mrs. Kiernan is making arrangements to send Patricia Howard to Europe this year, and the proceeds of this Recital will be used for this purpose.
>
> Seats: 7/6, 5/- & 3/-.

Once again, her accompanist was the excellent Dr. Percy Jones, and on the day of the performance, one of the newspapers printed a photograph of Delia seated at a piano, "practising for the recital". The next day, the concert was reviewed in a Melbourne newspaper by Thorold Waters: "Robust humors of a bubbling personality kept a big audience entertained when Delia Murphy ... devoted them last night to a Town Hall concert to help Patricia Howard, the young Sun Aria finalist, on her way to a career in Italy."

Whatever about his idiosyncratic use of the English language, the reviewer obviously knew a thing or two about Irish folk music, and observed, "Most of her ballads had a droll simplicity, eschewing the choicer folk styles which have been suited to the more fastidious ears by Herbert Hughes and other musicians. In *Down the Moor*, a Donegal song, she discarded her own succulent brogue for the sharper Harry Lauderish tang of the northern counties." And then Waters made a most interesting comment: "Moore's version of *She is Far from the Land* was hardly in her line." Why did Delia briefly abandoned her much loved ballads for a Victorian type 'drawing room' song? One wonders if she changed her uniquely effective singing style so widely appreciated, to try out some of the vocal technique her Italian maestro had taught her. If so, this apparent display of doubt about how 'legit' her singing really was, may be yet another instance of her inner conflict and the strain she was under.

Another reviewer, Thomas Culhane, of the Catholic paper, *The Advocate* was positively ecstatic in his praise for her performance that evening. "...it would be extremely difficult, if not impossible, to describe adequately the atmosphere and enthusiasm that marked this memorable occasion. From the moment she stepped on the platform, the vast audience was hers...Through every nuance of emotion which she portrayed in the many songs she sang, from the lovely *Spinning Wheel* down to the humorous *Legend of Glendalough*, her audience followed with an enthusiasm which was amply demonstrated by the thunderous applause that greeted her at the conclusion of each item."

The reviewer went on to say that Delia rightly believed that there was every reason to expect great advantage to Australian music from the knowledge and study of Irish folk melody. Whether this was what she had said on stage that evening, or something she spoke to him about personally, we do not know, but Thomas Culhane seems to be in no doubt about what Delia was trying to do: "She aims to spread in Australia the refining and cultural influences of the best musical tradition of Ireland and to weave into the texture of Australian life the heritage of good and noble things that have come down to us in the songs and music of Ireland."He goes on to place Delia in the same league as Ireland's finest traditional singers, but says that "there may be musical critics who have not been able to appreciate her songs." And he plainly takes Delia seriously, not just for her "artistry which is the fruit of long discipline", but also for the fact that she is a performer of the highest calibre, "a creative artist with imagination, and a power of interpretation. ... Mrs. Kiernan has a complete mastery of that art."

One of the few occasions where Delia was guest speaker was at a meeting of the Catholic Women's Social Guild, Canberra, on Wednesday, 28th August, 1947. She never really liked speaking in public, but like many people of artistic temperament, was happiest when she was performing. In a short address to the assembled ladies, Delia gave a humorous account of her reactions to Australia and its people. She and her husband had been to many European countries, she said, but there, she felt to some extent at least, that she was a stranger in a strange land. She felt a greater sense of homeliness in Australia, and she moved among them "feeling as much at home as if she were in O'Connell Street, Dublin." (applause) She told them how she often thought her driver had lost his way and had wandered into the bush by mistake. On her way to Canberra for the first time, she asked the driver if he was sure he knew where he was, and he assured her they were on the right track. (laughter)

More typical of the occasions on which Delia performed was the Sydney University Women Graduates' Association Christmas party. It was held in the common room of the Women's College, and more than eighty graduates attended. A Sydney newspaper reported: "She chose very old Irish folksongs, collected from all parts of Ireland." Then she gave an impromptu unaccompanied performance of three songs at a "St. Patrick's Day" concert in Melbourne, not on the saint's feast-day itself, but on 27th March, 1948. A newspaper report said about Delia that "she delighted the audience...and made a deep impression on her listeners, singing with great artistry and creating a vivid Gaelic atmosphere."

In a speech before the performances, Bishop J.P O'Collins, said that he hoped Dr. Kiernan would use his influence in getting more immigrants from Ireland. The Minister replied that while "there was still a certain amount of emigration from Ireland, some 11,000 leaving for England and Scotland each year...many returned to their country within a few months." Dr. Kiernan was still delivering the Government line, of course, which may well have been more optimistic that accurate, because over the next dozen years or so, approximately 400,000 Irish people emigrated.

The Kiernans had a fine collection of valuable paintings, and in May 1948, these were put on exhibition at the Velasquez Galleries in Melbourne, the Lord Mayor, now Sir Raymond Connelly, performing the opening. The Kiernans were entertaining Eamonn de Valera at the time, and he attended the opening with them. The exhibition drew favourable comment from the critics. One of them wrote: "Most of these works formed part of a group brought together by Dr. and Mrs. Kiernan, who are enthusiastic collectors, during Dr. Kiernan's recent diplomatic term at the Vatican. Those of greatest historical interest are a Madonna, attributed to Raphael, which was presented to Dr. and Mrs. Kiernan in Italy, and a big Domenichino, 'Charity'. A number of good contemporary Italians are also represented. Two of the most interesting works aesthetically are modern Irish – 'Going Into Exile', by Cecil Salkeld, a young Dublin painter, and 'The Wild Swans at Coole', by A.E. (George Russell)."

Delia recalled Dev's visit with some glee: "We were going to the Governor General's residence in the diplomatic car, and it was very dusty going along the road. Dev had dust all over his coat, so I handed him the only thing I had – a hairbrush. He got hair all over his coat. The only time I ever saw Dev thirsty was on that trip to Australia. It was in Melbourne, and he asked for a glass of beer and was refused."

After two years living in the hotel, the Kiernans moved into a house which was owned by the Chilean ambassador Huebner. Now they would be able to entertain properly. One of Delia's proudest boasts was that while she was in Canberra, she introduced a new style reception which became the talk, not only of the diplomatic circuit, but of the press corps, as well. "Barbecues were the Aussie way where people cooked outdoors and drank beer," Colm

Kiernan said. "Embassy receptions were the same staid affair they were everywhere else. My mother started the fashion of barbecue receptions on the diplomatic circuit, and it became very popular. The Aussies loved it because it was more democratic."

The Australian interpretation of what was 'more democratic' allowed guests to indulge in a most peculiar custom on these occasions: "There was a practice called 'souveniring'," Colm continued, "whereby visitors to receptions helped themselves to silver and things." Delia told the press that she had decided she wanted "to see the Australian spirit expand in its natural setting". Perhaps Delia had become familiar with 'souveniring', and by keeping guests out of doors, she was taking no chances! However, her explanation was that she was tired of seeing people sweating over cocktails, so when the Kiernans held their first party, they sent out invitations stating, "dress informal, toasting forks optional". It was to be a barbecue.

The French Ambassador's wife misunderstood her hosts' intentions and arrived with a dainty six–inch toasting fork, and presenting it to Delia, said: "Ze toasting fork, Madame." An Australian presented her with a six-foot fork, so she wouldn't burn her fair Mayo complexion. Diplomats and Government Ministers rubbed shoulders with members of the Salvation Army and priests of the Catholic Church. Someone remarked that there was enough Irish and Scotch whiskey to float a Parliament House. The barbecue grill was over a long trench, and a university professor supervised the whole operation in his shirt sleeves. It started at 6 p.m., and at midnight, guests were still wandering around singing Irish songs and ballads. Delia was in her element. The newspaper headlines declared:, "Diplomats at Barbecue", "Minister's Barbecue", and "A barbecue instead of Cocktails".

On 20th September, 1948, *The Sydney Telegraph* reported: "Diplomatic officials and their staffs yesterday sang *Waltzing Matilda* while they grilled lamb chops over open fires at Pymble. They were guests at a 'barbecue' arranged by the Minister for Eire (Dr. T.J. Kiernan) and Mrs. Kiernan. Mrs. Kiernan sang verses of *Waltzing Matilda* while the other guests, in accents ranging from Canadian to Chinese, joined in the chorus. More than 100 foreign diplomats and Australians attended the 'barbecue'. The guests drank Irish whiskey and beer, and sang Irish and Australian songs." Another paper said: "At last someone in Canberra has been courageous enough to give the formal cocktail party the go-by." Soon Delia was Canberra's favourite hostess and was known as the diplomatic circuit's most eccentrically clad woman. One journalist described her: "Half strangled by an enormous feather. She had a volatile personality, loved to sing lusty drinking songs, favoured informality, and liked people to be natural."

Delia travelled extensively during her time in Austraia. In Queensland one time, she asked an Irish priest if he could arrange for her to go and visit the Aborigine people. He did, and she set off.

"I went, as they say in Australia, back o' Bourke's, which is the 'outback', or the bush. I had been invited over to see a cane farmer's Aborigine foreman who was of an enormous age. We met, and he was grinning broadly, with his mouth back to his ears. When I asked him how old he was, he said he was here before the railway. I figured over eighty years. I asked him if he had a boomerang. He had, and I took a pin from my lapel and stuck it to a tree. He walked away about a mile and threw his boomerang, knocking the pin out of the tree."

En route to Sydney one time, she flagged down a boundary rider on horseback. He was wearing a broad slouch hat, she said, and he was tending to the wire fences. "They don't often talk to people for two years at a time," Delia declared. "Anyway, he noticed the tricolour on my car and he asked me where I got it. I told him I was the wife of the Irish Minister and he said that that could not be - thinking my husband was some sort of a clergyman. I think he was puzzled. He said, 'That flag will be flyin' forever,' and then he rode off."

On aother occasion Delia decided she wanted to experience what it would be like to go swimming off the beach near Sydney. She was entirely on her own, she said, and was totally unaware of the fact that the waters were infested with sharks. "Suddenly, an Aussie voice started swearing at me over the loudspeaker, telling me to get the hell out of there." Undaunted, Delia finished her swim and came out when she decided she had had enough enjoyment for the day. Whether or not she knew of the danger she was in, following the warning, she did not say, but Delia displayed absolutely no bravado whatever on another occasion when she encountered snakes. "It was at Toowoomba," she said, "and three snakes poked their heads out of the water. I ran a mile, and I wouldn't go back in the water."

When the family arrived for a visit in Freemantle, Western Australia's principal port, they were piped down the gangway, and the pipers led them in procession all the way to the Town Hall. "I was wearing a black dress with long sleeves," Delia recalled. "Unfortunately, one of the welcoming committee was so enthusiastic when shaking my hand, he pulled my elbow right out of my sleeve. There was a doctor there, and he cut both sleeves so that they matched!"

And she never lost an opportunity of picking up a new song if it took her fancy, and such an opportunity presented itself in Freemantle when she overheard a couple of sailors singing, *When I was a soldier of fortune in Freemantle*...She says she got the song from them and recorded it later in London. She recalled, too, that she had heard an Australian clerical student in Rome singing the well known song, *On the Road to Gundagai*, and when she visited the town of Gundagai, she ran into him again, and they "adjourned to a bar for a drink and sang the song".

Delia also said she got a variant of the song, *Coming home from the Wake*, or, *The Wake in Kildare*, from the Australian Prime Minister, Joseph Benedict (Ben) Chifley, whose people came from Ireland and who succeeded another Irish-Australian– John Curtin – as Prime Minister, in 1945.

"Prime Minister Chifley hummed the tune of *The Wake in Kildare* for me over dinner at the PM's lodge in Canberra. He told me his father was a blacksmith and that his mother had come out from Ireland to marry him. Chifley was very much a self disciplinarian and a non-drinker. He never stayed long at the barbecues. His driver, Arthur Treacy was Irish."

Meantime, Blon and her husband had arrived in Australia. The Kiernans had visited them in Johannesburg, South Africa, on their way to Australia, and the young couple were invited to come out later to Canberra for a holiday. Delia said that they "just sort of drifted into staying".

Later, Blon and Tony went to live in Sydney where she studied Law at Sydney University. "She would come to Canberra regularly to swat for her exams," Colm said. "She got good results, and was first in her group, one year. But she fell down a bit in the last year, because Tony - who had a preoccupation with cars - was working on the embassy car; there was a fire and he was seriously burned. He nearly died, and there were lots of visits to hospital." Colm Kiernan said that Tony used to drive the car for the family for a while, but not for money, but that he found it hard to make a go of things in Australia. "He was a foreigner and he had no particular skill. He was from a farming background in South Africa."

All the time, of course, Delia kept singing. "Irish Guest Set Them Singing" was the newspaper headline over a story that began, "Led by Mrs. T.J. Kiernan, wife of the Irish Minister to Australia (Dr. Kiernan), scores of women yesterday afternoon sang the song of *The Moonshiner*, an Irish ballad, with the refrain, 'I'm a rambler, I'm a gambler...'" Delia was the principal guest of the Catholic Daughters of Australia at an afternoon reception. "Mrs. Kiernan charmed her audience of nearly 400 by singing with an attractive brogue - and a great deal of Irish roguery, some Irish ballads, and *Waltzing Matilda*. Her songs were rendered without accompaniment, since she has collected them in her native country by persuading old women to sing them to her, and then jotting them down."

"The Gay Colleen who sings with the Commissar" was the headline in another newspaper, and this time she sang for a very different audience. The 15th March, 1950 edition of the British newspaper, *The People*, ran a story as part of the publicity she was receiving after she had returned from Australia to resurrect her singing career. The story was about Canberra, and the 'Commissar' in question was the Ambassador of the USSR, Nicholai Lifanov, who, along with his wife, had been invited to the Kiernans for a party. The newspaper report shows Delia in exuberant mood with her Russian friends: "Go on, Lifanov!" a lovely uninhibited Irish voice demanded. "Tell us more, ye liar." The Russian Ambassador to Australia, Nicolai Lifanov, precise of speech, fair-haired, straight-backed, laughed. The Soviet severity of manner vanished before the sparkling-eyed wife of Dr. Thomas Joseph Kiernan, Minister Plenipotentiary of Ireland in Australia. "Go on, tell us more," she cried, "and I'll tell me eleven sisters and me one little brother, scattered over the face of the earth though they be, and God bless them all."

"The Irish are not the only ones who can sing," the Russian Ambassador insisted. "Come, then," said Delia Kiernan, "come then and we'll sing a duet." The Russian Ambassador and the Irish Minister's lady sang *The Volga Boatman*. "Ah ha!" the joyous Irish lady cried at last, and brown eyes under long lashes were mischievous. "Ask me who are my favourite diplomatic friends and I'll say the Russians. Well, maybe the English. Oh, no, bother. I can't choose between them. And yet, the Russians are agin our religion, and the English agin our politics."

Toward the end of 1949, Delia decided that she was returning to Ireland. She later candidly admitted to friends in Canada that there had been a few occasions when she had 'over indulged' and caused a bit of a scene when she spoke her mind. Apparently she had developed a fondness for alcohol, which could cause embarrassment on occasions.

When word got about that she was planning to leave Canberra, the press became interested, and Delia spoke to one of them. She told him that many people had found that perhaps she was an exception to the rule, but that she believed people should come off their pedestals. "You are what you are in the sight of God," she said, "nothing more, nothing less. I am the way I am, and the way He sees me is the way I am! People should remember that no matter what their walk of life is, they are dealing with human beings, not animals," she declared.

One columnist said to her, "What am I going to write about now that you're going? All the colour has gone out of Canberra." He asked her if she had any regrets. Delia replied with an emphatic, "No." But then she added: "Perhaps I am a bit bovine, but the only regret I have in the world is that soon I will leave it all behind me." She said life was not long enough for her to do all the things she wanted to do. "When in Australia, my husband would be asked what my hobbies were, or what his wife was interested in, he always replied cryptically, "In living!"

One would dearly love to know more about how he felt at this stage of his life about Delia and her ways. There are indications alright that he was beginning to despair of her ever giving up her desire to pursue a singing career, and that when she decided to go back to Ireland - while he may have had mixed feelings - he just might have experienced a sense of relief that at last she was free to do her own thing away from the diplomatic scene. In the meantime, he would accompany her to Ireland for a holiday and a break from his duties as Minister.

But the reporters and columnists would certainly miss her. "For the most part the reporters were kind to me," she said, "and for Dr. Kiernan's sake I was glad. His job was difficult enough, without having to keep a wary eye on his wife. I hadn't set out to steal the limelight - ever. I knew I would share it, but it happened that most things I did or said tickled the fancy of somebody's pen or imagination."

Some of Delia's best friends were to be found among the 'gallery girls' – as the wives of the parliamentary correspondents called themselves – and they were the first to arrange a farewell get-together for her. They knew Delia was interested in collecting souvenir spoons of the places she visited, and they invited her to a tea-party at the Hotel Canberra. They presented her with another batch of tea-spoons, each spoon having the coat of arms of the town or city of each girl's home town.

One last bit of musical fun Delia had before leaving was to sit down and write a song called, *Farewell to Australia Forever*, a collaborative effort between her and Lina Di Mello of the Indian High Commission with whom she was very friendly. Colm Kiernan said that Lina and his mother made a recording together as a joke.

Meanwhile, Dr. Kiernan was doing research for his book, *Irish Exiles in Australia*. He had found Australians largely ignorant about modern Ireland, and therefore he had to travel extensively throughout the continent giving lectures in all six states. Dr. Kiernan said that his was very much a "people to people" representation, and that he had remarked drily, "And that just cannot be done by sitting at a desk in Canberra."

Colm Kiernan said that Australia was not the high point of his father's career at all. "His time as Director of Broadcasting, was one, Rome another, and the posting as Ambassador to Washington, was another. Australia was almost like being thrown into the wilderness. And one could ask why he was sent there at all. It wasn't a high point and he didn't like it very much. Delia hated it."

XI

A singing career is resurrected

In March 1950, Delia , her husband and Orla travelled to Ireland on the liner, *Orontes*. Colm was at boarding college in Melbourne, and Blon stayed on in Sydney where she was studying. Blon was an excellent student and won a prize in her third year for her studies in Private International Law. She eventually graduated in 1954. The newspapers reported that Orla was "going to study dietetics at the College of Surgeons, Dublin."

Delia had "trunkfuls of presents, including ornaments, a dining room table, and two pictures, one painted by Hans Heysen, and one by Natmatjira". Delia did not return to Australia, and her husband eventually came back to Canberra in November that year when he was appointed to a second term as Ireland's representative.

How did this separation affect them? Colm Kiernan is in no doubt: "Adversely, of course. I don't know what arrangement they came to achieve this. He then brought over a woman called Catherina who had worked for the family in Rome, and she was our housekeeper. But she spoke no English, and I had to bring her shopping all the time. She'd buy only a little at a time so you'd have to bring her shopping almost every day. When my mother was there she did the shopping and cooking more or less. Catherina regarded herself as a lady's maid and wasn't really a cook at all. She did cook in Australia, but with a bad grace."

With the other children grown up, Delia wanted to help Orla settle back into life in Dublin, where she was to study medicine. And then she summed up in a piece of plain speaking that is the most bluntly honest she had ever spoken, her reasons and her feelings for returning to Ireland.

"It seemed while they were all growing up that I never had time or opportunity to discover how popular or unpopular the ballads could become, and in those months I had to myself, before Dr. Kiernan returned to become ambassador to somewhere else, I was determined to record more ballad music and song." She says, "...in those months I had to myself..." The period in question was, in fact, the best part of four years. She continued: "For once, but just for a short time, I was free of the demands put on Her Excellency Mrs. Thomas Kiernan – free of the diplomatic merry-go-round where concerts are favoured, and Tin Pan Alley is frowned upon."

So then, Delia knew all along how her ballads and Come all ye's were regarded in certain quarters. But she never flinched for a moment in her determination to sing the songs she loved. And amazingly, she even puts herself in the category of a Tin Pan Alley performer, showing she had no illusions whatever about how 'precious' her material was from a cultural point of view. In other words, she knew perfectly well, that her material was for popular consumption, and that was alright with her.

We get some indication of how her husband probably regarded the Come all ye's and ballads Delia sang from this story of Bishop Thomas Ryan's during their time in Rome: "He loved her singing, but he had more elaborate tastes in music and singing than she had. But still he encouraged her to go ahead with her particular brand of traditional Irish music. "One night they were away on a holiday and they were listening to a programme from Switzerland, and they were listening to Bach or Beethoven, and the announcer on the radio said, 'We'll play you something now from Ireland,' and out they come with *Father O'Flynn.* "Dr. Kiernan, who wasn't a big man in stature, said he could feel himself sinking to the floor amongst the other guests at the thought of a prosaic Irish jig. But Delia didn't mind at all and later that evening she sang the *Three Lovely Lassies.*"

Novelist, Leo Cullen, Delia's nephew, feels that her need to perform had to do with, what he called, her lyrical expression.

"She was a song-writer, and she was a singer, and she liked singing in concerts, and she liked being on stage. But she was completely curtailed in her role as wife of an ambassador; she was constricted. It had to burst out some place. She couldn't contain herself, I don't think. The workaday situation wouldn't have allowed her much outlet for singing. She wasn't on stage, and she wasn't getting the feedback that she loved, I imagine. Anyone who is of a creative nature and has to forego it - it would have crippled them really, I'd imagine. So it was shown in her theatrical nature. She was always aware of herself."

So, despite frustrations and obstacles, Delia was ready to give her singing career one more go. "The ballads, I had decided, had been an elusive challenge for long enough; ever since the war broke out and we were sent to Rome. Now I was all set to split the seam of song and make the ballads of Ireland as well known as Galway Bay, and I was determined that next time, when I had a few months to myself, the ballads would not escape me, and I would get behind a microphone again in the recording studios of Dublin and London."

The first thing she did when she reached Dublin was to call up Martin Walton at Walton's Musical Instrument Galleries on North Frederick Street, and the song writer, Peadar Kearney. Martin had built up his music shop and recording and publishing business over two decades and was always interested in new material. He had a great regard for Delia, and saw that she had potential as a songwriter. He hoped that she and Peadar might collaborate on some new songs.

But the one thing that Delia wanted to do as much as writing songs, was to sing on stage. What was billed in the *Western People* newspaper as, "The First Public Appearance of Delia Murphy since her return from Australia," took place at the Central Cinema, Claremorris – her own native town – on Monday, 5th June, 1950. It was billed as a "Celebrity Concert" in aid of St. Colman's College. The programme (3d each) announced: *"Master of Ceremonies: Paddy McEllin, Solr., Accompanist: Mrs. Sinclair, Claremorris."*

Fr. Jarlath Waldron who was teaching in St. Colman's, had heard that Delia was home from Australia, and he suggested to his boss, Fr. J. Colleran, that they should ask her to come and sing for a fund-raising concert for their new college extension. "Priests are always interested in raising money, as you know," Fr. Waldron joked, "so Fr. Colleran went to her and she was very gracious, and she said she would sing for us."

Fr. Waldron looked after Delia before the concert and got to know her very well, and his impressions of her and the night itself are well worth quoting, because it gives us a very good idea of how she went about preparing for a concert. "Like a true artiste, she was very insistent about some things. She hadn't had a performance for years, and her voice had gone off a little, and she was anxious to have a rehearsal which she had in my room. I had a piano there and it was a pleasure to be with her for several hours over three or four nights. Delia was a mixture, you know, of two people, really. She was, on the one hand, a very gracious and dignified lady, a woman who had travelled widely, and was a refined and cultured woman who spoke a couple of languages. And then, on the other hand, when she came down to Mayo, she relaxed into the Mayo patois which was interspersed with a whole lot of Irish words. We're addicted in Mayo to the '-een' at the end of certain words. I mentioned this to her and she denied it, but then I told her the story of the priest who was completely against this use of '-een'. He was posted to a new parish where the curate was showing him around. The new priest asked the curate who lived in such and such a house, and he was told, 'Ah there's nobody there in that houseen except a maneen and a womaneen and two childeens.' So Delia had to admit that we were addicted alright."

"Before she appeared on stage that evening, I think she was a bit nervous, and I think she met somebody or other and had a little drink to give her some Dutch courage. When she had dressed for the concert, she came to my room in the college. Well, I saw her standing there in this dress, you see, and it had been made for a much slimmer and trimmer Delia – she was bulging out all over the place. I remember that it was a full-length polka dot dress. Well, I registered horror and disbelief, and she says to me, 'What's wrong with it?' And I said – in a cowardly way – Fr. Colleran would never let you out, he'll never let you appear in that. And then Delia said, 'Too much mate(meat)?' Exactly, Delia, says I! Anyway, off she went and came back in the long black dress she wore for the visit to the Pope, mantilla and all. The transformation was incredible. She was really a great lady, and could be, and dressed and spoke like one – when she wanted to."

Fr. Waldron also recalled how conservative and traditional things were at the time, because, he said, "The proprietor of the cinema, Jim Gallagher, had pictures every night of the week except Saturday. That was Confessions night. Nor was there any cinema on Christmas night or Good Friday. On Mondays in June he took a holiday, so that's why we were able to get the hall. It was a full house, of course." The *Western People* gave prominent coverage to this grand return concert of Delia's:

"Delia Murphy – Welcomed at Claremorris Distinction for Town, says Fr. Colleran.

"All of South Mayo was there," the reporter said. "To endeavour to describe her excellent rendering of the various songs would be like trying to paint the lily. Suffice to say that she sang them in her own 'Murphy style', with all the enchanting smoothness and richness of her voice that has made her such an outstanding singer of our traditional songs."

Meanwhile, Delia and Martin Walton set about "hunting for tunes, not fortunes, in that dusty mountain of music". She said that she found the tunes but that the fortune evaded her once more. "I know some people think I made a pile of money from my recordings and concerts. I didn't, and was never really able to work out what went wrong. Probably the root cause had been that I was too trusting." Once again, she neglected to appoint an agent, and admitted that anyway, she did not have much of a business head. But if there was no agent, she seems to have received some worthwile advice from someone about how to handle negotiations for money. Orla was engaged in driving her around the country to concerts here, there, and everywhere. But later, when studies prevented her from doing the driving, Delia called on her neighbour, John Killeen, from Killeens' Cross at Annesfield.

John said that it was remarked on locally why she had returned to Ireland: "She came back because herself and the husband weren't pullin' together. She wanted to do concerts but her brother-in-law, Mellett, went against her, as did her sister, Mary, his wife.

Delia said, 'It's my bread and butter and I'm doing the concerts.' "So we travelled far and wide, and she performed in places like Longford, Galway, Belcarra, Cummer, Killala, Kilmaine, Ballinrobe, Belmullet. I drove Delia in an Escort."

Delia's youngest sister, Tess, often accompanied them during the period John was with her – 1953 to 1954. He was in the box office along with whoever was taking in the money.

"The money was counted and the hall got half. That was the deal. The halls were always packed out. Her appearance in Galway was the best night, and she made three or four hundred pounds total. Two hundred in Belmullet. Tickets would cost about fifteen bob. Galway tickets were dearer. She always sang the same programme. There'd be a band there who played for her. When she'd be through with a concert the crowd would surround her and clap her on the back, but she was well able for them. 'Stop lads,' she'd say, 'and I'll sing ye another.' And she'd sing a bit for them which brought a bit of order. She'd sneak away then. These were dance-halls, and people were dancing. We'd go for the beer to the hotel after the concert was over, spend the night and come home the next day. The proprietor of the hall and friends would come back to the hotel. She was powerful sport. She would drink straight from the bottle sometimes."

In March the following year, Delia was "feeling very proud" of herself. "Walton and I signed a three party agreement with Sonny Cox of the London publishers, Box and Cox. My end of the bargain was to produce 500 songs." It seems an unbelievably large figure, but that is what she said. "For months I was busy recording along factory lines, and on one day recorded as many as forty songs in one session."

Delia is once again exaggerating more than slightly, because not only would it be physically impossible for any individual to sing that many songs in a day, the setting up and recording of each song requires at least a couple of 'run through' rehearsals for herself and the accompanists. "I loved the work. And more than anything, I wanted to begin and finish recording tunes that had gnawed at my soul for so long. After years of tune collecting, ever since I was a child, I suddenly found myself free to release the hundreds of songs that had waited like so many butterflies in a chrysalis. Songs like the *Connemara Cradle Song*."

The Melody Maker of 11th November, 1950, and other British publications noted the signing of the contract and Delia was photographed with many celebrities from the BBC and management people from HMV, following the signing. The caption to a picture in *The Melody Maker* says, "Famous Irish singer and folksong collector, Delia Murphy, is shown above surrounded by a group of admirers at a reception held in her honour by music publishers, Box and Cox at The Excelsior, Charing Cross Road, London, on Wednesday last week."

Obviously she was on the road to stardom once again, because in a newspaper article, broadcaster Godfrey Wynn talked about meeting her and playing her records on the BBC's Housewives' Choice. And someone was looking after her bookings, as well, because an English Sunday newspaper reported: "Mrs. Thomas Kiernan, wife of Eire's Ambassador to Australia, sat in a Manchester Hotel yesterday trying to get rid of a cold. Then she went to Hulme Hippodrome for her first stage appearance in England – top of the bill in tonight's recorded *Variety Fanfare* broadcast. And Mrs. Kiernan, otherwise song-writer Delia Murphy, sang her own songs. She filled the place of Irish tenor, Joseph Locke, who has a foot injury. She came from Canberra to record 20 of her latest tunes in London. Many are based on Irish folk-songs."

In *The Irish Review*, 1st May 1951, Terry Ward wrote about Delia's recent recordings with the Melodisc Recording Company. He listed the songs she recorded with them: *The Connemara Cradle Song, The Wake in Kildare, The County of Tyrone, Dance with Me, My Fair Maiden*, and *Come with me over the Mountain*.

A publicity sheet of the Songwriters' Guild (of Great Britain), dated, Sunday, 9th March 1952, announced a special concert at the Victoria Palace in London : "For the third year in succession, Our Friends the Stars". And there among the list of stars' names was that of Delia Murphy. Among the others on the bill were, Arthur Askey, Philip Green, the Luton Girls' Choir, Alfred Marks, Rawicz & Landauer, Tommy Reilly, and Anne Shelton. Delia had certainly 'arrived'. *The Daily Graphic* reported on 17th May that same year that the request that comes up most frequently on radio programmes was *The Spinning Wheel.*

Delia was happy that she was being reported in bigger and bigger type. "I was told that my reputation was growing, and I don't mind admitting that it was a proud moment for me when I saw the first of the 'House Full' signs go up outside one of those small west of Ireland halls. Maybe, though, I remember that first 'House Full' sign especially, because I met up with Tom Maughan again. "I was just starting to sing when there was a tremendous crash at the door of the packed hall. Unkempt and smiling, a man stood at the doorway demanding a seat, and when he saw there wasn't a seat to be had in the place, he gripped the steward and casually tossed the poor man out into the street! All the time the ruffian's eyes were glued on me, and when I had finished singing a familiar voice bawled out: 'Ye never changed a bit, Delia!' Of course, it was the voice of Tom Maughan. I promised to meet him the next day in the main street of Claremorris."

In the years 1950 to 1954, Delia sang at various venues all over Britain and Ireland. On Tuesday 27th February, 1951, she was at The Blarney Club, 31 Tottenham Court Road, for a Special Carnival Dance. Music for dancing was supplied by the Blarney Ceilidh Band, with P. Kearney (vocalist from Dublin), and the poster said that there would be a "Personal Appearance of the Celebrated Irish Singer, Delia Murphy."

A poster for the Harp Club, Putney Bridge in London, 1951, announced it was presenting "Delia Murphy, Ireland's Outstanding personality of Stage and Radio Fame on Sunday, December 16th, Dancing 8 till 11.30 p.m. – You can't miss hearing her sing your favourite Irish Songs."

Around the same time, she sang at a very different venue in Co. Tyrone. She was the highlight of a 'Celebrity Concert' which was part of the programme organised by the Cranagh Sports committee in Glenelly. Among the songs she sang, were *The Boston Burglar,* and "a new number, *Comin' Home from the Wake*", and she was called on for several encores.

Tipperary man, Jim O'Donnell, worked in Birmingham in the early fifties as a young man. He was associated with Gaelic League and they engaged artists like Michael O'Duffy, Patrick O'Hagan, Máirín Ní Scolaí, and Delia.

"It was around 1953 or '54 we booked her. I think it was at the Emerald Club near the Hippodrome. The night she was there, Guy Mitchell was in the Hippodrome and a big Irish contingent were going to go there. But when they heard about Delia they came instead to hear her. They came from places like Leamington Spa, Coventry and all around the Midlands. The place was packed. There was a contingent of Americans who supported the club, as well, and they were there, too. Delia sang all the favourite songs. During the concert a voice came from the back of the hall saying, 'Hey lady, would you sing *Dan O'Hara* – that's my name." She asked him where he was from and he said Boston. She invited him up on stage. She sang and he played the mouth-organ. She sang on stage that evening unaccompanied – just a microphone – for an hour and a quarter, non-stop. Afterwards she came down off the stage and joined the rest of the dancers in The Siege of Ennis, The Walls of Limerick, The Bridge of Athlone, and was happy with all the crowd there." She more than enjoyed herself, and was back at the same venue six months later."

Mrs. Kathleen Duffy from Dundalk was Delia's piano accompanist when she sang at a concert in the town's St. Nicholas' Hall. "She was on stage for about one and a half hours. She apologised to me for the tattered and torn state of her sheet music, and said that she didn't intend to replace it. It was the music that she had when starting out on her singing career. It had been around the world with her and had been lucky for her. The hall was packed to capacity... She brought me up on stage at the end of the concert and asked the audience for a big hand for me."

Ivor Browne was a young medical student in Dublin at the time Delia returned from Australia. People who knew him at the time describe him as a beatnik-type figure long before the beat generation materialised in Ireland, and he would be seen busking on the streets of the capital. It was either 1951 or '52, and he was planning to go to the Galway races and do a bit of busking when he ran into Delia and Orla. They gave him a lift all the way.

"I only wanted a lift, and really wanted to get away from these two strangers, because I really didn't know who Delia was. I felt a bit shy anyway, but I got caught up in this feeling of activity, because once she hit the Galway Races, she really came alive. She seemed to know everybody, with these old fellows reciting long poems. But she never seemed to be fed up, or for that matter, hogging the limelight. She'd sit for hours in that sort of situation.

"So here's a person not long back in the country, most of her life out of it, yet once in any house around Galway, it was just as if she'd never left. And I don't think she stood out as being a personality. She was just totally at home. And the reason I think that she didn't boot me out was that I was singing on the street. I remember she was fascinated with me meeting the tinkers at the Galway Races. She loved the idea of it.

I left them for a day during the races, and the next day I met her again, and Delia said, 'Right, up to the races,' and I put on a suit. But the previous day I'd been playing with a tinker lady who was collecting money for me. I remember that what appealed to Delia was when she heard someone say, 'There's the big hairy bugger that was up here yesterday with no shoes on.' That really took her fancy.'

Soon, a friendship grew up between Ivor and Delia, and he got to know her very well. Did he think she was aware of the fact that she was making a unique contribution through her singing?

"Not at first, but probably later. She was aware of being Delia Murphy. I saw her in relatively informal situations in small halls in the West, in Achill, etc. She was at her very best and was totally at home. The people all knew her. In that sense she was part of every Irish household. She was a great entertainer because she was being herself, just by being part of the people's own lives. The nearest example is what Jimmy O'Dea was to the Dublin people. She had that kind of relationship. So, in a sense, she was hardly entertaining." However, he also said that Delia had a great need to be recognised, and recalled being on the Holyhead boat with her one time, and she said to a group of Irish people, 'Do you know who I am?' "If they didn't, she soon let them know, and then the talking would start."

Ivor and Delia were on their way into the National Library one morning at about 11 o'clock when they met Brendan Behan on his way out. It was the first and last time Ivor met him, but it would prove to be an unforgettable experience.

"We went to have a drink, but I didn't know who he was from Adam. I remember the big red neck, and he had the same kind of infectious air about him as Delia. Now, with the two of them, we just went round Dublin all day long, and all sense of time, or thought of anything I should have been doing, was completely gone. I don't think she had ever met him before either. They got along perfectly, and I remember howling with laughter, particularly at Brendan. I wasn't aware of his reputation at that time – or of hers, for that matter, although my mother used to listen to her records on the radio. They were both full of life and to hell with what was going to happen next. I don't remember them being in competition. Delia couldn't tolerate the little girls with the harps. This was anathema to her. I remember one thing Brendan Behan said that day was to do with these girls with the pioneer pin on and a chastity belt. That absolutely charmed her. She had utter contempt for this pseudo polite Irish thing. Some felt that way about McCormack, but she had tremendous respect for him. She was a great friend of Margaret Burke Sheridans, too."

Brendan Behan was courting Beatrice Salkeld at the time. She was the daughter of Blanaid and Cecil Salkeld, friends of Delia's. Delia always referred to Cecil as, "Dear Cecil in Christ", because an American priest friend of his used to address him as such in his letters.

"Delia had a marvellous sense of humour," Ivor Browne said, "and a sheer joy in a particular kind of humour that knocked any falseness. Humour that brought people down to earth. She had no feeling that she had to shock people, but she very much liked the thing that was down to earth. In telling any story she didn't dwell on the storytelling and deal with it systematically. She'd flit around from this to that."

But when passing an opinion on someone whose style of singing she did not like, Delia was blunt and to the point: "Jaze, sure yer man can't sing at all – he has no balls!" This was her view of the legion of John McCormack imitators in Ireland and abroad who warbled reedily and nasily through sad songs about poor ould Ireland and Mother Machree. And Delia applied the same phrase to describe women singers, too. She had no time for the type described by the American journalist and humourist, George Ade, as "a town-and-country soprano of the kind often used for augmenting grief at a funeral."

Delia's father died on 25th March 1952. Before his death, his daughter Mary and her husband Paddy (Mellet) supervised the farmwork.Tess was still at home and she looked after her father for the last couple of years of his life.

Leo Cullen was about four years of age at the time, and he has an amazingly clear memory of the events at Mount Jennings House when all the family gathered for funeral. "There was a strong atmosphere of women around the place, and I know these women were Papa's daughters. Delia was one of them, and Tess who was the youngest, and my mother, Angela. They were going around in black, and they drove in big cars to the funeral.

"And I remember we were in an upstairs room looking at them going out. And I think Tess stayed with us. But I remember even then an atmosphere about Delia. That she was somebody important. I vaguely remember Papa. He was by all accounts quite a character. And I can even testify to that myself, because of some presence of him, even when he was dead and I went back to the house, I could still feel it there. Of course the house was empty afterwards – after he died. They all just scattered away. Paddy was in America, and Laura, and Lizzie. They all married and ended their days there. And Tess, too, later on."

Paddy was the eldest son, and although he never had an interest in the farm, and was making his own way in the U.S., he inherited the Mount Jennings property. John Killeen said that Paddy gave the place to Tess to run more or less as she wished.

"Angela, who was married in Templemore, came down and she created hell when she heard Tess got the place. She was there for about two years when Paddy came home to fix things up, and he brought Tess back with him to America." John said that he and Tess had been 'very friendly'. In other words, they were in love. All he would say was that "it didn't work out".

Tess sent papers to John that would allow him to go to America, but John said that Paddy Murphy discouraged him from going. He never did go. "Tess was too good-natured for her own good, and money meant nothing to her." Then, in 1956 Paddy himself died suddenly, and his wife then owned the farm. In 1960, the Land Commission acquired the property for a mere £500 and it was divided up between the neighbouring farmers. The beautiful house remained empty for a few more years and eventually the roof was taken off and the lead sold to a builder from Ballinrobe. Most of the large trees had already been cut down and sold for £1,500.

Leo Cullen continued to go down to Hollymount area to spend part of his summer holidays with his Aunt Mary. He used to go to Mount Jennings House and explore its vast interior. It made him feel very sad to see it empty and abandoned.

"The house was just amazing. It had atmosphere, and the atmosphere contained Papa, my mother, and it contained Delia. There had been a big photograph of Delia and her husband, 'Mac' Kiernan, in the sitting room, beside the fireplace, and it kind of took over that room. But my mother's presence was there, and Papa Murphy's was there. There was this story about him which will give you the feeling of the atmosphere of Papa in the place. When the house was being sold and the land was divided up by the Land Commission, there were two big stone lions outside the house. Lots of things were taken away. But these people tried to take the lions away, and as soon as they started lifting them this voice from the heavens said, 'Leave them there.' And it was Papa apparently, shouting at them. And everyone round there believed it. That's what happened. I believed it."

XII

Farewell to the ballads & abroad again

When Dr. Kiernan was appointed Ireland's Ambassador to Bonn in 1955, Delia went with him. She had had a great deal of enjoyment on what she called "a whirlwind tour" of theatres and small halls all over Ireland and Britain; but life on the road is not an easy one, and eventually she seems to have had enough of it. Other kinds of music were becoming more popular among the new generation. Certainly, her records would continue to have wide popular appeal, but the life of a travelling entertainer no longer held the appeal it once had, and she was tired of it all. Besides, she was getting older, and her voice had dropped a semitone. But her interest in collecting songs and "cobbling together" new material, was as strong as ever.

The Kiernans set up house at Godesburg on the banks of the Rhine, outside Bonn. "There I found a font of music," she said, "and at the famous University of Bonn I mingled with the bearded students of that great German city, learning more of their music and song." Again, one would love to have been around to hear a Delia–student song-swap in a German beer cellar, and was she in the company of bearded students? Colm said that his mother picked up a bit of German, much more than his father did.

Photographs of her during her time in Bonn show Delia back in her familiar role as hostess, and she looks quite contented. There is no talk now about sing-songs and entertainment. Perhaps there was no audience for her kind of material, but it is hard to imagine her remaining silent at parties and not singing; that would not be Delia's form.

She did say she got a chuckle out of their first St. Patrick's Day reception in Bonn, because when some of the Germans were handed sprigs of shamrock, they ate them! She also got a laugh out of some of the German surnames and gave as examples, Untezhernschidt and Kranscheidt. Colm was studying at Cambridge from 1954-56, and he spent his holidays with the family in Bonn. "It was one of the nicer of Ireland's embassy residences abroad," he remembers.

After two years in Bonn, Dr. Kiernan was posted to Canada's capital, Ottawa, in eastern Ontario. According to Delia "It was while I was there I was to discover what became for me, God's country – rich, wide open spaces such as I had never seen before in my life. I knew instinctively that this was the country where I would want to settle and end my days; a land where I could be at peace with myself. I never really found out what I wanted in life till I came to Canada."

Her life had been influenced by the lives of so many other people, and their way of life, she said. She had had a bee in her bonnet about the stage, and now that she had exorcised that particular ghost, she was able to find in the Ontario countryside a contentment and joy that she had not known for many years, where she felt no pressures and where there were no prying eyes.

Colm said that his mother would refer to the first eight years of her marriage as 'the golden years'. "That would offset some of the later years which by comparison were less so," he added. "It is unusual to find two talents like theirs locked together...."

So, finally, in the Ontario farmland country, she could be herself. "Half the time I was Her Excellency Mrs. Thomas Kiernan, wife of the Irish Minister to here there and everywhere; somebody who learned how to sink a thousand diplomatic cocktails. Some of the time I was plain Delia Murphy, a woman from Co. Mayo, in love with the traditional music and songs of Ireland. And the rest of the time, I was a bit of both. It's confusing right enough, but so were the years that have passed."

While they were in Ottawa, the Kiernans were joined once again by Blon and her husband, Tony, and their children. The Hodgsons bought a farm near Jasper, and later on, Blon went to work as a lawyer with the Ontario Government. Delia and her husband used to visit them regularly, and enjoyed getting out of Ottawa to be away from the constant attentions of people who sought access to them. In fact, Delia said she spent as much time on the farm in Jaspar, as she did in Ottawa, and the area appealed so much to her that she decided that that was where she wanted to live, and eventually bought a small holding nearby. The house was a sturdy stone building, situated near the Rideau Canal. It was typical of the farmhouses of Ontario, built by Scottish stonemasons in the last century. The most dominant feature of the big living room was the grand piano which was in a prominent position, not up against the wall, but smack in the centre of the room.

There were many fine paintings on the living-room walls by Harry Kernoff, Paul Henry, and others. But her pride and joy, she would often say, were the large green curtains which came from the old Abbey Theatre. When the Abbey burned down in 1954, they were salvaged from the burning building, and her husband acquired them. First-time visitors to Delia's home were also shown another prized possession – the Chinese Ming vase presented to her by Sir D'Arcy Osborne.

But there was sadness, too, in her life at this time. Blon and her husband, Tony Hodgson, were going through a difficult time. To say the least, Tony and Delia did not hit it off well, and it seems he developed a deep dislike of her. It must have affected their marriage badly, because, suddenly, he absconded to South Africa with the children – two girls. Blon eventually found out where they were, but the girls wanted to stay with their father, and that was that.

But generally, times in Jasper were happy years for Delia. One of those who knew her well at this time was physician, Dr. Michael Brennan, a Dubliner, with a medical practice in Smiths Falls. He had been a fellow student of Ivor Browne's at the College of Surgeons, Dublin, in the early fifties. Dr. Brennan used to visit the Irish Embassy in Ottawa on St. Patrick's Day and became friendly with Delia. He invited her to dinner at his home in Smiths Falls. She came on her own and they talked about the Dublin artists, writers, and poets they knew. Afterwards, she brought him a portfolio of Harry Kernoff's woodcuts as a gift.

"She was compulsively generous," Dr. Brennan said. Delia did not live with T.J. at this time. "He was very professorial, highly intelligent. Delia had disgraced herself at a few receptions here and there, and they agreed that they would separate. She had no bitterness in her about this, and they had a great deal of affection for one another."

Neither Delia nor her husband would talk about those episodes which caused embarrassment, as for example, when she had had a few drinks at a pleasant evening somewhere, she was liable to turn to someone next to her and say, "You're an awful f—-ing phoney." Delia hinted at another source of conflict when she said that servants in the various places to which they were posted were always a difficulty for her. "Having servants," she told Dr. Brennan, "was like paying your enemies to come and live with you." She was very fond of Michael Brennan, and he said he had the honour of helping her home on a few occasions.

She told him she had 'memorabilia' that she had 'acquired' at various receptions, like an item from the White House on the occasion of the christening of President Kennedy's son, John John. "She had enormous charm and warmth," Dr. Brennan recalled. "But her capacity for drink amazed me. She could consume a lot. It sometimes led to interesting and embarrassing situations."

A friend of Dr. Brennan's who knew the Canadian writer Farley Mowat asked him once to treat Farley's wife for a minor medical complaint. Later, Michael Brennan invited Farley and a number of friends to his house for a party so that they could meet Delia.

"It proved to be memorable evening. Farley was wearing a kilt, and sang Newfoundland songs. Delia would respond with Irish songs, and gave the Irish history of every Newfoundland song he sang. Eventually, in frustration, Farley burst into an Inuit song and danced to the tune, jumping up and down and banging the floor with his feet. I noticed Delia growing paler, and she became quite sombre. Suddenly she got up and headed into the kitchen." Dr. Brennan followed her and asked her what was wrong. "

"That great big dirty thing of his keeps jumping up at me when he's dancing," she says. "Can you get me a seat somewhere else?" It seems Farley was not wearing anything underneath the kilt!

She genuinely enjoyed life in the Smiths Falls area, and most of her friendships were made through the Brennan family. It seems Delia had ambitions to make a big comeback and felt that Dr. Brennan was the man who could make it all happen.

"She had completely unjustified confidence in my skills as some kind of person who might manage her artistic return. She wanted to get on the Ed Sullivan Show and she felt I would be able to get her on it. But I didn't have what was needed. She did have an ambition to make money, but like many Irish people, was touched with fantasy – with the possibilities – and was not practical. I told her there were agents in NY who would be delighted to take a look at what she could do, but she said, 'Oh no, no, no. You know me.' And that again is an Irish thing. You know, someone you know and trust is better than somebody that can do the job."

In 1960 Dr. Kiernan received his last posting and was appointed to the highly prestigious position of Ireland's Ambassador to Washington. A few months later, John Fitzgerald Kennedy was elected U.S. President. Colm Kiernan said his father developed close personal ties with J.F.K. "Mind you, any Irish ambassador would have, and because the President wanted to develop the Irish connection, my father was very eager to help, because he realised that a great deal of good could come of it for Ireland."

While Dr. Kiernan was still ambassador to Washington, he visited Dr. Brennan, in Smiths Falls, and he talked about life in the U.S. capital, and the differences between Kennedy and Eisenhower. Michael confirmed Colm's statement about how well his father and the President got on together. "Dr. Kiernan was a delightful, erudite man. Relations between him and Delia were cordial, but I don't think he could handle her."

Delia did not spend a lot of time in Washington, and lived on the farm in Ontario. One Irish diplomat said that he remembers her being at the embassy only once while he was there, and that was on the occasion of a visit from the head of the Irish Government, Taoiseach Seán Lemass.

But when she was in Washington, Delia did what she did everywhere she lived – she collected songs – and tells how she met an old Irish woman in a store in the city, who knew the ancient Child ballad, *Babes in the Wood*. Delia took the old lady aside, and there and then wrote down all the words of the song.

Delia recalled that the day of Kennedy's inauguration was bitterly cold. She was under a special covered-in area for the diplomats' wives and wore a fur coat to keep warm. She said she felt a lot more comfortable than those wives from Eastern countries who were dressed in their silk saris. "Then a St. John's Ambulance woman passed out and I had to give her brandy to revive her. She'd never had a drink in her life and when she came round she just couldn't stop talking!" Delia did not say whose brandy it was, or how she got her hands on it.

In 1961 Delia met the renowned folksong scholar, Dr. Kenneth Goldstein, producer and publisher of hundreds of recordings of traditional songs from the U.S., Britain and Ireland. Only a couple of years earlier, he had produced the first ever recording by three young men from Carrick-on-Suir, Co. Tipperary, the Clancy Brothers, and a fourth young man from Keady, Co. Armagh, named Tommy Makem.

It did not take a lot of persuading to get Delia to agree to recording a long play album of songs, and Dr. Goldstein arranged a recording date for her in New York. The result was an LP entitled, *The Queen of Connemara*, the only LP she ever did, and the last record she made.

He was impressed at how well organised Delia was. "Since she didn't accompany herself, she asked for some musicians to accompany her and perhaps an arranger, as well. She said she had fairly strong ideas about this, and that she wanted fairly simple arrangements." Dr. Goldstein called on his friend, Walter Raim, to do the arranging.

"I immediately realised that Delia was far more of a professional than her simple voice and demeanour would indicate. She knew exactly what she wanted, and told Walter in no uncertain terms what kinds of background she wanted for the songs. So he got her to record the songs unaccompanied, and a week later he had the arrangements done."

The musicians were an accordionist, a bass player, and Walter Raim himself played guitar and banjo. The album illustrates Delia's uncanny ability to choose songs that not only suited herself, but which had the same popular appeal of her first successful recordings twenty-three years earlier. She had not lost the magic touch.

The sleeve notes for the album were written by Arthur Argo, singer and folksong collector. He also notes Delia's method of "cobbling together" songs from those she collected "from the highways and byways of the world", and he goes on: "Her approach to collecting is not that of the academician or folklore scholar who will usually note a song exactly as it is found. She candidly admits to editing and adjusting songs to suit her own taste and style. The majority of the songs on this album have undergone this process of change."

Dr. Goldstein's collection of books and broadside ballads in the English language was probably one of the finest in the world at the time, and he invited Delia to his house to show them to her and exchange views on various Irish folksong collections.

"In the course of our discussion, she asked if I knew of such-and-such a book, and I'd show her the actual book. But then I remembered that there was one book I didn't have and I asked her if she knew of it – *Songs of the Wexford Coast* by Joseph Ransom. I had used a copy in the Harvard Library, and as far as I knew, there were only three copies in the whole of the U.S." Not surprisingly, the generous-hearted Delia wasted no time in getting a copy which she had in her own collection, and she made Dr. Goldstein a present of the book.

Delia said that she and Mrs. Jacqueline Kennedy used to have "many fundamental chats" while she was in Washington, but she did not say when or where or under what circumstances. She tells the story of her first visit to the White House. The Kennedy children were there and perhaps Jacqueline was with them. One of the children asked her what her name was. "Call me Irish," I told them. The child looked at the President, and said, "Just like you, Dad," and he replied, "That's right – Irish, just like me."

Colm Kiernan recalled that his father accompanied John Kennedy when he visited Ireland in June of 1963. "He and John Kennedy were largely instrumental in setting up the Ireland-America Foundation, and when my father retired in 1964, he was put in charge and worked out of the head office in New York." Dr. Kiernan worked with the Ireland-America Foundation until 1967. He became ill that year and returned to Dublin and died a few days after Christmas.

When I visited Delia for the first time in August the following year, she appeared to be in a deeply nostalgic mood, and spoke fondly of her husband who was so understanding of her, saying that he allowed her to live on the farm in Canada while he slaved away in his office in New York.

To listen to Delia, one might have gained the impression that she was into cattle ranching in a big way. In fact, it was quite a small operation, and she had fewer than a hundred cattle. By all accounts it was quite successful, and she made a bit of money at it.

Seán Ó Cillín of the Department of Geography at University College Galway was teaching in Ottawa in the late 1960s and got to know Delia very well. He visited her regularly at her farm in Jasper. What were his impressions of Delia at this time?

"There was a duality about her, I would say. On the one hand she was very shy, and on the other, she was quite a rabelaisian character. She really cherished her privacy, but at the same time, when she came to trust you, you would see the other side. She didn't want anyone except those closest to her, those who were her few friends in Smiths Falls, to know that side of her. Blon always tried to keep that side from people, as if there was some sort of shame in this beautiful, Rabelaisian side of Delia.

"When I'd get homesick for Ireland I would head for Jasper and visit Delia; it was like a piece of Ireland to me. And Delia would take out the bottle and she would sing far into the night, and have friends around to share the fun. She was very much an existential being, and in the right company she just let her hair down, creating a great conviviality and warmth around her. Blon was a lawyer and lived in Toronto, but I always felt she was the boss, and that Delia toed the line when she was around. You'd just love to walk into Delia's house. Her face would light up and she'd start singing right away, head for the freezer and take out a couple of steaks."

In 1969 I (the author) was in a part-time folk group called, The Cobblers, which included my wife, Joyce, and two others – Sandy

Carson and Ron Magee. We had been guests on a folk music series on CBC radio (the Canadian Broadcasting Corporation) in Ottawa, presented by folk singer, Tom Kines. I spoke to Tom about Delia, and since he knew of her earlier reputation, agreed that she should be asked to be a guest on the series. She readily agreed. Of course, we were slightly apprehensive about the prospect, as much for Delia's sake as for the programme's, because we could not be sure how well things would go for her, a woman not far short of seventy, and perhaps a little bit out of vocal condition.

Well, once again, we need not have worried, because she was totally relaxed and in the best of good humour. At rehearsals we would look at one another and smile at how calm she was and so completely in control. In fact, we who were relatively inexperienced in studio recording work, felt much more at ease because of Delia's assured, professional approach, and we learned a lot from her. The backing musicians and the technical crew were full of admiration at how competently she went about her business in the rehearsals and then in the final 'take' for broadcast.

The show itself was broadcast in May that year. The producer, Peter Shaw, was so taken with the whole programme, and in particular Delia's contribution to it, that he decided on a 'live' repeat performance in the CBC's July Summer Festival series of outdoor concerts at Camp Fortune in the Gatineau Hills, Quebec, north of Ottawa. Once again Delia agreed.

The day before the performance Seán Ó Cillín and I went down to fetch her at the farm. She was slightly nervous about the prospect, but looking forward to it all the same. At the last moment a friend of hers from Smiths Falls decided that he wanted to go to the concert, and he drove her in his open top MG sports car.

I have an unforgettable picture of Delia in the passenger seat of the MG, her hair blowing in the wind as we sped along the highway towards Ottawa. At one stage, I decided to pass them, and as I pulled out I could see her gesticulating and laughing and she was singing her head off. Delia was like a small child out on an excursion for the day and was thoroughly enjoying herself.

The following night at Camp Fortune's natural amphitheatre, a large crowd assembled in the open air for an "Evening of Folk

Music from Ireland". *The Ottawa Journal* and *The Ottawa Citizen* each sent a reviewer. They had a fairly basic disagreement about the number of people in the audience, the reviewer from the *Journal* estimating the crowd at 400, while the *Citizen* reviewer thought there were 8,000 present! Of course, newspapers can add a zero or leave one out very easily, and maybe that is what happened in this case. In fact there were somewhere in the region of 1,000 people present. However, neither reviewer was in any doubt about who the 'star' of the show was. It was Delia Murphy.

Considering that Delia had not done anything like this before, nor that she had performed before so large an audience in many years; that she was in her sixty-seventh year, and a complete unknown to the great majority of those in attendance, it is a remarkable testament to her skills as a performer that she held the audience spellbound from the moment she set foot on stage.

"The presence of Miss Murphy was an especially inspiring bonus," wrote the *Journal's* reviewer, "...since the Camp Fortune concert represented something of a comeback for her....But, as her performance Wednesday evening indicated, she remains a magnetic performer, capable of winning an audience with a word or a gesture. Her singing was animated by a kind of ragged grace, and the more she sang, the better she sounded." Seán Ó Cillín said that for days afterwards Delia kept on talking about the concert and how much she enjoyed it. "What was it that lad shouted from the audience?" she'd ask Seán. "Fine girl you are still, Delia, was what he shouted," Seán told her, and she would laugh again and repeat the line, "Fine girl you are." Seán said that the whole experience made her feel young again and that it really put a spring into her step.

When Delia announced at the concert that she was going to sing *Comin' Home from the Wake*, the host, Tom Kines asked her which version, she smiled and said, "I think I'd better sing the clean one." When Delia cobbled together new songs from those she had collected, very often she "cleaned up" several of them. She knew very well that some of the rather explicit references in the songs would be too much for 'polite ears', and therefore she watered them down for general audiences.

She still liked to sing the 'unexpurgated' and unsanitised versions at parties, and was giving more than a broad hint to the audience at Camp Fortune that the spicier version of *Comin' Home from the Wake* would be too much for a family gathering like theirs. But by referring to the rawer version at all, of course, she enabled the audience to make up their own minds about what had been changed, and they enjoyed it all the more. It was not what she said, or how much she said, but the way she said it, and how she brought out the fun in her singing, that did the trick.

In the winter of 1968-69, I brought Delia along to the Capitol Theatre in Ottawa to hear the Clancy Brothers and Tommy Makem. I knew they had never met her, and were looking forward to the meeting. Many people attribute the phenomenal success of the folk revival of the sixties to the Clancys and Tommy, but Liam says they could never have done it but for the influence of Delia and her songs. He still speaks with great pleasure at the memory of their meeting in Ottawa.

"No four people were more surprised than the four of us, because she had been a great inspiration. We idolised her, and she was exactly as I thought she would be. Y'know, totally down to earth. I remember we had a bottle of whiskey back there and we offered her a drink and she jumped at it, and within ten minutes she was singing *The Queen of Connemara*, and my father's favourite song, his party piece for years and years, *Dan O'Hara*. One thing that never made sense to me was that she was married to the Irish ambassador, because I couldn't imagine anybody with that kind of shut-eyed singing sitting at an ambassadorial dinner out in Australia or wherever. But when she came back stage that time, she was exactly as I thought, and I then had to rewrite my opinion of the ambassador. I thought he must have been a great man to fearlessly take this woman around who was singing these old Come-all-ye's, and so on.

One winter's evening in early 1969, I was a dinner guest at Delia's house. Also present were Blon and Seán Ó Cillín. After dinner we sat around talking and singing, and I sang a verse from the song, *The Wayward Boy*, which is sung to the well known tune of *The Girl I left behind me*. Right away Delia responded with glee, "That reminds me of the Dublin children's rhyme which is sung to the same tune," and she sang:

Oh, as I looked over Dublin's walls, I saw King William shitin',
So I got a coal, and stuck it up his hole, and he ran home like lightnin'.

There was much laughter, of course, but what was impressive was the speed with which she could come up with a verse to the same tune – a ridiculous piece of nonsense, but typical of the sort of coarse material found in children's rhymes. But again, it shows that Delia did not turn her nose up at such material and saw it as reflecting an aspect of the people's sense of fun and rough good humour in poking fun at a much despised figure in Irish history.

A few weeks later, when I was at Delia's place with Seán and Blon, in the course of the evening I recalled her verse about King William, and I told her that I had been at a house party where most of those present were members of the Ottawa Little Theatre. The person who invited me along was my next-door neighbour, a friend of the man in whose house the party was held. I told Delia that my neighbour, who was Irish, had got great enjoyment out of the verse about King William, and not much more was said about it – except that I thought I detected a hint of a disapproving look on Blon's face. In any case, the result was that there was just a slight cooling off in Delia's dealings with me for a while.

Subsequently, I heard that Blon, or Delia, or both, were somehow under the impression that the story was told to a roomful of people in Ottawa, and that 'everybody' would be saying things about Delia that were not very complimentary. Not so, of course. I had told the story to just one person, and in any case, it is doubtful if anyone else at the party would have had a clue who Delia Murphy was. The fact is that many people in the Smiths Falls area and in Ottawa who knew Delia had heard her singing songs at parties which were full of sexual *double entendre* and worse – a not unknown feature of many folksongs. But it never bothered anyone, and in large measure this side of her character added enormously to her appeal among her many admirers.

Inevitably, there had always been the detractors right from

earliest days who regarded her style of singing, choice of song, and the fact that she enjoyed a drink, as being totally unsuitable for an Irish Catholic mother and the wife of a distinguished Irish diplomat. I have good reason to believe that Blon – who was understandably concerned for her mother's image – was being somewhat over-protective of Delia in this instance, and had spoken to her mother about it.

Later in July I returned to live in Ireland, and I did not see Delia again. She was not really in the best of health and was being treated for high blood pressure. Seán Ó Cillín says she did not think she had "long to go" and that members of her family persuaded her to return to Ireland. "I'm sure Blon persuaded her in the end. I'd say anywhere Delia was she would make the most of it, because that's the sort of person she was. I don't think she was ever lonely in Smiths Falls, for instance, because she had lots of friends there. She was very much her own person and a very strong person in a quiet sort of way, strong minded and strong willed."

All the time she was in Jasper, Delia continued to write. She composed a number of new songs, some of which she had included in what she called a ballad opera that she had written called *Granuaile*. "I have put the story of the pirate queen of Connaught into words and music, a work that has taken all my spare minutes between watering and feeding the cattle. My make-believe story of Granuaile begins in Westport; make-believe, because I like to believe I shared some of the blood and spirit of Granuaile.

"Soon, I hope, somebody will publish it. But whether or not, I am glad it is written. You see, for me it was a release of so many pent-up emotions that had ached an exit line." Delia said she had sent a copy to the movie director, John Huston, but it seems nothing came of it.

XIII

'I'll live till I die...'

In November 1969, Delia sold the farm for $30,000. She bade a sad farewell to all her friends in the Smiths Falls area, and having settled all her affairs in Ontario, returned to Ireland. Ivor Browne was very kind to her and he and Delia's daughter, Orla, helped her acquire the small but comfortable Liscannor Cottage, in the Strawberry Beds, in the Liffey Valley, near Chapelizod, where she would live out the last year of her life. Ballyfermot man, Tommy Phelan, had long been an admirer of Delia's singing, and when he heard that she had returned to Ireland, he was most anxious to meet her. He knew Ivor Browne, and the two of them went out one afternoon to visit her. Tommy brought his tape recorder with him, and recorded a chat with her.

"I asked her if she would consider singing for an old folks' party I was helping to organise, and she agreed without any bother. It was at the Shelbourne Hotel. The conductor of the band said it was his privilege to conduct for Delia Murphy. She was as bright and breezy as ever, and the old people really enjoyed her singing."

When word got out that Delia was home again, Pan Collins the researcher on the *Late Late Show* on RTE enquired if she would like to be a guest on a forthcoming programme. Her surprise appearance early in 1971 was the first time a large Irish television audience had had a chance to see and hear herß. Pan said they were delighted with the reaction.

Many people were amazed to find out she was still alive. For the first time she spoke of her work in helping Allied POWs escape from Rome, and admitted that she had taken a calculated risk in using the legation car many times in this work. Unfortunately, only two pieces from that year's *Late Late Show* series have been retained in the RTE Archives. Neither piece is of Delia's guest appearance. Her health deteriorated shortly afterwards and she was taken to St. Kevin's hospital– now St. James. . Delia, who 'lived just for today', would not have been a good patient, and in typical fashion began planning a holiday abroad.

On Thursday 11th February, she was sitting up 1n bed, just a few days afer arriving at St. Kevin's, surrounded by travel brochures of the Canary Islands, when suddenly she had a massive heart attack and died. She was just four days short of her 69th birthday. There were several tributes to her in the newspapers, and the obituary columns announced that the remains would arrive at the Church of SS. Alphonsus and Columba, Ballybrack, on Monday evening, 15th at 5.30. That the funeral was the following day after 10 o'clock Mass to Dean's Grange Cemetery, where she was aid to rest alongside her husband. The simple inscription on the gravestone states:

Dr. T.J. Kiernan 1897-1967
Delia Murphy Kiernan 1902-1971
May they rest in peace.

That Monday after I paid a half-hour tribute to her in my *Morning Airs* programme on RTE radio. Listeners from all over the country phoned in and wrote letters expressing their sadness at the news of her death, and saying how much they appreciated the contribution she had made to their lives through her songs. Several said how ironic it was that she should have died so soon after her *Late Late Show* appearance, and one listener remarked that it was almost as if she had planned it as a last farewell to the people of Ireland.

A year later I presented a documentary tribute to Delia on radio in which old friends like Martin Walton, Leo Maguire, and Liam Redmond recalled her life and times. The journalist, broadcaster, and opera buff, Tommy O'Brien, himself no mean judge of singers and performers, reviewed the programme for the Cork *Evening Echo* and was delighted with it. However, writing of Delia's voice, he said: "You could not fit it into any of the familiar categories – soprano, mezzo-soprano, contralto; it was none of these. In fact, there was little that was feminine about it and nothing at all that suggested demure femininity. Rather, it was a strange instrument with a rather masculine quality on which Delia played to such unique effect that, once you had heard her, you could never associate her music with anyone else."

Not exactly a flattering assessment, nor one that many people would agree with, but does he have anything more positive to say about her? He then quoted a review from *The Record Guide* published in the early 1950s, by Edward Sackville-West and Desmond Shawe-Taylor, who said of Delia's singing, "In the most attractive of these (Irish songs), *The Spinning Wheel,* she conjures up, with her deep brogue and lazy drawl, a peasant scene as vivid and haunting as a dream – the blind grandmother drowsing in the corner, the girl at her spinning wheel, the young man tapping at the window."

As we are left wondering what he was getting at, Tommy added, "A description which, I think, could not be well bettered. And yet it conveys little of the performance. To fully appreciate what the genius of Delia Murphy would make of a song, one simply must hear the recording, after which, one simply forgets all others."

The Irish Times reviewer, P.K. Downey, noted that it took RTE over a year to broadcast a commemorative programme on Delia, after her death. "When you consider the speed with which other deceased entertainers or, for that matter, retired ones - Frank Sinatra, for example - are featured in special programmes, the lapse of a year in this instance was a slight to the singer's memory." He kindly added that I was exempt from any blame, and that perhaps it might never have been done but for my relatively brief friendship with her.

In 1973 I returned to Canada and spent the next five years there and I gave little further thought to the subject of Delia Murphy. When I returned to Ireland in 1978, I became host of the RTE 1 programme, *Fáilte Isteach,* and discovered that listeners still requested her music, and in their letters they occasionally expressed their admiration for Delia. It was good to know she was not forgotten.

In 1981, a committee of local people in Hollymount/Roundfort area of Mayo, began raising funds to erect a memorial to Delia. The chairman was V. Rev. W. Walsh, P.P. Roundfort, Doreen Hennelly, secretary, and Rev. E. Concannon, C.C., treasurer. Funds for the project were raised through concerts, and voluntary subscriptions, and much of the voluntary work was done by local people. The committee outlined what they had planned: "The Memorial is of Wicklow granite, with the theme of a Blackbird, from one of Delia's best known songs. The base is of Liscannor stone."

The Memorial was designed and sculpted by E.P. Hughes & Sons, Claremorris, and Michael Mellett, Hollymount, was the engineer on the site. Fr. Éamon Concannon asked me to write a souvenir programme for the occasion, and to include as many photographs as possible. On Sunday, 25th April 1982, a crowd estimated at over one thousand people turned up to see the broadcaster, Donncha Ó Dúlaing, unveiling the Memorial at Annefield Crossroads, near Mount Jennings House. The newspapers published a photograph of Orla, Colm, the actor, Liam Redmond, Donncha, and V. Rev. W. Walsh, standing at the Memorial.

Beautifully carved into the polished granite are the words, "*If I were a Blackbird*" and "Delia Murphy, Ballad Queen, 1902-71" and in smaller letters at the bottom, "Erected by neighbours, relatives, friends, and admirers".

The Committee members were quite amazed at the size of the attendance, which included not only local people, but many who came from all over the country. They thought they were being more than prepared for demands for the pamphlet by running off 1,000 copies, at £1 each, but they could easily have sold at least twice that number. Speeches were made, and songs were sung. Dr. Colm Kiernan that the organising committee were to be congratulated for doing an excellent job, and said that although his mother had travelled the world, her roots were always in Mayo.

Following this event, I felt I had to get to work on a TV documentary on Delia, and when I checked to make sure that no one had done anything on her for television, I approached the documentary unit at RTE 1 soon after, and Seán Ó Mórdha, Head of Features, agreed that something should be done.

After many frustrations and delays, RTE finally agreed to shoot the film documentary in 1987, and appointed the experienced TV producer, Joe O'Donnell as director. The programme was entitled, *The Ballad of Delia Murphy*, and was scheduled as the final one in the *Tuesday Documentary* series in February, 1988. It was to be a commercial hour in length, but for reasons best known to themselves, RTE shortened the last few programmes in the series by fifteen minutes.

In the May 1953 edition of *Hibernia*, R.M Fox wrote a piece called, "Delia Murphy: Ballad Singer of Ireland" in his column, "Portrait of an Artiste":

> One of my most vivid memories is of Delia Murphy standing on the stage of a Dublin theatre while the audience, ranged in tiers from pit to gallery, roared its appreciation of her songs and demanded more. Dark-eyed and dark-haired, with strong expressive western features, Delia is an artist of temperament. When she sings Irish ballads she puts the passion of this folk music into her eyes, voice and manner. Thousands have heard her singing over the radio, many have listened to her gramophone recordings, but luckiest of all are those who have seen and heard her in person, giving full expression to the mood of the song – plaintive, sad, humorous, rakish.

Liam Clancy paid her the following tribute: "I think her main contribution was that she made us all feel that we could respectably sing our own songs. The sean- nós never died out in Connemara, nor down in Ring. But it had never become hugely popular like she did. I would thank her directly for giving people myself and the brothers and Tommy Makem the encouragement to discover more about the songs and to keep singing them. Delia made it all possible."

These were just some of the attributes and qualities people everywhere admired in Delia. Some of those qualities, I hope, have been brought out in this account of Delia's life, from the statements of friends and relations who knew her well, and from what she said about herself, too. I have no doubt that she would be more than happy to share it all with 'the real people of the gods' for whom she sang.

Discography

in chronological order

In a 1930s HMV recording session, a Matrix (the 'mother' plate or disc) number was given to every performance ('take') and these numbers were prefixed by the letters, OEA & OEL. The Matrix cards give the actual date a recording was made and how many 'takes' there were. For example, the song, *Coortin' in the Kitchen* has the Matrix number, OEL 154-3. The -3 indicates that the third 'take' is the matrix from which the records were pressed. The date of the recording of the song is given as 31st August, 1940, and the Gramophone Company gave it the catalogue number, HMV IM777. The card also states what accompaniment there was: fiddle, accordion, guitar, and 'arr. A. Darley' means that the music arrangement was by Arthur Darley.

Where the Matrix card has been lost, I have looked for the earliest reference to the recording in an HMV catalogue. The abbreviation (C) means this is the first catalogue reference date found for the recording.

I am deeply grateful to Nicholas Carolan of the Irish Traditional Music Archives in Dublin for all his assistance.

There are 72 songs in this list. ND=No Date.

1. *The Castle of Dromore*
   Probably 1938 or '39 1940(C), HMV IM676, accordion, guitar.
2. *Down by the Glenside* (P. Kearney) OEA7571   Sept. 1938, HMV IM 662 With piano, accordion, guitar
3. *If I were a Blackbird* OEA7570   Sept. 1938, HMV IM662 With Piano, accordion & guitar
4. *Molly Bawn & Brian Og* OEA6710   Sept./Oct. 1938(C), HMV IM576. With Richard Hayward

5. *What will you do, Love* OEA6707 Sept./Oct. 1938, HMV IM576 With Richard Hayward

6. *After Aughrim's Great Disaster* OEA7567 1st March 1939, HMV IM676 Studio No. 3, Abbey Rd., London, guitar & accordion, arr. Arthur Darley.

7. *The Spinning Wheel* OEA7567 July 1939(C), HMV IM646. Trad. arr. A. Darley, guitar. Re-issued on HMV BR56 & BD 1256

** NOTE: Previously issued in England as HMV BD1256 & 7EG 8295

8. *The Lovely Sailor Boy*

Oct. 1939(C), HMV IM668, with Richard Hayward, piano, accordion, guitar, arr. R. Hayward.

9. *Three Lovely Lassies* OEA7569 Oct. 1939, HMV IM646, Trad. arr. A. Darley, guitar. Re-issued on HMV BR56 & BD 1256

** NOTE: Previously issued in England as HMV BD1256

10. *As I walked out* OEL158-3 31st Aug. 1940, HMV IM822, with fiddle, accordion, guitar.

11. *Coortin' in the Kitchen* OEL154-3 31st Aug. 1940, HMV IM777, with fiddle, accordion, guitar, arr. A. Darley

12. *My bonnie Irish boy* OEL156-1 31st Aug. 1940, HMV IM816, with accordion & guitar

13. *The Roving Journeyman* OEL155-3 31st Aug. 1940, HMV IM747,with fiddle, accordion & OEL151 guitar, 1940 HMV IM747 & BD 1268 (London).

14. *The Lady Fair* OEL167-3 3rd Sept. 1940, HMV IM815, with Michael O'Higgins arr. A. Darley, guitar.

15. *Nora Creina* OEL165-3 3rd Sept. 1940, HMV IM749, with Michael O'Higgins, fiddle, accordion & guitar.

16. *Thank you Ma'am, says Dan* OEL168-3 3rd Sept. 1940, HMV IM749, with Michael O'Higgins, fiddle & guitar

17. *The Girl from Donegal* OEL179-3 5th Sept. 1940, HMV IM751fiddle, accordion, guitar. Oct. 1940 HMV IM751 coupling no. OEL198-3; Mar 1941 HMV IM808 coupling no. OEL199-1

18. *The Shepherd's Lamb* OEL180-1 5th Sept. 1940, HMV IM818, fiddle, accordion, guitar.

19. *Whistle, daughter, whistle* OEL182-1 5th Sept. 1940, HMV IM821, fiddle, accordion, guitar, arr. A. Darley.

20. *The Boston Burglar* OEL185-1 6th Sept. 1940, HMV IM777, fiddle, accordion, guitar.

21. *The Humour is on me now* 1940(C), HMV IM 618 With Richard Hayward, piano, accordion, guitar, arr. R. Hayward

22. *The Lowlands of Holland* OEL183-1 6th Sept. 1940, HMV IM819, guitar.

23. *The Moonshiner* OEL151 1940(C), HMV IM 747, Dublin, accordion & guitar; BD 1268 & 7EG 8295 (London).

24. *On the banks of my own lovely Lee* OEL198-3 8th Sept. 1940, HMV IM751, fiddle, accordion, guitar.

25. *The Peeler and the Goat* Sept. 1940(C), HMV IM775, with Michael O'Higgins, guitar, arr. A. Darley.

26. *Reilly the Fisherman* Sept. 1940(C), HMV IM775 fiddle, accordion, guitar, arr. A. Darley.

27. *Send back my Barney to me* OEL199-1 8th Sept. 1940, HMV IM808 fiddle, accordion, guitar.

28. *Whiskey in my tea* 1940(C), HMV IM618

29. *The Bantry Girl's Lament* OEL 129-3 7st Feb. 1941, HMV IM820 Trad. arr. A. Darley, guitar.

30. *The Cailín Deas* OEL201-3 7th Feb. 1941, HMV IM813, guitar.

31. *Good-bye, Mick, & good-bye, Pat* OEL127-3 7th Feb. 1941, HMV IM821, accordion & guitar, arr. A. Darley.

32. *I wish that I never was wed* OEL133-3 7th Feb. 1941, HMV IM813

33. *Reynard the Fox* OEL29-3 7th Feb. 1941, HMV IM817, with accordion and guitar. arr. Arthur Darley

34. *The Star of Donegal* OEL128-3 7th Feb. 1941, HMV IM822, with George Walsh, accordion & guitar

35. *The Cailín Ruadh* OEL170-3 10th Feb. 1941, HMV IM818, with Michael O'Higgins, fiddle, guitar, arr. A. Darley

36. *The Enniskillen Dragoon* OEL166-3 10th Feb. 1941, HMV IM814 , with Michael O'Higgins

37. *I was told by my aunt* OEL153-3 10th Feb. 1941, HMV IM816, with fiddle, accordion & guitar

38. *Jackets Green* OEL157-3 10th Feb. 1941, HMV IM817, with fiddle & accordion(Blon Kiernan)

39. *Johnny the daisey-o* OEL134-3 10th Feb. 1941, HMV IM814, with fiddle, accordion & guitar

40. *The Croppy Boy* OEL184-1 11th Feb. 1941, HMV IM820, guitar A. Darley

41. *The Green Bushes* OEL171-3 11th Feb. 1941, HMV IM819, with Michael O'Higgins, fiddle, guitar.

42. *The Ballad of O Bruaidir* June-Jly 1946, HMV IM1147

43. *Dabbling in the Dew* 1946(C), HMV IM1146

44. *The Legend of Glendalough* June-Jly 1946, HMV IM1147

45. *Three Brave Blacksmiths* 1946(C), HMV IM1146 fiddle & accordion, arr. D. Murphy.

46. *The Captain with the Whiskers* 1951, Melodisc P203

47. *Cloughmills Fair* OEP 217-1(622455) c.1951 Glenside W 164

48. *Connemara Cradle Song* 1951, Melodisc P202

49. *County Tyrone* 1951, Melodisc P203

50. *Dan O'Hara* OEP219-1(622457) c.1951 Glenside W165

51. *From Liffey's Side* Nixa 7623, with James Moody (piano).

52. *My Beloved and I* OEP 214-1(622452) c.1951 Glenside W 164

53. *Return to Freemantle* c.1951 Nixa 7623, with James Moody (piano).

54. *Sailors don't care* Nixa 7621 with guitar accompaniment.

55. *Sarah* c.1951 Nixa 7624 accomp. dir. Nat Temple

56. *Shamus Rafferty* c. 1951 Nixa 7624 accomp. dir. Nat Temple; also, 1961, Prestige Irish 35002

57. *Shores of Lough Bran*   OEP218-1(622456) c. 1951 Glenside W165

58. *The Trip we took over the Mountain* 1951 Melodisc P202(RR132)

59. *The Wake in Kildare* 1951 Melodisc P201(RR132)

60. *Where sleeps my love* c. 1951 Nixa 7621, with guitar accompaniment

61. *The Wild Colonial Boy* 1951 Melodisc P201(RR 132)

62. *The Bold Granuaile* 1961, Prestige Irish 35002

63. *Cold Blows the Wind*   do.

64. *Down the Moor*   do.

65. *The Irish Rover*   do.

66. *Mary of the Wild Moor*   do.

67. *The Queen of Connemara*   do.

68. *Slievenamon*   do.

Other songs Delia recorded (source is RTE Gram Library):

69. *Wars of America* ND & 70. *The Cobbler* ND   Glenside

71. *Fairy Lullaby* ND & 72. *Walking through the fair* NDGlenside

Re-issues, etc.:

The Bonnie Irish Boy

I was told by my aunt 1951 Regal Zonophone MR 3536

The Boston Burglar

Courtin' in the Kitchen 1951 Regal Zonophone MR 3427

The Cailín Deas

I wish that I never was wed 1951 Regal Zonophone MR 3548

Down by the Glenside

If I were a blackbird 1951 Regal Zononphone MR 3379

The Enniskilling Dragoon with Michael O'Higgins

Johnny the Daisy-o 1951 Regal Zonophone MR 3535

 Goodbye Mike and Goodby Pat

Whistle, daughter, whistle 1951 Regal Zonophone MR 3589

The Green Bushes

The Lowlands of Holland 1951 Regal Zonophone MR 3646

Jackets Green

Reynard the Fox 1951 Regal Zonophone MR 3549

Molly Bawn & Brian Og (with Richard Hayward)

1951 Regal Zonophone MR 3220

The Moonshiner

The Roving Journeyman 1951 Regal Zonophone MR 3426

Nora Creina

Thank you Ma'am, says Dan 1951 Regal Zonophone MR3460

The Spinning Wheel

Three Lovely Lassies 1951 Regal Zonophone MR 3274

What will you do, Love

1951 Regal Zonophone MR 3025, with Richard Hayward

1976, 12" LP, "Souvenir of Ireland", Dublin, Talisman(EMI)
STAL6006, Trk. A7: *The Spinning Wheel.*

1976, 12" LP, "Voices of Radio, 1926-1976", RTE/EMI, RTE50,
Delia Murphy on one track - *The Roving Journeyman.*

1977, "The Legendary Delia Murphy", 12" LP, Dublin, Talisman
STAL1055 (*With Michael O'Higgins):

Side 1	Side 2
The Spinning Wheel	Three Lovely Lassies
If I were a Blackbird	Down by the Glenside
I was told by my aunt	The Moonshiner
I wish that I never was wed	Coortin' in the Kitchen
Roving Journeyman	The Croppy Boy
Boston Burglar	Good-bye Mike & Good-bye Pat
*Thank you Ma'am says Dan	*Nora Creina

1977, "The Spinning Wheel", 12" LP, England, Grasmere GRALP
16 (Same content as "The Legendary Delia Murphy", above)

1977, "Delia Murphy", 12" LP, Dublin, Talisman(EMI) STAL1055
(Same content as "The Legendary Delia Murphy", above)

1977 "Delia Murphy", Fiesta label, 1619 Broadway, NY, (Same content as "The Legendary Delia Murphy", above)

1986, "The Golden Years of Irish Music", Vol.1, 12" LP, EMI(Ireland)   GAL 1004, Trk B8 *Coortin' in the Kitchen*

N/D 12" LP, "Songs from the Emerald Isle", MFP(EMI) England DL1104, Trk A2 *The Spinning Wheel*, and Trk A6 *Coortin' in the Kitchen*

1992, Audio cassette, "Ireland & its Melodic Powers - Voices & Melodies of Ireland, 1923-1955". Notes by Liam Breen, EMI TC EMS1459, Trk A2

1992, CD EMS1459 (Same content as "Ireland & its Melodic Powers - Voices & Melodies of Ireland, 1923-1955", above)

1993, CD, "My Irish Home Sweet Home", Empress RAJ CD809, Trk 10 *Down by the Glenside*, Trk 14 *The Spinning Wheel*, Trk 18 *Three Lovely Lassies*

1995, CD, "Irish Cream - Great Singers and Songs of Ireland, 1913-1955", EMI 7243-8 32657 2 5. Notes by Liam Breen, Trk 2 *The Spinning Wheel*, Trk 12 *Enniskillen Dragoons*, Trk 19 *The Bantry Girl's Lament*

N/D CD, "An Ireland of Treasures - Voices & Melodies of Ireland, 1913-1948. Notes by Liam Breen, Capitol/EMI CDP7 965772, Trk 2 *The Spinning Wheel*, Trk 12 *The Enniskillen Dragoons*, Trk 19 *The Bantry Girl's Lament*

N/D 7" LP, "The Delightful Delia", HMV(Ireland) Trk A1 *The Spinning Wheel*, Trk A2 *Three Lovely Lassies* Trk B1 *The Moonshiner* Trk B2 *If I were a Blackbird*

N/D 12" LP, "Souvenir of Ireland" Vol. 2, Shamrock series, Talisman EMI STAL 6021, Trk B2 *The Moonshiner.*

Primary Sources

RTE Radio Documentary, *I Sing for the Real People of the Gods* — 4th June, 1972.

RT.E. Documentary, *The Ballad of Delia Murphy*, Tuesday Documentary, RTE I, February 1988.

Conversations of Author with Delia Murphy – 1968/69, (in possession of the Author).

Typed notes of Barbara Hutchinson with Delia, (in possession of the Author).

Taped interviews with Leo Maguire, Billy Carter, Liam and Barbara Redmond, Ivor Browne, Albert Healy, Stella Seaver, Leslie Thorne, Mary Cassidy, Eve Cullen, Hubert Valentine, Frs. Tom Twomey, Michael Lee, Eamon Concannon, Dr. John Carr, Leo Cullen, Sean O Cillin, Mike and Tom Killeen and Dr. Michael Brennan, (in possession of the Author).

Newspaper cuttings, photographs and other material supplied by Orla Browne for T.V. documentary 1988, (in possession of Orla Browne).

Taped accounts from Liam Clancy and from Dr Kenneth Goldstein, (in possession of the Author).

Taped interviews done by Mel O Hara (author's brother) with informants in Ontario & Quebec, (in possession of the Author).

Newspapers

The Irish Press.
Irish News.
Western People.
Connacht Tribune.
Connacht Telegraph.
Leitrim Observer.
The Belfast Telegraph.

Secondary Sources

Chapter One

Brennan, T. Ann, *The Real Klondike Kate,* Goose Lane Editions, Fredericton, New Brunswick, Canada, 1990.

Colum, Mary, *Life and the Dream*, Dolmen Press, Dublin, 1966.

Colum, Pádraic, *My Irish Year*, Mills & Boon, London, 1912,
 Ch I p.p 8 & 15.

Ellmann, Richard, *Oscar Wilde*, Hamish Hamilton, London, 1987.

MacGowan, Michael, trans. Valentin Iremonger, *The Hard Road to Klondike*, Routledge and Kegan Paul, London, 1973, p.92.

Chapter Two

O'Hara, Bernard, ed. *Mayo*, The Archaeological, Historical & Folklore Society, RTE, Galway, 1982.

Quinn, J. F., *History of Mayo*, Vols. 1&2, J. Quinn.

Chapter Three

Ó Broin, Leon, *...just like yesterday*, Gill and Macmillan, Dublin, 1985.

— , *No Man's Man*, Institute of Public Administration, Dublin,1982.

Chapter Four

Foster, R. F., *Modern Ireland 1600-1972*, Penguin Books, London, 1989.

Gorham, Maurice, *Forty Years of Irish Broadcasting*, The Talbot Press, Dublin, 1967.

Tobin, Fergal, *The Best of Decades*, Gill and Macmillan, Dublin, 1984.

Chapter Five

MacDonagh, Donagh, and Arthur Darley, *Ballads with Words and Music*, The Parkside Press, Dublin, N/D (1940s).

Mac Lochlainn, Alf, "Mellow the Moonlight" in *Ceol Tíre*, 1974, The Newsletter of the Folk Music Society of Ireland, Dublin.

Ní Laodhóg, Nóirín, ed. *A Heritage Ahead - Cultural Action and Travellers*, Pavee Point Publications, 1995.

Ó Lochlainn, Colm, *Irish Street Ballads,* The Three Candles Limited, Dublin, 1939.

— , *More Irish Street Ballads*, The Three Candles Limited, Dublin, 1965.

Chapter Six
Capuchin Annual, 1940.

Chapter Seven
Keogh, Dermot, *Ireland and the Vatican*, Cork University Press, 1995,
   p. 161

Chapter Eight
Gallagher, J. P., *The Scarlet and the Black*, Fount Paperbacks, London,
   1983, p.p. 109/110
Keogh, Dermot, *Ireland and the Vatican*, Cork University Press, 1995, p.
   198.

Chapter Nine
Johnston, Denis, *Nine Rivers of Jordon*, Derek Verschoyle, London
   1953.
Gallagher, J. P., *The Scarlet and the Black*, Fount Paperbacks, London,
   1983, 62, 74.

Chapter Eleven
The Irish Review, 1st May 1951.
The Melody Maker, 11th November 1950.
Walton's 132 Best Irish Songs and Ballads, Walton's, Dublin.

Additional
Andrews, C. S., *Man of No Property*, The Mercier Press, Cork & Dublin,
   1982.
Healy, James N., *Comic Songs of Ireland*, The Mercier Press, Dublin &
   Cork, 1978.
—, *The First Book of Irish Ballads*, The Mercier Press, Cork, 1968.
—, *The Second Book of Irish Ballads*, The Mercier Press, Cork, 1968.
Lockwood, Glenn, ed. John D. Munro, *Kitley, 1795-1975*, © G.
   Lockwood, & J. Munro, 1974.
MacManus, Francis, ed. *The Years of the Great Test 1926-39*, The Mercier
   Press, Cork, 1967.
Moody, T. W., F. X. Martin, eds. *The Course of Irish History*, The Mercier
   Press, Cork, 1967.

INDEX

Derry, Major Sam 113,116,124, 125,----- 138
Doherty, John 83
Doherty, Margaret 62
Doherty, Mickey 83
Doherty, Simon 83
Donoghue, Thomas 94
Doran, Felix 83
Doran, John 83
Dowdall, Fr. 138
Downey, P. K. 190
Doyle, Lynn 65
Duffy, Kathleen 170
Dulanty, John 141
Dunne, Pecker 83
Earles, Tommy 66
Eisenhower, Dwight 179
Fanning, Anna Agnes (Delia's mother) 21, 143
Farmer, Jock 63
Fee, Fr. 96
Fenning, Máirín 75, 76,77, 92
Fields, Gracie 74
Fitzpatrick, Seán 76
Flaherty, Robert 56, 91
Flanagan, Fr. Joe 88
Flower, Robin 48
Flynn, Renee Godolphin 75
Forbes, Moira 123
Forde, Cecil 90
Forsythe, Fr. Ben 138
Foster, Roy 61, 202
Foster, Stephen 31
Fox, George 86, 90
Fox, R. M. 192
Furey Brothers 83
Furey, Ted 83
Fursey, Sr. 31, 32, 33
Gaffney, Mary 74, 81
Gaffney, Sylvester see Leo Maguire

Gallagher, J. P. 116, 117, 128,132, 203,
Gallagher, Jim 166
Gallaghers 83
Gardiner, Bridie 42
Gertrude, Sr. 32
Goldstein, Dr. Kenneth S. 180, 181
Green, Philip 168
Gregory, Lady 23, 48, 51, 52, 77
Greig, Gavin 83
Grey, Julia 75
Gwynn, Professor Denis 46
Gwynn, Stephen Erwin 48
Hanley, Delia (Mrs. Clarke) 21
Harty, Sir Hamilton 48
Hayward, Richard 65, 66, 69, 70,75, 96
Healey, Albert 63, 64, 66....93
Hennelly, Doreen 191
Hereward, Pac 33
Heuston, John 187
Heysen, Hans 162
Higgins, F. R. 92
Hodgson, Anthony 142, 144,177
Hoffmann, Dr.121
Hogan, Dr. John 55
Houlihan, Andy 143
Howard, Patricia 151
Huebner, Ambassador 154
Hughes, E. P. & Sons 191
Hughes, Herbert 48, 49,65, 152
Hughes, Séamus 76
Humilis, Br. (Fr. Michael Lee) 116....119, 120, 131, 134, 137.
Hyde, Douglas 23,
Irwin, Robert 75
Ives, Burl 84
Jenings, Charles Benjamin 23
Johnston, Denis 135
Jones, Basil 151